Defining Democracy

Peter Emerson

Defining Democracy

Voting Procedures in Decision-Making,
Elections and Governance

Second Edition

 Springer

Peter Emerson
The de Borda Institute
36 Ballysillan Road
Belfast BT14 7QQ
Northern Ireland
pemerson@deborda.org

ISBN 978-3-642-20903-1   e-ISBN 978-3-642-20904-8
DOI 10.1007/978-3-642-20904-8
Springer Heidelberg Dordrecht London New York

Library of Congress Control Number: 2011939483

1st edition: © Peter Emerson 2002, published by The de Borda Institute
2nd edition: © Springer-Verlag Berlin Heidelberg 2012
This work is subject to copyright. All rights are reserved, whether the whole or part of the material is concerned, specifically the rights of translation, reprinting, reuse of illustrations, recitation, broadcasting, reproduction on microfilm or in any other way, and storage in data banks. Duplication of this publication or parts thereof is permitted only under the provisions of the German Copyright Law of September 9, 1965, in its current version, and permission for use must always be obtained from Springer. Violations are liable to prosecution under the German Copyright Law.

The use of general descriptive names, registered names, trademarks, etc. in this publication does not imply, even in the absence of a specific statement, that such names are exempt from the relevant protective laws and regulations and therefore free for general use.

Printed on acid-free paper

Springer is part of Springer Science+Business Media (www.springer.com)

To the intellectual diversity of our species, even if its place in the spectrum, which ranges from the stone to the divine, is so very very small.

Foreword: To the Second Edition

I am delighted to see that Peter Emerson has continued to advocate consensual politics. This second edition, with its additional information on Rwanda and elsewhere, is an even more potent argument for reform of the adversarial structures which still serve in so many parliaments and international gatherings.

As the reader may know from my writings elsewhere, I have long since been an advocate of proportional voting. Given the current difficulties in Belgium, however, not to mention the precarious state of the power-sharing arrangements in so many conflict zones, I am drawn more and more to consider the potential of the more pluralist voting procedures outlined in these pages.

Arend Lijphart
La Jolla
California
USA

January 2011

Foreword: Democracy versus Majority Rule

I am very pleased to write this foreword to Peter Emerson's important and stimulating new book *Defining Democracy*. My research has focused on the comparative study of democratic institutions for many years, and I often find that the concept of democracy is defined and used either much too broadly or much too narrowly. An egregious example of the latter is that while, in principle, there is virtually unanimous agreement that one of the most basic criteria of democracy, if not *the* most important criterion, is universal suffrage, in practice many people use the term to describe political systems where the right to vote is not, or not yet, truly universal.

For instance, in his celebrated book *The Third Wave* (Norman, University of Oklahoma Press, 1991), Samuel P. Huntington argues that the first wave of transitions to democracy started as early as 1828, although in the entire nineteenth century there was only one country – New Zealand – that adopted truly universal suffrage, that is, the right to vote for both men and women *and* for the Maori minority; this happened toward the very end of the century, in 1893. However, women did not have the right to be candidates for public office in New Zealand until 1919 – a violation of another important democratic criterion: the right not only to vote but also to be elected. We must therefore conclude that it was not until the twentieth century that any democracy was established. (I must immediately add that I have ignored the right-to-vote criterion myself by, for instance, including Switzerland and the United States in my comparative studies of democracy even before the Swiss adopted full women's suffrage in 1971 and before the 1965 Voting Rights Act was passed in the United States.)

The main example of the term democracy being used too narrowly is when people define it, all too often, as the equivalent of majority rule. *Defining Democracy* is a most welcome and very forceful challenge and antidote to this widespread tendency. It is full of excellent alternative suggestions – written in a lively style – concerning preferable methods of voting in mass elections and better decision-making methods in legislative and other multi-member bodies.

In my own intellectual development, I have gradually become more and more critical of the majoritarian form of democracy. I started out, in my undergraduate and graduate student days in the late 1950s and early 1960s, as a great admirer of the Westminster majoritarian model of democracy; at that time I regarded multi-party democracy with proportional representation, coalition cabinets, and so on – the kind of democracy practised in my native country of the Netherlands and to which I later attached the label of "consensus democracy" – as clearly inferior. In a later phase, from the mid-1960s to the mid-1980s, I became strongly aware of the dangers of majority-rule democracy for religiously and ethnically divided societies, but I still believed that it was the better choice for more homogeneous countries. Only from the mid-1980s on did I become more and more convinced that the consensus model of democracy was superior to the majoritarian model for all democracies and in almost all respects. Many commentators have pointed out that there are serious contradictions between what I have written in different publications and at different times. And they are quite right: I have changed my mind very radically on these matters!

As I read Peter Emerson's work, I think that he basically feels that majority rule is not, or only barely, democratic. I would not go so far as to argue that majoritarian democracy is really not democratic at all, but I do believe that consensus democracy is considerably *more* democratic than the majoritarian type. I hope and trust that *Defining Democracy* will help in furthering the knowledge and appreciation of the many excellent and perfectly democratic alternatives to majority rule.

Arend Lijphart
La Jolla
California
USA

June 2001

Preface

> *Any civilization... will present a number of bizarre features which [people] accept as perfectly natural because they are familiar.*
>
> (Miłosz 1985: *xv*)

The Simple Theory

Like many another civilization, the European version has acquired, adopted, or simply just failed to question, a number of extraordinary beliefs. On the economic side, for example, we have slowly but surely converted what was the old vice of usury into the modern virtue of credit. As a result, most countries, banks and people are in debt, and all are intertwined. It is in fact bizarre.[1]

Another myth relates to that which we call democracy, arguably one of the vaguest terms in common usage. Some have tried to tie it down with what they regard as specific expressions like "democratic centralism" (Máo Zédōng), "democratic dictatorship" (Sékou Touré) and "democratic collectivism" (Jawarharlal Nehru). Others have spoken of "bourgeois democracy", "proletarian democracy" (Vladimir Ilych Lenin) and "political democracy" (Fidel Castro). And then there are some other phrases like "majoritarian democracy", "consociational democracy" and "consensus democracy".

All of these terms, and especially the last three, refer to various interpretations of the word "democracy", and all envisage different structures of government. Little wonder, then, that today's democracies cover a wide spectrum of practice with but the one thread common to many of them: somewhere, at some stage or other, people cast a vote, and something, or someone, gains a majority.

---

[1] The banking crisis of 2009 has caused some people – not many – to now question this practice; suffice here to say that these words also appeared in the 2002 first edition.

This, apparently, is the key, which makes it all "democratic". It might involve an either/or vote on options A or B, or it might be just a vote on A, yes or no. As long as there is a vote which results in a clear majority, however, many people appear to be satisfied. Democracy is equated with majority rule and majority rule is assumed to be best effected by a majority vote. As we shall see, this too is bizarre.

> [People] are captivated... by what may be called the mystique of the majority; it is often thought to be the foundation of democracy that the will of a majority should be paramount.
> It is *not* the foundation of democracy, however... (Dummett 1997: 71)

Majority Voting in Practice

Decision-Making

In many instances of political decision-making, the "A-or-B?" question is the equivalent of the following: "Are you left-wing or right-wing?" The actual majority opinion, however, is often somewhere in the middle, in the realm of a silent majority. A better term would perhaps be the *silenced* majority, silenced by being presented with only two options, neither of which adequately represents their viewpoint? In some cases, then, the outcome of a majority vote will not even correspond with the real majority opinion, let alone "the will of the people".

Elections

Elections are also a little bizarre. Our elected members, it is said, represent their constituencies. As often as not, however, they primarily represent their party, and during the course of their tenure in office, they will probably do more for their party supporters in other constituencies than they will for many of their own electorates.

Governance

In theory and sometimes too in practice, a parliament represents *everybody*, albeit with varying degrees of fairness. Invariably, however, the elected chamber then splits into two and the executive represents only the bigger "half".

The Book

The first edition of this book was published as a *samizdat* in 2002. Since then, I have worked in East and Southern Africa; undertaken a study tour in Lebanon; lectured in the United States and across Western Europe; observed many elections for the Organization for Security and Co-operation in Europe, OSCE, in Central and Eastern Europe, from Kosovo to the Kyrgyz Republic; and most recently, in the wake of the Vladimir Putin / Mikhail Saakashvili war of 2008, I was a member of the EU monitoring mission in Georgia. Although these experiences have improved my knowledge of politics abroad, there are still many parts of the globe about which my knowledge is minimal. This may explain some inadequacies in the text, but I cannot use it as an excuse for them all.

The following pages examine the weaknesses of current "democratic" structures, and then consider some rather better procedures. The two chapters in Part I discuss decision-making, first the defects of present practice, and then a more inclusive *modus operandi*. In Part II, Chapters 3 and 4 examine electoral systems in a similar sequence, while Part III brings all of these ideas together in structures of government. In conclusion, the Epilogue then asks why such an inclusive ideal is not yet on most people's agenda. There are, in addition, four appendices, illustrating both what is wrong and occasionally what is right in voting procedures, and I have also added a chronology of mainly Western democracy, to show when and where it all developed, and where too it suffered so many setbacks.

Just one small note on the nomenclature: options and candidates are lettered from the beginning of the alphabet, *A, B, C* and so on; voters of alternate gender are called J, K, L etc.; and political parties are named *W, X, Y* and *Z*.

Thanks

I would like to offer my thanks to those who, yet again, have helped to turn my thoughts into what I hope has become a coherent text. In particular, I wish to offer my appreciation to Alan Quilley, whose diligent red pen on both drafts often took up more space than my black print. My friendship with Phil Kearney also goes back many years, and it is often his ideas which then have the semblance of being mine; the title, to take the first example, is his.

Next I would like to thank all those who continue to give their support to the work I do in the de Borda Institute: first and foremost, to the patrons and committee members, all of whom have given their time and energies on a voluntary basis. Of these, Professors Elizabeth Meehan of Queen's University Belfast and John Baker of University College Dublin deserve especial mention, for she has given her name to many events, often in the role of chair, while John has done umpteen hours of technical work, developing computer programs and then analyzing votes. Another patron is Professor Arend Lijphart of the University of California, whose own personal journey away from majoritarianism has given him the perfect basis on which to write the foreword to this work. I must also thank those individuals and organizations that have helped to fund our endeavours, not least Stephen Pittam of the Joseph Rowntree Charitable Trust, which gave the Institute its first grant; there are very few such NGOs which have survived for ten years and more on the basis of a lump sum of just £3,000.

Thanks too are due to those friends in like-minded associations such as the Society for Social Choice and Welfare, SCW, where Professors Hannu Nurmi (Turku), Don Saari (California) and Maurice Salles (Caen), have been very supportive. Without their explicit endorsement, the de Borda Institute would not have been able to wield as much influence as it now does. Meanwhile, at a local level, John Robb, Wes Holmes and other colleagues in the New Ireland Group, NIG, have often blown my trumpet, and it has been a joy to work with them. Another organization in which I have found much support and friendship is the Irish (and Northern Irish) Green Party, GP, where, thanks to Phil Kearney *et al,* consensus voting is now used on a regular basis. (Baker J 2008: 431–40) Hopefully, colleagues like Perry Walker of the New Economics Foundation and Gordon Burt in the Conflict Research Society will help to spread the practice in Britain. May I also mention a few brave hearts in the media, Roy Garland and William Graham of the *Irish News*, and Andy Pollak, formerly of the *Irish Times,* for they have supported some of the events which we have organized over the years, and questioned with their own pens the media's otherwise impregnable belief in majoritarianism. Acknowledgement too goes to Springer-Verlag for publishing this work and in particular to their editor, Barbara Fess; not everyone in the trade will take on a text which criticizes the bizarre. Lastly, yet most importantly, I want to say thanks indeed to those other friends not mentioned among the above, who have always given this very *un-Sovietski* dissident much needed support and encouragement.

Peter Emerson
Belfast
Northern Ireland

26 January 2011

References

Baker J (2008) Election of the Green Party *Cathaoirleach*, 2007. *Irish Political Studies,* Vol. 23, 3, 431–40.
Dummett M (1997) *Principles of Electoral Reform.* OUP, Oxford.
Miłosz C (1985) *The Captive Mind.* Penguin, London.

Contents

Foreword vii
Preface xi
List of Figures xxi
List of Tables xxiii
Abbreviations xxv

Part I Decision-Making

1 The Myths of Majority Rule 3
   1.1 An Historical Perspective 3
      1.1.1 From Majority Rule to the Majority Vote 5
      1.1.2 Illogicalities of Majority Voting 5
   1.2 Horrendous Consequences of Majoritarianism 15
      1.2.1 Rwanda, the "Land of a Thousand Hills" 15
      1.2.2 The Middle East 16
      1.2.3 The Right of Self-Determination 17
      1.2.4 International Diplomacy 18
      1.2.5 The Minority of the Minority 20
      1.2.6 Repeat Referendums 21
   1.3 Conclusions 22
   References 23

2 Pluralist Decision-Making 25
   2.1 Decision-Making: the Ideal Defined 25
   2.2 Majority Voting: Theory and Practice 27
      2.2.1 Variations on the Majoritarian Theme 28
   2.3 Multi-Option Decision-Making: Theory 30
      2.3.1 A Three-Option Continuum 30
      2.3.2 A Four-Option Conundrum 32
      2.3.3 The Wording of Motions 33

	2.3.4 Single-Peaked Preferences	35
2.4	Multi-Option Decision-Making: Practice	36
	2.4.1 Plurality Voting	36
	2.4.2 The Two-Round System, TRS	38
	2.4.3 Approval Voting	38
	2.4.4 Serial Voting	38
	2.4.5 AV, STV or IRV	39
	2.4.6 Pairings, a Condorcet Count	39
	2.4.7 Points System or Borda Count, BC	39
2.5	Consensus Voting: The Modified Borda Count, MBC	40
	2.5.1 The MBC: Theory and Practice	41
	2.5.2 An Example	43
	2.5.3 Other Applications of the MBC	43
2.6	Conclusions	44
2.7	Democratic Decision-Making Defined	46
References		46

Part II Elections

3 Party-ocracies 51
   3.1 The First Elections 51
      3.1.1 An Old English Tale 52
      3.1.2 L'état, C'est Quoi? 53
      3.1.3 The "New World" 54
      3.1.4 The Collapse of Soviet Communism 55
   3.2 Today's Elections 56
      3.2.1 The Politics of Adversarial Electoral Systems 58
      3.2.2 The Mathematics of Adversarial Electoral Systems ... 63
      3.2.3 The Application of Adversarial Electoral Systems ... 65
   3.3 Today's Elections: Practice 67
      3.3.1 FPP 68
      3.3.2 TRS 69
      3.3.3 FPP and PR-List 71
      3.3.4 TRS or PR-List 71
      3.3.5 PR-List 72
      3.3.6 SNTV 73
   3.4 Conclusions 73
   References 74

4 The Candid Candidate 75
   4.1 Free and Fair Elections 75
      4.1.1 Electoral Principles 76
   4.2 A Comparison of Various Electoral Systems 81
      4.2.1 Plurality Vote or FPP 82

Contents

	4.2.2 TRS	82
	4.2.3 Approval Voting	83
	4.2.4 AV or STV or IRV	83
	4.2.5 SNTV	83
	4.2.6 PR-List	83
	4.2.7 PR-STV	85
	4.2.8 Condorcet	86
	4.2.9 BC/MBC	86
	4.2.10 Top-Up	87
4.3	Consensus Voting for a Parliament: QBS	87
	4.3.1 QBS: Theory and Practice	87
	4.3.2 Inclusive Counting Procedures	90
4.4	Consensus Voting in Parliament, Electing a Government: The Matrix Vote	91
	4.4.1 The Matrix Vote: Theory	91
	4.4.2 The Matrix Vote Count	92
	4.4.3 The Matrix Vote: Practice	92
	4.4.4 The Matrix Vote for Use in Committees	93
4.5	Conclusions	94
4.6	Democratic Elections Defined	95
References	96

Part III The Art of Governance

5 The Elected Dictator 101
  5.1 Party Structures of Governance 101
    5.1.1 The One-Party or No-Party State 102
    5.1.2 One-Party Dominant States 105
    5.1.3 The Two-Party State 106
    5.1.4 Multi-Party States 107
    5.1.5 All-Party States 109
  5.2 Governments and their *Modus Operandi* 113
  5.3 Government Structures 114
  5.4 The Debate 115
    5.4.1 People Power 116
    5.4.2 International Government 117
  5.5 Conclusions 118
  References 119

6 Governance 121
  6.1 First Principles 121
  6.2 The Debate 122
    6.2.1 The Consensors 123
    6.2.2 Composite Resolutions 124

6.2.3 The Art of Compromise	124
6.3 Inclusive Government	125
6.3.1 Power-Sharing	125
6.3.2 Consensus Coefficient	126
6.3.3 Collective Responsibility	127
6.3.4 Direct Democracy	128
6.3.5 Human Rights	128
6.4 A Comparison of Some Democracies	129
6.5 Conclusions	133
6.6 Democracy Defined	134
References	135

Epilogue: Majoritarianism in Focus ... 137
  E.1 A Bizarre Absence of Dissent ... 137
  References ... 142

Appendix A: The Dictators' Referendums ... 143
  A.1 Introduction ... 143
    A.1.1 France ... 144
    A.1.2 Italy ... 145
    A.1.3 Germany and Austria ... 145
    A.1.4 Romania ... 146
    A.1.5 Haiti ... 147
    A.1.6 Chile ... 148
    A.1.7 Iran ... 148
    A.1.8 Croatia and Serbia ... 149
    A.1.9 Iraq ... 149
  A.2 Conclusions ... 149
  References ... 150

Appendix B: The People Have Spoken ... 151
  B.1 By a Whisker ... 151
  B.2 Conclusions ... 153
  Reference ... 153

Appendix C: Won By One ... 155
  C.1 Introduction ... 155
    C.1.1 Ireland ... 155
    C.1.2 Russia ... 156
    C.1.3 Britain ... 156
    C.1.4 India ... 157
    C.1.5 USA ... 157
  C.2 Decisions ... 158
  C.3 Elections ... 160
  References ... 161

Appendix D: Some Multi-Option Referendums 163
    D.1 Introduction 163

A Chronology of (Western) Democracy 167

Glossary 175

Index 183

List of Figures

Fig. 2.1	A voters' profile	26
Fig. 2.2	A profile of tastes	31
Fig. 2.3	A more complex profile	32
Fig. 2.4	A choice of questions	34
Fig. 2.5	A seven-option ballot	34
Fig. 2.6	Another seven-option ballot	35
Fig. 2.7	Single-peaked preferences: *D-C-E-B-F-A-G*	36
Fig. 2.8	Decision-making systems	37
Fig. 2.9	An MBC five-option ballot	41
Fig. 3.1	A voters' profile	64
Fig. 4.1	A voters' profile	82
Fig. 4.2	Electoral systems	84
Fig. 4.3	A QBS five-candidate ballot paper	88
Fig. 4.4	A QBS analysis	89
Fig. 4.5	A partial vote	90
Fig. 4.6	A matrix ballot	92
Fig. 4.7	A matrix vote ballot paper for a five-person executive	94
Fig. 6.1	Democratization	130

List of Tables

Table 1.1	Some actual and possible secessions	21
Table 4.1	The quota	77
Table A.1	Napoleon's referendums	144
Table A.2	Mussolini's referendums	145
Table A.3	Hitler's referendums	146
Table A.4	Antonescu's referendums	147
Table A.5	Duvalier's referendums	147
Table A.6	Pinochet's referendums	148
Table A.7	Some Iranian referendums	148
Table A.8	Some Yugoslav referendums	149
Table A.9	Saddam Hussein's referendum	149
Table D.1	Some multi-option referendums	164

Abbreviations

ACE	Administration and Cost of Elections
AGM	Annual General Meeting
AMS	Additional Member System
ANP	Awami National Party (Pakistan)
AV	Alternative Vote
BBC	British Broadcasting Corporation
BC	Borda Count
BCE	Before the Common Era
BJP	*Bharatiya Janata Party* (India)
CDP	Conservative Democratic Party, (Switzerland)
CDU	Christian Democratic Union (Germany)
CIS	Commonwealth of Independent States – *Sodruzhestvo Nezavisimykh Gosudarstv, SNG*
CPA	Comprehensive Peace Agreement (Sudan)
CPC	Communist Party of China
CPSU	Communist Party of the Soviet Union
CSU	Christian Social Union (Germany)
CUP	Cambridge University Press
CVP	Christian Democratic People's Party (Switzerland)
DAP	*Deutsche Arbeiter Partei,* German Workers' Party
DM	Deutsche Mark (Now replaced by the Euro, €)
D-R	Democratic-Republican (Party) (USA)
DRC	Democratic Republic of the Congo
DUP	Democratic Unionist Party (NI)
EC/EU	European Community or Union
EISA	Electoral Institute for the Sustainability of Democracy in Africa
EP	*Yedinaya Rossiya,* United Russia
FDP	Free Democratic Party (Germany and Switzerland)
FF	*Fianna Fáil* (Ireland)
FG	*Fine Gael* (Ireland)
FIS	*Front Islamique du Salut* (Algeria)

FPP	First-Past-the-Post
GNU	Government of National Unity
GP	Green Party (Australia, England and Wales, Ireland, Germany)
HDZ	*Hrvatska demokratska zajednica*, Croatian Democratic Union (Bosnia and Croatia)
ICC	International Criminal Court
ID	Identification
IMF	International Monetary Fund
INC	Indian National Congress
IOC	International Olympic Committee
IRA	Irish Republican Army
IRV	Instant Run-off Voting
KLA	Kosova Liberation Army
KPD	*Kommunistiche Partei Deutschlands* (Germany)
MBC	Modified Borda count
MLA	Member of Legislative Assembly
MMP	Multi-Member Proportional
MP	Member of Parliament
MQM	Muttahida Qaumi Movement (Pakistan)
NATO	North Atlantic Treaty Organization
NGO	Non-Governmental Organization
NI	Northern Ireland
NIG	New Ireland Group
NRM	National Resistance Movement (Uganda)
NURC	National Unity and Reconciliation Commission (Rwanda)
NSC	National Security Council (USA)
NSDAP	National Socialist DAP, Nazis, (Germany)
OSCE	Organization for Security and Co-operation in Europe
OUP	Oxford University Press
PM	Prime Minister
PML	Pakistan Muslim League
PNG	Papua New Guinea
PPP	Pakistan People's Party
PR	Proportional Representation
QBS	Quota Borda System
RPF	Rwanda Patriotic Front
RTÉ	*Radio Telefís Éireann* (Ireland)
SCW	Society for Social Choice and Welfare
SDA	*Stranka demokratske akcije*, Party of Democratic Action (Bosnia)
SDLP	Social Democratic and Labour Party (NI)
SDP	Social Democratic Party (Bosnia)
SDS	*Srpska demokratska stranka*, Serbian Democratic Party (Bosnia)
SF	*Sinn Féin* (Ireland, NI)
SLA/M	Sudan Liberation Army/Movement

Abbreviations

SNP	Scottish National Party
SNTV	Single Non-Transferable Vote
SPD	*Sozialdemokratische Partei Deutschlands* (Germany)
SPLA/M	Sudan People's Liberation Army/Movement
SPS	*Sozialdemokratische Partei der Schweiz* Social Democratic Party (Switzerland)
SR	Socialist Revolutionary (Russia)
STV	Single Transferable Vote
SVP	*Schweizerische Volkspartei*, Swiss People's Party
TRS	Two-Round System
UCD	University College Dublin
UK	United Kingdom
UMP	*Union pour un Mouvement Populaire* (France)
UN	United Nations
UPA	United Progressive Alliance (India)
USA	United States of America
USSR	Union of Soviet Socialist Republics
UUP	Ulster Unionist Party (NI)
VAT	Value Added Tax
WWI/II	World War I/II

Part I
Decision-Making

Chapter 1
The Myths of Majority Rule

...and what is the best condition for the state to be in (whether we assume that participation in the state is desirable for all or only for the majority)?

(Aristotle VII ii, 1324a13)

Abstract This chapter examines the history of democratic decision-making, a tale in which a Western interpretation has come to dominate other less adversarial methodologies. It next considers some of the illogicalities of placing so much emphasis on the two-option majority vote. Finally, it chronicles some of the horrendous consequences of majoritarianism, not least as applied to the right of self-determination.

1.1 An Historical Perspective

In numerous societies around the world, people have come to the almost archetypal conclusion that absolutism is wrong. Instead of being subjected to some autocratic dictator, many aboriginal communities devised practices in which the elders imposed restraints on their rulers. The same was true in Europe, where the *archons* of ancient Greece, or the barons and boyars in the Middle Ages, set limits to what might otherwise have been despotic monarchies.

Western society was sometimes slow to reject its autocratic rulers, especially in pre-reformation days, partly because the equally autocratic church leaders were often in cahoots with royalty – a practice which was indeed bizarre. At the time, however, it was blessed by a doctrine now known to have been wrong, the "divine right of kings." Thus by the time the peoples of Europe eventually saw the development of more advanced forms of governance, societies were often split, not only along the old divide between rich and poor, but also along a new fault line between a middle and a working class. In such circumstances it seemed to many that unanimity could not be achieved, which was probably true; any mechanism for achieving a compromise was, alas, also ruled out.

Life, after all, was a battle between good and bad, right and wrong, justice and injustice. On the democratic front, western Europeans pursued a logic, which was less archetypal: theirs was a propensity to reduce every complex dispute to a dichotomy, or to a series of such binary choices. Admittedly, it fitted in with the religious tendency to consider beliefs as true or false, practices as righteous or evil, and choices as between heaven and hell. But perhaps it goes back further, to the very earliest days of democracy, for even in the fifth century BCE, the 'language of opposites – word/deed, hot/cold, wet/dry, left/right, mind/body and so on – had come to obsess Greek thought and expression...' (Davies 1993: 24)

Elsewhere in the world, a more inclusive approach was apparent. In China, an equally if not more advanced society, any 'rivalry between different philosophical systems... took an altogether less adversarial and exclusive form. While criticism of others' views was often voiced, a common way of doing so was to suggest that one's rivals had found only *part* of the Way, the Dao, not the *whole*.' (Lloyd 2008: 54–5)

In Africa, too, a different practice evolved: 'According to tradition... if someone... is quarreling with someone else, then the court convened beneath the tree... will set itself the sole task of ending the conflict... while granting to each that he is in the right.' (Kapuściński 2002: 315) Similar practices were used in many parts of Swahiliphone Africa, as evidenced by the word *baraza*; in Rwanda, the term is *gacaca*, in Sudan, *judiye*; and in French-speaking Africa, *palambre*. Indeed it seems that, throughout the sub-Sahara, 'Majority rule was a foreign notion.' (Mandela 1994: 25) Likewise, in the Americas, 'The tribes then gathered and discussed the issue at hand, listening and speaking until common understanding had been reached... [a] practice of government by consensus.' (Nerburn 1999: 138)

Europe, it seems, was the exception, both in ancient times and in more recent centuries. Disputes here were to be resolved via a choice of two seemingly mutually exclusive opposites. If, then, minority rule were wrong, its opposite was bound to be right. The argument was supported by the benign supposition that most people try to be right for most of the time. Therefore, it was surmised, the majority opinion will be right; thus was born not just majority rule but the *right* of majority rule, a right enshrined in such wholesome phrases as 'the greatest good of the greatest number'.

As will be seen in Chap. 2, this was definitely a step in the right direction, but it would be wrong to think that it marked the pinnacle of democratic evolution. Nevertheless, today, almost every party politician believes that a 'core value of democracy... is to ensure majority rule'.[1] With Western culture now dominating so much of today's world, this belief is now virtually ubiquitous.

---

[1] The quotation comes from an official US government website. <http://usinfo.org/enus/government/overview/docs/ang.pdf > (accessed 23 May 2010). It then adds a second core value, namely, 'to protect individual rights and civil liberties.'

1.1 An Historical Perspective

1.1.1 From Majority Rule to the Majority Vote

The belief itself may be sound, but from it emerged a fatal flaw. Both in ancient Greece and in modern Europe, what followed was neither logical nor archetypal: it was decided, or more likely just assumed, that a majority opinion could be identified, or at least confirmed, by a majority vote. Countless statements are now made with this sentiment: 'the very principle that lies at the heart of democracy itself, [is] the notion that all citizens are equal and that decisions are to be reached and disagreements resolved by *majority vote*.' (Lloyd 2008: 52)

Equality is fine, but all too little is to be found in today's ballot boxes. Alas, in the media and academia, among politicians and the general public, the frailties of majority voting are not fully understood, and this pertains despite many words of caution that have been voiced over the years, words such as these: 'however democratic simple majority decision initially appears to be, it cannot in fact be so.' (Riker 1988: 65) Majority rule may indeed be a solid principle but, paradoxically, the majority vote is not an accurate way of identifying the majority opinion, if, as often is the case – or *should* be – more than two options are possible.

Almost by definition, on any contentious question and in any democracy which aspires to be plural, there will invariably be more than two possible options. Given this truism, majority voting is inadequate. Accordingly, before considering a better form of decision-making in Chap. 2, some of the contradictions inherent in using the two-option majority vote will be examined.

1.1.2 Illogicalities of Majority Voting

The most glaring fault of the majority vote is its inapplicability for use in conflict resolution work. Accordingly, priority will be given to this fault, and the more mathematical deficiencies will be examined from Sect. 1.1.2.2 onwards.

1.1.2.1 The Question is Closed

In conflict resolution work, no matter whether the dispute be domestic, industrial or political, the professional mediator will invariably rely on questions which are open. Initially, she will talk to the various parties in order to identify just what options exist. Next, in a phase often termed shuttle diplomacy, she may seek everyone's consent on some refinements to these proposals. Finally, she will ask those concerned for their preferences and thus identify the option that enjoys the highest level of support from all concerned.

Whereas in mediation the emphasis is on *open* questions, it is unfortunate that in politics resort is invariably made to the *closed* question, the two-option majority vote. This is especially sad when applied to conflict zones. In theory, the political process should be a means by which disputes can be resolved peacefully. In other words, as traditionally in Africa, as for example in a *gacaca*, (Sect. 1.1) the political process should be a type of mediation process, involving perhaps a win-win voting procedure, but certainly not a win-or-lose contest.

1.1.2.2 The Majority of the Majority

If a majority wins the election, how do the members of that majority then decide what policies to pursue? Naturally enough, believing as they do in majority voting, they take a majority vote. But this means the policy adopted may have the support of only a majority of the majority, and 51% of 51% is only 26%. To be sure of a real majority, they would need 71% of 71%... and they would hardly ever get that. The conclusion may be unexpected: in practice, majority rule rarely pertains in practice.

> In December 2001, delegates to the Ulster Unionist Council, voted (for the twelfth time) to maintain their support of the Belfast Agreement, albeit by only a small margin. As a result, the Northern Ireland Assembly survived yet another hurdle, but only because it gained the support of the majority of the majority of the majority: the Council majority, of the Ulster Unionist Party, UUP, majority, of the unionist majority. If, perchance, a minority of that majority of the majority of the majority had changed sides...

1.1.2.3 Votes of Confidence

In a multi-party parliament, the government of the day may occasionally lose a vote. Policy A of party W might not get a majority; nor might policies B, C and D of parties X, Y and Z. In such circumstances, party W might no longer enjoy the confidence of the House, but nor might parties X, Y and Z. The conclusion is that, in theory, majority rule might work in a parliament consisting of only two political parties; in any pluralist forum, such a voting mechanism could lead to a stalemate. Taking majority votes on the basis of "option A, yes-or-no?" is therefore not perhaps the best methodology. (See also Sect. 3.2.1.7, Chap. 4 note 8, and App. C, C.1.3, C.1.4, C.2.1927, 1963, 1972 and 2010 Italy.)

In an effort to counter such a scenario, which had so damaged the Weimar Republic, the German parliament now uses the so-called "constructive vote of no-confidence." It has now been introduced elsewhere as well: in Belgium, Papua New Guinea, PNG, and Spain for example. (Lijphart 1999: 101) This rule 'requires that parliament can dismiss a cabinet only by simultaneously electing a new cabinet.' (*Ibid*: 304) Thus the Bundestag takes such votes on the basis, not of "option A, yes or no?" but of "option A or option B?" It is a distinct improvement from having just one option.

Sadly, in many jurisdictions, questions of the one-option variety are still being asked. The will of all the people, however, cannot be identified if many voters are only saying 'no'. In 2003, 99% of the people of Gibraltar told the world what they did not want; 1 year later, in a UN-sponsored referendum, 76% of the Greek Cypriots did the same; while for years, Northern Ireland was in a state of political *impasse*, as Rev. Ian Paisley and company led the "Ulster says no" campaign. If, however, the objective of the democratic process is to identify what the collective actually wants, the individual voters must first say something about their own aspirations which is *positive*.

1.1.2.4 Pluralism

Perhaps a multi-option question would be better, but this raises a problem. In a world which believes in majoritarianism, what happens when there are more than two options "on the table?" Consider the decision of the International Olympic Committee, IOC, on the venue for the 2012 games. Five sites were short-listed: London, Madrid, Moscow, New York and Paris. A very *sovyetski* chair could have called for a majority vote on "Moscow, yes-or-no?" but the outcome would have been pretty meaningless. Another might have suggested "Paris or New York?" but that too would have been inadequate. In other words, reducing a multi-option debate to a two-option majority vote may well introduce a distortion.[2]

A more serious example occurred in October 2002 when the UN Security Council debated Resolution 1441 on Iraq. The debate was complex. The outcome could have involved any combination of more/fewer sanctions, inspections, diplomatic efforts and/or threats or promises of war. Yet only one resolution was on the table: "1441, yes-or-no?" In effect, and in retrospect, that use of the majority vote was one of the many causes of the 2003 war. (See also Sect. 2.5.2)

Not only did the UN practise majoritarianism, so too did the protagonists. Without knowing all the facts which were at Prime Minister Tony Blair's disposal, the UK parliament took a majority vote on whether or not to go to war.[3] Meanwhile, in the enemy camp, Tariq Aziz, the Iraqi Foreign Minister said, 'Being a member of the government, I had a moral responsibility to defend the government. I asked

---

[2] The IOC used three plurality votes followed by one majority vote, with the supposedly least popular option dropping out at each round. Doubtless because of the frailties of such a procedure, the results of all but the last round were kept secret.

[3] On 18.3.2003, the House of Commons voted by 412 to 219 to say (a) it 'regrets... it has not proved possible to secure a second Resolution in the UN,'– yet a second resolution was not even debated, not, that is, in formal session; and (b) it 'supports the decision [to] use all means necessary to ensure the disarmament of Iraq's weapons of mass destruction.' Two days later, Iraq was invaded.

Hansard, http://hansard.millbanksystems.com/commons/2003/mar/18/iraq-1
(Accessed 19 Jan. 2010).

Saddam Hussein not to invade Kuwait, but I had to support the decision of the majority.' (The *Guardian*, 6.8.2010)

1.1.2.5 The Will of Parliament

How, then, can the collective will of, let us say, a parliament be identified? In effect, should the question posed in the Preface be asked: "Are you left-wing or right-wing?"

Consider an example on the cost of a dog license, and assume that the two extreme options mooted in debate are £100 and zero. If I want to know the average will of parliament, I could ask all the individual members to state their preference – to the nearest pound would be sufficient – and then work it out. Or I could do it democratically, by asking them to vote.

Now I could resort to a majority vote and pose the choice: 'Should it be £100 or nothing?' If I do this, however, then no matter what the outcome or how big the majority, the answer is almost bound to be wrong. So I could ask a different question: 'Is the average opinion £40?' If a majority says 'yes', then perhaps this is the correct answer. *Perhaps.* So a majority vote can perhaps be used to *confirm* a majority opinion – although, even then, one cannot be sure – but the point is this: majority voting cannot be used to *identify* the consensus opinion of the House; in fact, it cannot even facilitate the identification of the *majority* opinion. The identification takes place earlier, if at all, in some committee room, when someone either guesses or decides, for whatever reason, that a dog license fee of £40 would or should get majority support.

In politics, then, a majority vote is often a methodology by which a few can decide what they want the will of parliament to be. All too often, the answer is the question; majority voting gives far too much power to those who set that question.

1.1.2.6 Bitter Arguments

Not for these reasons alone, decision-making by majority vote is often very adversarial. It is yes-or-no, for-or-against. It "forces" people to take sides. No wonder the methodology is so alien to other cultures.

> '"The elders sit under the big tree and talk until they agree." This "talking until you agree" is the essential of the traditional African concept of democracy.' President Julius Nyerere. (Sigmund 1966: 197)
> 'Every village practices democracy. But do they in these village meetings apply the practice of voting? Of free-fight liberalism, where half plus one is always right? No... Everybody says something different until at one time a compromise is achieved out of all these different opinions, without voting.' President Sukarno. (*Ibid*: 62)

In most political forums, the nature of the debate is in part determined by the decision-making process to be used at its conclusion. If everyone knows it is going to be a two-option, zero-sum contest in which the winner wins everything and the loser gets nothing, the debate itself will invariably be bitter and polarized.

We are subjective creatures. But we set the objective rules and procedures. In other words, we ourselves determine that which then determines us. If an adversarial voting system is used at the end of the debate, the debate itself (of which more in Chap. 5) will also be adversarial. If resort is made to an improved decision-making process, (for which see Chap. 2), a more constructive exchange might develop (see Chap. 6). Before all of that, however, a few more of the serious consequences of majority voting must first be considered.

1.1.2.7 Turkeys for Christmas

In many plural societies, and especially in many conflict zones, the protagonists believe in the right of the majority. So they fight over the location of their constituency boundaries.

> When the Balkans started to implode, one Vladimir Gligorov asked, 'Why should I be a minority in your state, when you can be a minority in mine?' (Woodward 1995: 108)

In 1988, Ante Marković wanted an all-Yugoslav referendum, but Slovenia applied the veto and 2 years later held its own poll instead. (Emerson P 1999: 62) At that time too, in Northern Ireland the unionists wanted a vote in NI only while the republicans argued for an all-island electorate. Perhaps the most bizarre use of the referendum in this regard took place in 1991 in the USSR when Mikhail Gorbachev held an all-Soviet vote on the subject of maintaining the Union: six republics boycotted the poll while four changed the question and, despite winning the vote with a majority of 105 million, he still lost the Union. (See also chronology, 1991, Armenia.)

Once the constituency boundaries have been resolved by fair means or foul, the majority will vote "yes" because they know they will win. And the minority will probably not vote. After all, what is the point in voting if you know you are going to lose?

In the 1973 border poll in Northern Ireland, the Social Democratic and Labour Party, SDLP, organized a boycott. In Croatia's referendum in 1990, the Serbs abstained. The Croats did the same one week earlier in the *Krajina*, (three predominantly Serb-populated areas of Croatia, until two of them were "ethnically cleansed" in 1995). In Bosnia's ballot, it was again the Serbs who abstained. In Serbia's poll, the Kosovars stayed at home. In Kosova, the Serbs were inactive. While in Macedonia, both the Albanians and the Serbs abstained. Used in this way, the majority vote is hardly a tool of reconciliation, and yet it is still being promoted as such, as in the 2002 Machakos Protocol on South Sudan and the Abuja talks on Darfur. (See Sect. 1.2.4.2)

1.1.2.8 The Answer is Indeed the Question

Given that a majority vote cannot be used to *identify* "the will of the people" or "the will of their parliament" – indeed, it cannot even be used to identify "the will of a majority" – the actual business of policy making must lie elsewhere, in the cabinet or some inner party caucus. Admittedly, there might then follow a majority vote, either in a national referendum or in a parliamentary division. Usually, however, the supposedly democratic outcome sheds remarkably little light on what is actually the opinion of society or its parliament.

Take, for example, the Welsh referendum of 1997. The people were given the choice of voting either for policy **A**, the *status quo*, or for policy **B**, devolution. In the event 51% voted for option **B**, and 49% for option **A**. So **B** won.

What would have happened if a third policy **C** had been on the ballot paper? *Plaid Cymru*, the Welsh Nationalist Party, had actually asked for a four-option ballot and pointed out that, 'A simple "Yes/No" to an inadequate assembly is no choice at all.' (Wigley 1996: 11) Well, if just three per cent had opted for option **C**, then, in a plurality vote, **B** might have gained only 48%, so **A** might have won instead. Logically, therefore, the actual vote says very little. Perhaps 3% wanted **C** or possibly all 51% wanted **C** and maybe nobody wanted **B** at all. But **B** won. From the results themselves, we simply do not know what the people wanted. The outcome of that vote reveals only one thing which is definite: it does not say, "The Welsh want autonomy"; rather, it says, "Blair wants the Welsh to want autonomy."

The conclusion is stark: the majority vote is not very democratic. It is a means by which those in power may, and often do, manipulate the rest. Sometimes, admittedly, they do it benevolently; it is still manipulation. At other times, they are distinctly malevolent: two-option referendums have been used by such notable figures (in reverse chronological order) as Slobodan Milošević, Augusto Pinochet, Adolf Hitler, Benito Mussolini and Napoleon Bonaparte. (For a summary of these "democratic dictators," see App. A.)

Now maybe the most popular opinion in Wales in 1997 was indeed option **B**, but *maybe* it was not, and that is the crux. In society's attempt to identify the Welsh consensus, or even the Welsh majority viewpoint, the two-option vote did not really help for the answer tells us so little. (App. B gives a full list of referendums where 51% or less beat 49% or more; and for a brief view at how a difference of only one vote can sometimes change the course of history, see App. C.)

If the outcome is tight, the answer means next to nothing; but even if the outcome is a majority of 90% or more, the answer may still mean very little. In Algeria in 1962, on an 80% turnout, a majority of 96.7% said they wanted what Gen. Charles de Gaulle wanted them to want, namely, an independent Algeria with French economic privileges and military bases and nuclear test sites. As history very quickly showed, they actually wanted something else. (Emerson R 1966: 75)

Admittedly, in a nation-wide poll, there is at least a chance that the people will refuse to be manipulated, and thankfully, a few "democratic leaders" have failed to get their way, as the following examples show.

1.1 An Historical Perspective

- Chile. Augusto Pinochet lost a referendum in 1988 and so fell from power; (to be a dictator who cannot dictate properly must be a little humiliating). (App. A)
- Zimbabwe. In 2000, Robert Mugabe lost a referendum on the constitution by 55–45%, but the vote was non-binding.
- Canada. Quebec's Jacques Parizeau failed to manipulate thrice, in 1980, 1992 and 1995. (Sect. 1.2.6 and App. B)
- Ireland. Éamon de Valera lost and won in 1959. He tried to persuade the Irish to vote both for his presidential candidacy and to change the electoral system from proportional representation – single transferable vote, PR-STV, to first-past-the-post, FPP. The people, however, liked him but not this policy, so he was elected but his referendum was lost. This vote 'indicated an independence of mind and a degree of political maturity which should be welcomed even by those who disagree with the decision.' (Lakeman 1974: 267)

1.1.2.9 Order, Order

As noted above, some country-wide polls may mean very little, especially if conducted by majority voting. In those parliaments where, in addition, the party whips come into play, many majority decisions mean even less. If the cabinet chooses a policy, and if the government (party X) has a majority in the House, parliament can debate the issue if it wants to. Alas, when it comes to the vote, party X votes for option A, anybody else may vote against, but because party X has a majority, party X (nearly) always wins.

Originally, as mentioned in the beginning of this chapter, democracy was meant to be a means by which society could distinguish between right and wrong, between the correct and incorrect ways of organizing its affairs. Today, in contrast, though still in the name of democracy, MPs in many European jurisdictions are often asked to vote not according to their consciences but in line with the dictates of the party whip. Others elsewhere, like Uganda's President Yoweri Museveni, prefer a different system: 'On the question of how issues are decided on in parliament... the members should vote as individuals, according to their own judgment on the issue – what is called a "free vote" in a multi-party system.' (Museveni 1997: 195)

1.1.2.10 A Further Disorder

Imagine a parliament in which party X has a majority of 60% and party Y just 40%. If 70% of party X vote in the party ballot for policy A, the cabinet may well adopt policy A and put it to parliament for the vote. Needless to say, because of the whips, it will probably win any vote by the above margin of 60 to 40.

If, however, 30% of party X and say 90% of party Y are opposed, perhaps the answer should be different. After all, 30% of 60% = 18%, and 90% of 40% = 36%, so a total of (18 + 36) = 54% is opposed to policy A. Yet under a whipped majority vote, policy A still wins.

> ...*as M. Calonne could not depend upon a majority of this Assembly in his favour, he very ingeniously arranged them in such a manner as to make 44 a majority of 140: to effect this, he disposed of them into seven separate committees, of 20 members each.* [In four committees, he appointed 11 of his own + 9 others; and to the other three committees he appointed 0 of his + 20 others.] *Every general question was to be decided, not by a majority of persons, but by a majority of committees; and as 11 votes would make a majority in a committee, and four committees a majority of seven, M. Calonne had good reason to conclude... he could not be outvoted.* (Paine 1985: 97) This tale comes from the not quite democratic goings on in the Assembly of Notables in France in the 1780s.
>
> *In 1994... the central government... re-drew the administrative boundaries of Darfur... The reform divided the Fur, the largest tribe in Darfur, among the three new states and made them minorities in each...* (Flint and de Waal 2008: 56–7)

In many countries, in umpteen parliaments and in numerous companies, organizations and associations, there are those who use and abuse their positions of power to manipulate the wording of motions. As will soon become clear, they can also manipulate the agenda.

1.1.2.11 Murphy's Law

Sometimes, of course, those in power have a very small majority, and even for the likes of M. Calonne, this can make manipulation a little difficult. If, for example, the House has 100 members and the majority of Party X consists of just 51 of them, a switch of but one individual member would be enough to reverse the balance. This is even more likely in a hung parliament when no one party has a clear majority, and such a scenario could make the democratic process vulnerable to the not-so-scrupulous. After all, to take an Irish example, it only requires one or two bribes to get one or two members to abstain or absent themselves, in order to reverse a decision... so no wonder the brown envelopes were passed under the council chamber tables of Dublin Corporation![4] Murphy's law – "What can go wrong will go wrong" – also applies to majoritarian politics.

The United States system is not so strict when it comes to party discipline so US elected representatives have a different practice: logrolling. It works like this: if Ms **J** is interested in nuclear power and Mr **K** is concerned about dog licenses, then both can come to a mutual understanding: Mr **K** votes for **J**'s nukes if Ms **J** votes for **K**'s dog licenses. The conclusion should be another rider to Murphy's law: in majority voting, the outcome of a debate sometimes depends upon those who know or care least about the resolution in question.

---

[4] In the late 1990s, many planning applications were approved in rather dubious circumstances, and a number of politicians received 'payments' equivalent to thousands of pounds.

1.1 An Historical Perspective

> *You must vote yes or no... with the knowledge that it's unlikely to be a compromise that either you or your supporters consider fair or just. In an era of indiscriminate logrolling... you can also rest assured that no matter how many bad provisions there are in the bill, there will be something... that makes the bill painful to oppose.*
> (Obama 2006: 130)
>
> *At Westminster, 'you cannot abstain; [you can] only vote yes or no, [that] or not turn up at all. It prevents MPs from registering that there are alternatives to full support or outright opposition, and is symptomatic of a parliament based on two-party conflict.'* Caroline Lucas MP. (The *Guardian*, 10.9.2010)

1.1.2.12 The Simple Truth?

Because a two-option vote limits the voter's freedom of choice, there are sometimes a number of justifiable, tactical reasons why people vote for "this" and not for "that," (as well as the less justifiable reasons, of course). Going back to Wales for a moment, we can well understand the *C* (independence) supporters who voted for *B* (devolution), given that *C* was not on the ballot paper and that *B* was their obvious next preference. There again, some *C* supporters might have concluded that it would have been better to vote for *A* (the *status quo*), for in the event of *B* losing, the *B* supporters would doubtless have continued to campaign for a further poll, and maybe then there would be *C*, the third option. So a simple majority vote is often not simple at all.

1.1.2.13 The Split

> *The first item on the agenda of any [Irish] Republican organisation is the split.*
> Brendan Behan's famous proverb.

Sooner or later, those who practice majority voting tend to fall into two parties or, if they are already members of a party, into two wings. In Europe at least, 'public opinion seems to manifest a deepseated tendency to divide into two rival major factions...' (Duverger 1955: 387) Sometimes, whole nations divide into two, and not only the US and the UK, for 'The "two blocs" myth... is [also] so prevalent in France...' (*ibid*: 388) and elsewhere.

Where societies are already split, each of the opposing factions tends to divide into two as well. In NI, for instance, the division on one side is made manifest by the Ulster and the Democratic Unionist parties, the UUP and the DUP, while on the other side there is the SDLP and Sinn Féin, SF. In Macedonia, 'Both the Macedonian and the Albanian sides are divided into two', (Šedo 2010: 171). In like manner, in Bosnia, to take a third example, there were invariably two Bosniak parties, two Croat, and two Serb. (Emerson and Šedo 2010: 13) Similarly, in the Middle East,

Palestine divides into Fatah and Hamas; while Israel, despite enjoying a more pluralist electoral system, has its Kadima and Likud parties.

If the final decision is going to be a majority vote between options A and B, each side will try to ensure that it has the internal unity required to outnumber the opposition. What happens, then, when someone in the A camp suggests an alternative policy, option A'? In theory, the supporters of A and those of A' are allies in their struggle against those of B. In practice, it is often the opposite, and majoritarian politics exemplifies the old adage from history: "your neighbour is your enemy, and your enemy's enemies are your friends." The result is often an unholy alliance between the B supporters and either the A or A' supporters; normally, it is between the B supporters and the more extreme of the A or A' supporters. It must also be said that B has a vested interest in creating dissension in the A camp. As will be shown shortly, such policies of divide and rule are an intrinsic part of majority voting.

> *The split between the [German] Social Democrats... and the Communists... paralysed the political strength of the German working class when it alone could have barred Hitler's road to power. ...Stalin must be held to bear his share of responsibility for... Hitler's triumph.* (Deutscher 1982: 400–1)

1.1.2.14 The Unholy Alliance

Sometimes there is an unholy war between the supporters of A and those of A', and an unholy alliance between those of B and A'. On other occasions, such alliances only become apparent after the relevant vote.

Going back to the earlier example of dog licenses (Sect. 1.1.2.5) we could use a majority vote to ask if every MP thought the cost should be £40. This could mean, of course, that those who thought this price was too high would then form an unholy alliance with those who considered it too low, and both would vote against. This is yet another disadvantage of majority voting.

> *[In Switzerland] the 1992 campaign against membership in the International Monetary Fund, [IMF], and the World Bank, for example, was waged by an alliance of opposites.* (Kobach 1994: 134)
>
> *[The 1992 referendum in Ireland on abortion] aligned liberals and ultra-conservatives against moderate conservatives.* (Gallagher 1996: 97)
>
> In the 1998 NI, referendum the 29% minority who voted against the Good Friday Agreement included extreme nationalists like Ruairí Ó Brádaigh and extreme unionists like Paisley – a most unholy alliance.

1.1.2.15 The Two-Option Dichotomy

Alliances both holy and unholy exist, and tactical voting occurs, mainly when people are unable to vote sincerely – i.e., as they would really wish to vote – because their particular first preference options, option C or perhaps D, are not included on the ballot paper. In short, majoritarian politics often reduces what should be a multi-option question into a two-option choice, and many political debates are seen in terms of *either* black *or* white, even when there is no question of right or wrong, and often when there is a considerable amount of grey.

There are, in fact, very few political questions which are inevitably of a two-option variety. One glaring exception, which is definitely black or white, is the question: "Which side of the road shall we drive on?" Only one country, Sweden, has ever put this question to the people in a referendum. Yet even then, the electorate had the offer of a third option: left, right, and blank. Thus in 1955, 82.9% said, let us stay on the left; 15.5% said, we should drive on the right; while 1.6% handed in a blank ballot, thereby to suggest, perhaps, that though they supported the democratic process, on this particular question they were indifferent. (Not that any of this mattered because the politicians had already decided that Sweden would drive on the right, regardless.)

In practice, then, many political questions are drafted in a two-option format and, as a result, they are often loaded one way or the other. If the question were asked correctly, however, there could well be more than two options "on the table." Policies on hanging, for example, should not be resolved via the yes-or-no closed question: "Should capital punishment be used for those convicted of first degree murder?" Instead, the question should be re-phrased on perhaps the following lines: "How should society deal with the convicted first degree murderer?" If such were the case, there could then be a pluralist debate on such issues as civil service orders, open/closed prison terms, restorative justice etc., and not only on executions.

Similarly, policies on nuclear power need not be subject to questions of a "do-or-do-not" variety. The topic should be covered in a more comprehensive manner and alternative energy sources, for example, could be considered at the same time. Indeed, if there had been such a debate – to take the UK example – the outcome could well have been very different from that which has transpired, a most extreme nuclear option: fission power *and* fusion power *and* atomic bombs *and* nuclear re-processing.

1.2 Horrendous Consequences of Majoritarianism

A number of countries have suffered from the divisive nature of majoritarian decision-making structures: some have descended into violence at the prospect or as a consequence of a referendum; others have divided without any vote at all.

1.2.1 Rwanda, the "Land of a Thousand Hills"

In 1892, at the Battle of Mengo in today's Uganda, a violent clash took place between two groups of Africans. One was the *wafaranza,* who spoke French; they had been converted to Christianity by the White Fathers so they were Catholic.

Those in the other 'tribe' had been educated by Scottish Presbyterians: the *waingereza*, English-speaking Protestants. (Pakenham 1991: 424–6) The result was war: Catholics fighting Protestants, not unlike twentieth century Belfast, a battle caused by a (religious) mind-set which was entirely European.

The background to a more recent tragedy started in 1926 when the Belgian authorities in Rwanda introduced ID cards. By this means, they perpetuated a system of minority rule, a pyramid in which they stood at the top. The next layer down, the middle class, they called the Tutsis, and these were often very tall people; the rest, the workers, were the stockier Hutu. (A third tribal group, if indeed such distinctions were/are possible, were the Twa, but they constituted a very small minority and were ignored.) So cards were issued on the basis of a closed question: are you tall or small? In cases of doubt, for people of average build, a second question was asked as if it were closed: how many cows do you have? If ten or more, the interviewee was declared to be Tutsi, if nine or less, Hutu. (Reader 1998: 616)

Thus, in a country where so many villages were mixed, where almost uniquely in sub-Saharan Africa, everyone spoke the same language – Kinyarwanda – and where over the years countless had intermarried, a social distinction was turned into a tribal one.

After WWII, we Europeans changed our minds: we now advocated not minority rule but its polar opposite, majority rule, democracy. So the losers of yesterday could become the winners of to-morrow. When the *Interahamwe* launched their dreadful genocide in 1994, the slogan they used was, *'Rubanda nyamwinshi'*, the majority people. (Prunier 1995a: 183) To a large extent, therefore that massacre was caused by a (political) mind-set which was entirely European.[5]

1.2.2 The Middle East

A belief in majoritarianism is an underlying obstacle to the ideal answer of the Middle East question: a one-state solution. Both Palestine and Israel consider majority rule to be the basis upon which a democracy should operate. In consequence, neither considers the one-state option, and nor will they unless perhaps they

---

[5] In the hope of overcoming the legacy of the genocide, the Rwandan Government has initiated a process called *gacaca* (Sect. 1.1) based on their traditional methodology of conflict resolution. Like mini-Peace and Reconciliation Commissions, these meet throughout the country in order to identify not the leaders but the foot soldiers of the *Interahamwe*, then to administer restorative justice to the guilty. To see how the process was being received, the National Unity and Reconciliation Commission, NURC, initiated a nation-wide survey which was funded by the British and Swedish governments. The report, a European's analysis of several binary questions (Republic of Rwanda 2003: annex 4) was published in 2003 at a press conference in Kigali, which the author attended. When the debate was opened to the floor, one participant remarked, 'Asking yes-or-no questions in very unAfrican'.

1.2 Horrendous Consequences of Majoritarianism   17

think they are in a permanent and unassailable majority. Thus many Israelis insist 'that implementation of the Palestinian right of return is not compatible with the survival of a democratic Jewish majority state.' (The *Guardian*, 25.1.2011) The phrase is oxymoronic, twice: the state cannot be democratic (1) if it is only for the Jews or (2) if it is only for the majority.

For the moment, it seems the best that can be hoped for are two mutually antagonistic theocratic states (worshipping the same deity), both of which claim the mantle "democratic." If for no other reason than to help the resolution of this ancient conflict, the word "democracy" definitely needs to be more precisely defined.

1.2.3 The Right of Self-Determination

With multi-option voting, even on divisive constitutional issues, the collective decision is unlikely to be the worst of all options: war. In two-option voting, in contrast, violence is often a direct consequence of such ballots. Indeed, in situations where voters are known to be divided by strong feelings of ethno-nationalism and/or religion, the holding of a two-option plebiscite may be most unwise, for the consequences of a stark *A* or *B* question may be, and often are, dreadful. Are you Catholic or Protestant? Serb or Croat? Hutu or Tutsi? These were all questions of war, as too was the choice during the Cold War: are you communist or capitalist?

The disadvantages of such two-option referendums are obvious. Anyone who might wish to vote for a compromise is, as it were, disenfranchised. Furthermore, the democratic process itself sometimes acts as an instrument of "ethnic cleansing": if you are clean (sic) you can vote, one way or the other; if, however, you are the partner in, or the child of, a mixed marriage, or if you are a member of another minority, you are not entitled to a free, sincere vote. The democratic process "forces" people either to abstain or, as in war, to take sides. In the Balkans, for example, 'the EC's [European Community's] insistence on referendums... provided the impetus... to expel people from their homes and jobs on the basis of their ethnicity and to create ethnically pure areas through population transfers and expulsions as a prelude to a vote.' (Woodward 1995: 271) The final cost was horrible: 'all the wars in the former Yugoslavia started with a referendum.' (*Oslobodjenje*, Sarajevo's now legendary newspaper, 7.2.1999.)

Thus the prospect of a referendum and this belief in majority voting often provoked people to commit acts of ethnic cleansing before the vote, so to ensure that they would then gain the necessary majority. In the Caucasus,[6] the vote usually

---

[6] In 1990, at the invitation of the late Zurab Zhvania MP, the author gave a press conference in Tbilisi, in Russian, on the need for a non-majoritarian form of governance.

came after the war: in Abhazia[7] and South Ossetia in Georgia,[8] and in Nagorno-Karabakh[9] in Azerbaijan.

Similar tensions from government-sponsored transmigration and religious battles have been witnessed in Indonesia where too there has been talk of referendums in Ache, Ambon and West Papua (Irian Jaya). Ignoring the dangers of contagion both within the archipelago of over 3,000 inhabited islands let alone further afield, it was nevertheless decided to hold a ballot in Timor-Leste (East Timor). In effect, in a jurisdiction where there has been considerable friction between Moslems and Christians, this 1999 referendum allowed the Catholic Timorese to be separate from the Moslem Timorese. I do not wish to ignore the horrors of the 1975 invasion; I simply stress the frailties of the two-option majority vote. In the wake of the poll, violence erupted.

1.2.4 International Diplomacy

Despite all its inadequacies, the two-option referendum is still advocated as a suitable tool in some, but not all, peace processes. It was most definitely not included in the 1995 Dayton talks on Bosnia, but it was on the agenda in Northern Ireland in 1998, in discussions on Kosova in the same year, and then, in July 2002, in the negotiations on the civil war in Sudan.

1.2.4.1 Kosova or Kosovo?

In February 1999, talks on the future of Kosovo took place in Rambouillet, and hence the agreement of that name.[10] It included a clause to suggest that Kosovo should hold a referendum on independence. Kosova had in fact already held such a poll, in 1991, at which time 99% of an 87% turnout – i.e., the Albanian speakers – had voted in favour. The West had refused to recognize that particular ballot, but now, apparently, they had changed their minds on the matter: so they proposed a further plebiscite in 3 years time. Knowing what the outcome was bound

---

[7] On 3.10.1999, in an 88% turnout, 97% of the electorate in Abhazia voted for independence; the presidential elections were held on the same day and, in a throw back to Soviet times, there was only one candidate. He won by 99%.

[8] South Ossetia has had four referendums since 1990, two of them in 2006: the South Ossetians voted for independence in one and boycotted the other, while the Georgians voted to federate with Georgia in the second ballot and boycotted the first.

[9] By the time of the vote in Nagorno-Karabakh, the minority was in exile, or dead. On 10.12.1991, in an 82% turnout, 108,615 people voted 'for' and only 24 voted 'against' independence: that is 99.89% to 0.02%.

[10] Kosova is the preferred Albanian spelling; Kosovo or Kosovo-Metohija is more frequently used by the Serbs.

to be, Milošević refused to sign, and doubtless his immediate successor, Vojislav Koštunica, would also have objected. NATO, the North Atlantic Treaty Organization, went to war. Milošević still refused. NATO continued to bomb. Eventually the Russian foreign minister, Viktor Chernomyrdin, went to Belgrade, the clause on the proposed referendum was dropped from the agreement, and Milošević now signed.[11] In this respect, then, the war achieved nothing. (Emerson P 1999: 49 *et seq*.)

1.2.4.2 Sudan

With British officials in attendance, the two sides to the civil war in Sudan – the Khartoum government and the Sudan People's Liberation Army, SPLA, along with its political wing, the SPLM or Movement – signed the Machakos Protocol. *Inter alia*, this was to give South Sudan the possibility of a referendum on secession, later scheduled for January, 2011. So what were/are the consequences?

First, if one part of Sudan can have its own way, why not another? A recipe for Balkanization. Sure enough, 6 months after the Machakos Protocol was signed, there was renewed violence in the already troubled region of Darfur, this time from a carbon copy of the SPLA/M, the SLA/M, the Sudan Liberation Army/Movement. Originally, 'Darfur was an ethnic mosaic, not a land divided along binary lines of fracture.' (Prunier 2005: 23) Today, albeit with splits and factions almost too numerous to count, the conflict has taken on an Arab versus Bantu character. Therefore, any use of a two-option vote in Darfur would be foolhardy at best, yet this was the methodology chosen by delegates at the Abuja talks of 2006 – not on secession this time but on autonomy – where again British diplomats were in attendance.

A second consequence is that 'if the South were to secede this would open a Pandora's box in the whole of Sudan.' (Othieno 2007: 280–1). And maybe too elsewhere. At the time of going to press, with the Jan. 2011 ballot still being counted, a further referendum has already been scheduled and postponed for Abyei, an oil-rich area straddling the North-South border which was given special administrative status in the 2005 Comprehensive Peace Agreement, CPA. Some violence has already been reported there. At the same time, the districts of South Kurdufan and Blue Nile are due to hold popular consultations, which may lead to a further break-up of Sudan.

Thirdly, the religious divide in Africa is made more stark as North Sudan moves closer to a more comprehensively sharia state, (The *Guardian*, 20.12.2010).

A fourth consequence relates to other countries in Africa and the first knock-on effect has already taken place: Somaliland wants to break away from the rest of Somalia, again by referendum. What the consequences might be in Côte d'Ivoire,

---

[11] Admittedly, there were many other points of contention. The present text relates only to the referendum.

where a postponed and disputed 2010 presidential election has led to violence and fears of renewed civil war, remain to be seen. (Sect. 3.3.2.2) In Nigeria, too, there are tensions between a Moslem North and a Christian South, with much recent loss of life in the city of Jos, which straddles the two. As in Sudan, so too here and elsewhere in Africa, politicians may seek to use the referendum, this most unAfrican methodology, to take advantage of religious and tribal divides. The effects in the Democratic Republic of the Congo, DRC, for example, or even South Africa, could be horrific.

Now it may be that the referendum in South Sudan is peaceful, that as expected a huge majority opts for independence, and that the transition to independence takes place smoothly. Let us hope so. That is not to say that a resolution of the South Sudan problem could not have been achieved by a more peaceful voting methodology. Twenty years earlier, many thought the 1990 referendum in Slovenia was also successful; for Yugoslavia as a whole, in contrast, it was a disaster.

1.2.5 The Minority of the Minority

In numerous charters and declarations, leaders and lawyers have stressed that, 'All peoples have the right of self-determination. By virtue of that right, they freely determine their political status...'[12] Unfortunately, to put it at its mildest, it has invariably been assumed that such a right is to be exercised by a majority vote, even though the voters are hardly *free* to choose as they would wish if those in power have restricted their choice to just two options.

In practice, this right means that if a majority in a large country wants to live in that state, then they may. However, if a minority in a small part of the large country wants to opt out and have their own small nation, then, if a majority of that minority so decides, they may. This might leave a disgruntled minority of that minority. And if, in a tiny bit of the small nation, a majority of the minority of the minority want to opt out of opting out and opt back in again, then they may too. So it goes on, like those famous Russian dolls,[13] *ad infinitum*, until there is a majority of two and a minority of none, i.e. until throughout the world every couple is an independent nation state of only two people!

---

[12] Article 1.1 of the International Covenant on Civil and Political Rights was adopted by the UN General Assembly in 1996. The right of self-determination was first introduced by President Woodrow Wilson as one of his fourteen points in 1916. He later reflected, 'I never knew that there were a million Germans in Bohemia.' (Eban 1998: 38)

[13] In Russia, the term used is '*matrioshka* nationalism'. (Reid 2002: 136)

1.2 Horrendous Consequences of Majoritarianism

Table 1.1 Some actual and possible secessions (possible secessions are shown in brackets)

Large	Average	Small
UK	Ireland	NI
USSR	Georgia	Abhazia
		South Ossetia
		(Ajaria)
	Azerbaijan	Nagorno-Karabakh
	Moldova	Trans-Dnestr
Yugoslavia	Croatia	*Krajina*
	Bosnia	*Republika Srpska*
		(Herzeg-Bosna)
	Serbia	Kosova
		(*Sandžak*)
		(*Preševo* Valley)
Indonesia	(Timor)	Timor-Leste
	(Ache)	–
	(Ambon)	–
	(Papua)	West Papua or Irian Jaya
Sudan	North Sudan	(South Kurdufan) (Blue Nile)
	South Sudan	(Abyei)
	(Darfur)	–

It should also be pointed out that this right of self-determination was originally intended for the resolution of an external problem, colonialism, not for the facilitation of a settlement in any internal conflict.

1.2.6 Repeat Referendums

Despite its many faults, people still believe in and use majority voting. Sometimes, as has been noted, it does not give the politicians the answer they want, but that's democracy. Or is it? For in such scenarios, the government of the day sometimes just waits awhile, tweaks the ballot question a little, and has another vote.

- Denmark needed two votes to adopt the Maastricht treaty.
- Ireland required two to get its divorce legislation through.
- Canada. Quebec (Sect. 1.1.2.8 and App. B) has had three referendums on independence already, and there is some demand for another.
- Northern Ireland. According to the Belfast Agreement, NI will have one, or two, or as many polls as are necessary, a referendum every 7 years or so until eventually there is a united Ireland. Such a process, a 7-year-itch if you like, is not so much a referendum but a "never-end-um."[14]

---

[14] The phrase was first used by some wit on BBC Radio 4.

1.3 Conclusions

A majority vote is fair, probably, if and when only two options are possible. Such occasions are, or should be, rare. Majority voting does work to some extent, of course. In the Welsh debate of Sect. 1.1.2.8, it is possible to say that, when confronted by a straight choice between *A* and *B*, the people preferred *B*, (we think), for reasons either tactical or sincere.

Consider another example. In 1989, the Swiss held a referendum on whether or not to scrap the army. By 64 to 36%, the answer was no. However, the mere fact that quite a large number wanted to abolish it suggested to the powers that be that a reduced military budget might be advisable. Such a conclusion implied, of course, that it might have been better to have held a multi-option vote on a range of military budget proposals, an alternative that will be considered in Chap. 2.

There is one further possibility: the two-option majority vote need not be a means of manipulation if the authors of the question were either the judges in a truly independent commission or, indeed, members of the public. Both of these measures belong to an improved democratic framework.

> *Majority rule works only when the minority has such confidence in the ultimate reasonableness of the majority and such conviction of the ultimate community of majority and minority interests that it can afford to respect the right of the majority to rule without undue obstruction... Indeed, majority rule has no valid claim of legitimacy apart from the existence of a basic moral consensus.* Inis L. Claude Jr.. (Emerson R 1966: 331)

Given the many defects of majority voting, why is it that parliaments and international forums still use this methodology? Part of the answer is all too simple: vested interest. 'The IMF and World Bank... allocated power not on the basis of "one country, one vote," like the UN General Assembly, but rather on the size of each country's economy...' (Klein 2007: 163) 'To pass a substantial resolution... requires an 85% majority. The US alone, which possesses more than 15% of the stock in both organizations, can block a resolution supported by every other member state.' (Monbiot 2003: 16) Thus the US, with a 17% share of the vote, has the ultimate power of veto, not least on any suggestion as to changing the rules on decision-making.

Other vested interests rule in parliaments, such that the beneficiaries of a rotten system can vote against any attempts at modernization. Sometimes, however, they are the victims of their own bigotry. In 2003, when the British parliament debated the question of Lords reform – a topic that has been discussed umpteen times over the course of the last century – there were seven options. So the House intended to take seven majority votes. In the debate beforehand, Lord Meghnad Desai intervened: 'The proposed voting procedure is the daftest I have seen in a long time and will not result in a decision being arrived at. The right way... is to ask all of us to rank the seven options from one to seven and then add up those rankings. If one's most preferred option is ranked one and one's least preferred option is ranked seven... the option with the lowest ranking is the preferred option.' (*Hansard*,

22.1.2003) In other words, he proposed a Borda count, BC. His suggestion was ignored.

The Commons refined the seven options to a list of five: all elected, all appointed, and in between 80/20, 50/50 and 20/80. They then took five majority votes. All were lost. Crisis, they said. (Emerson P 2005: 276) Shortly afterwards, the late Robin Cook MP tried to introduce (an unspecified form of) preference voting, but in vain: most politicians are firmly wedded to the majority vote. He later explained that his reform 'would have involved the technological development of a pencil and a piece of paper, which was far too big a step for our parliament and its medieval procedures.'[15]

References

Aristotle (1992) The politics. Penguin Classics, London
Davies JK (1993) Democracy and classical Greece. Fontana, London
Deutscher I (1982) Stalin. Pelican, Harmondsworth
Duverger M (1955) Political parties. Methuen & Co., London
Eban A (1998) Diplomacy for the next century. Yale University Press, New Haven
Emerson P (1999) From Belfast to the Balkans. The de Borda Institute, Belfast
Emerson P (2005) Reforming the house of lords: choosing from the options. Representation 41(4):276–285
Emerson P, Šedo J (2010) Electoral systems and the link to the party systems. In: Stojarová V, Emerson P (eds) Party politics in the Western Balkans. Routledge, Abingdon
Emerson R (1966) From empire to nation. Beacon, Boston
Flint J, de Waal A (2008) Darfur, a new history of a long war. Zed Books, London
Gallagher M (1996) Ireland: the referendum as a conservative device? In: Gallagher M, Uleri PV (eds) The referendum experience in Europe. Macmillan Press, London
Kapuściński R (2002) The shadow of the sun. Penguin, London
Klein N (2007) The shock doctrine. Penguin, London
Kobach KW (1994) Switzerland. In: Butler D, Ranney A (eds) Referendums around the world. The AEI Press, Washington
Lakeman E (1974) How democracies vote. Faber and Faber, London
Lijphart A (1999) Patterns of democracy. Yale University Press, New Haven and London
Lloyd GER (2008) Democracy, philosophy and science in ancient Greece. In: Dunn J (ed) Democracy, the unfinished journey, 508 BC to AD 1993. Oxford University Press, Oxford
Mandela N (1994) Long walk to freedom. Little Brown and Company, London
Monbiot G (2003) The age of consent. Flamingo, London
Museveni YK (1997) Sowing the mustard seed. Macmillan, London
Nerburn K (1999) The wisdom of the native Americans. New World Library Novato, California
Obama B (2006) The audacity of hope. Three Rivers Press, New York
Othieno T (2007) Democracy and security in East Africa. In: Matlosa K et al (eds) Challenges of conflict, democracy and development in Africa. EISA, Johannesburg
Paine T (1985) Rights of man, Part II. Penguin, London
Pakenham T (1991) The scramble for Africa. Abacus, London

---

[15] From an interview conducted in February 2005. <http://www.unlockdemocracy.org.uk/wp-content/uploads/2007/01/2-robin-cook.pdf> Accessed 23 May 2010.

Prunier G (1995) The Rwanda crisis. C. Hurst and Co., London
Prunier G (2005) Darfur, the ambiguous genocide. C. Hurst and Co., London
Reader J (1998) Africa. Penguin, London
Reid A (2002) The Shaman's coat, a native history of Siberia. Phoenix, London
Republic of Rwanda (2003) Participation in gacaca and national reconciliation. NURC, Kigali
Riker WH (1988) Liberalism against populism. Waveland Press, Long Grove
Šedo J (2010) The party system in Macedonia. In: Stojarová V, Emerson P (eds) Party politics in the Western Balkans. Routledge, Abingdon
Sigmund PE (ed) (1966) The ideologies of the developing nations. Frederick A. Praeger, New York
Wigley D (1996) A real choice for Wales. Plaid Cymru, Cardiff
Woodward SL (1995) Balkan tragedy. The Brookings Institution, Washington

Chapter 2
Pluralist Decision-Making

It is a superstition and an ungodly thing to believe that an act of a majority binds a minority.
Mohandas K Gandhi. (Sigmund 1966: 81)

Abstract Chapter 1 showed that, in many circumstances, majority voting is both inadequate and inaccurate. It is 'fit for purpose' (a) if the subject is not controversial and the minority is willing to accept the outcome; (b) if and when only two options are possible, and such occasions should be rare in any democracy which aspires to be plural. Accordingly, this chapter starts by trying to define decision-making.

There are better ways of resolving disputes. The text first looks at the theory and practice of improved forms of majority voting, before next conducting a similar analysis of the best known methodologies of multi-option voting. Then consensus voting in all its roles is examined. Finally, the text offers a draft definition of democratic decision-making.

2.1 Decision-Making: the Ideal Defined

If democracy is for everybody and not just a majority, if in other words it is more than just majority rule, and if a democratic opinion can best be *identified* by something more accurate than a two-option majority vote, then what *should* be the basis of a democracy, and how best should its principles be effected?

In his 1863 Gettysburg address, Abraham Lincoln famously said that 'Government of the people, by the people and for the people shall not perish from the earth.' The phrase 'of, by and for' refers to everyone, not just the largest faction. In theory, therefore, democratic decisions should be in line with public opinion, *vox populi*, or what Jean-Jacques Rousseau called the general will, *la volonté générale*. Unfortunately, however, 'Though he was at pains to stress that the general will was not

Fig. 2.1 A voters' profile

	Preferences							
-	1st	2nd	3rd	4th	5th	6th	7th	8th
Ms J	*F*	*D*	*G*	*B*	*H*	*A*	*C*	*E*
Mr K	*A*	*B*	*D*	*E*	*H*	*F*	*G*	*C*
Ms L	*C*	*H*	*G*	*D*	*E*	*B*	*A*	*F*

necessarily the will of the majority, the term passed quickly into normal usage as meaning just that.' (Doyle 1990: 53)

A general will or common consensus often involves an accommodation or a compromise, and it is probably fair to say that in questions which do not involve a stark choice between right and wrong – in other words, in numerous if not indeed most political controversies – an accommodation should be both feasible and advisable. To take a hypothetical example, consider a committee of three people, Messrs J, K and L, choosing one of eight possible options: *A, B, C, D, E, F, G* and *H*, and let us suppose their preferences are as shown in Fig. 2.1.

Because Ms J's second preference is the same as Mr K's third preference and Ms L's fourth, that particular option, *D*, shown in tint, would seem to be the obvious choice.

In theory, the democratic process should allow all participants, (a) to freely express their opinions, and (b) to have an equal influence on the final decision. In the above example, with Messrs J, K and L all having their say, such a process should lead to the most acceptable outcome, where perhaps nobody wins everything but everybody wins something.

This sort of outcome can sometimes be achieved without voting at all, by just talking the matter through "under the big tree" until all agree to a compromise, a process sometimes known as a verbal consensus. As will be shown below, it can also be expedited by a voting process. Either procedure is feasible; they are both democratic; and, if done correctly, both should facilitate the identification of (roughly) the same outcome.

These principles prompt the following definition of democratic decision-making. Subject to certain limitations which should be laid down in human rights legislation, democratic decision-making is a process which identifies:

(a) either the unanimous viewpoint (where such exists);
(b) or, on more controversial issues, the average opinion or consensus;
(c) or, on very contentious issues and especially in any plural society, the most acceptable compromise.

In (b) and (c), the process involves both a willingness to compromise and a degree of give and take. So those who believe that "politics is the art of the possible" should find a consensus democracy fairly attractive. Accordingly, consideration will now be given, first to some improvements on the simple, two-option majority vote, and secondly, to some multi-option voting procedures. The best of these might indeed form part of a consensual polity.

2.2 Majority Voting: Theory and Practice

As noted in the conclusions to Chap. 1, majority voting *can* work, when those who set the question are benevolent and/or intuitive, or when the question is posed by a neutral player such as a really independent commission – some independent commissions are not quite as independent as they should be[1] – or via a group of concerned individuals mounting their own citizens' initiative. This last-named procedure consists of a petition which, if sufficiently well supported, then goes to a binding referendum on the issue raised.

In these citizens' initiatives, there is little to stop certain interests, including the political ones, from getting involved as well. Indeed, experience suggests they often do exactly that. Nevertheless, on balance, it seems the availability of the initiative is a very useful adjunct to a healthy democracy, not least because it tends to dissuade the politicians from passing laws in their own rather than the people's interests. After all, in a democracy, the people are sovereign. If, therefore, the political structure is to allow for checks and balances, it would seem logical enough to allow for this additional measure.

> *Legislating in Switzerland is the art of avoiding the referendum.* (Koback 1994: 150)
>
> *Both the logic of the referendum-plus-initiative and the example of how it has worked in Switzerland support the conclusion that it can be seen as a strong consensus-inducing mechanism...* (Lijphart 1999: 231)

Only Italy and Switzerland plus a few states in the US have these citizens' initiatives, although lots of other countries have other variations on the referendum theme. Several allow for constitutional referendums, for any proposed changes thereto. Some have positive referendums, where the proposer asks for a new law to be introduced. And a few have negative ones, by which the people may demand that certain measures be repealed.[2] Finally, while some referendums are binding, others are only advisory.

---

[1] In 1997, for example, the British government asked Lord Jenkins to chair a supposedly independent commission for a referendum on Britain's electoral system. As stipulated by the terms of reference, he was told to make only one proposal. A more independent commission would have allowed for a multi-option approach, as was the case in New Zealand. (Sect. 2.6 and the epilogue.)

[2] This sometimes leads to the rather confusing situation where those in favour of something vote "no" and those against vote "yes", for that is what you have to do when you want to retain or repeal that something in what is called an abrogative referendum, as in Italy.

2.2.1 Variations on the Majoritarian Theme

It would be even better if the electorate were offered a multi-option referendum. Some countries already cater for such, and three Scandinavian countries use multi-option voting in their parliaments (Fig. 2.8). These are huge improvements on simple majority voting, if only because they allow the debate to revert from an *A* versus *B* *argument* into an *A* or *B* or *C* or *D* *discussion*.

Multi-option voting is dealt with in Sect. 2.3; first comes an examination of those better forms of the two-option vote in current use, either in national/regional referendums and/or in parliaments and committees.

2.2.1.1 A Weighted Majority

Reference was made earlier to the vote of no-confidence in situations where, in theory, no one policy enjoys majority support (Sect. 1.1.2.3). In other circumstances, there might be some similar or even different majorities in favour of several different policies. That is, there could well be a majority in favour of option *A*, another majority in favour of option *B*, and so on.

In Northern Ireland, for example, there is probably a majority in favour of staying in the UK. There could also be a different but no less valid majority for the main provisions of the Belfast Agreement under a form of joint authority. There might even be a majority in favour of some well-conceived federal Ireland, as long as such a structure gave the North a considerable measure of autonomy. So which majority, if any, represents the general will?

Another example is Kosova where there is definitely a huge majority in favour of independence (Sect. 1.2.4.1); if a different question were posed, there could well be another huge majority in favour of a united Albania, or yet another in support of a greater Albania. As implied in Sect. 1.1.2.8, the answer depends upon the question, and the outcome of a majority vote may indeed mean next to nothing.

One way to be a little more certain of the general will is to use a weighted majority vote when, say, a 67% or 75% majority is required.[3] The advantage – if we take the 75% model – is that in a divided society with, let us say, 60% belonging to "this" group and 40% to "that" faction, any 75% majority would clearly consist of voters from both "this" and "that" community. The disadvantage is equally apparent: any minority of 25% or so could veto any or even everything.

---

[3] The largest weighting in use is a five-sixths majority, the requirement for certain constitutional amendments and/or fiscal policies in the Finnish parliament (McRae 1997: 290).

2.2.1.2 A Minimum Majority

In some parliaments and committee meetings, decisions can be taken only if a certain minimum number of members, a quorum, is present. Similarly, in some countries like Denmark, certain minimum levels of participation are laid down by law for referendums. In such instances, any proposal will be adopted only if it enjoys the support of a majority of the voters *and* if the turnout passes a certain minimum percentage of the electorate. The Danish requirement is 40%.

2.2.1.3 A Double Majority

In a few countries such as those constituted on federal lines, referendums depend not only upon a majority of votes cast, but also on the support of a majority of regions or cantons, to take the Swiss example.

2.2.1.4 The Veto

The greater the number of majoritarian provisos imposed on the use of a majority vote, the more likely it is that one or other group may resort to a veto. If a minority party which chooses to veto does so by an internal party majority vote then, while the majority of the minority might indeed want to veto, the minority of the minority might prefer to veto that veto. This is another inherent snag in any majoritarian process: the minority of the minority of the minority... (Sects. 1.1.2.2 and 1.2.5)

2.2.1.5 A Consociational Majority

Another form of majority voting is the consociational vote, a method of decision-making which has been used in a politically divided society at peace (Austria), in societies divided by different nationalities (Czechoslovakia)[4] and (Belgium), and in a post-communist plural society in transition (Bosnia).[5] It is also a part of the Belfast Agreement. For many of the politicians involved, consociationalism is a quantum leap beyond the simple majority vote.

To take the Czechoslovak example, any vote would have been conducted simultaneously in the two constituencies and, if a majority of the Czechs *and*

---

[4] Interestingly enough, the Czechoslovak model was initiated by one Joseph Stalin, a politician not always associated with democratic reforms. Furthermore, throughout Stalin's reign, this system of decision-making never failed because, in those grim days, no major decisions were taken in Prague anyway; everything of importance was decided in the Kremlin.

[5] 'The three national parties had secretly agreed before the [1990] elections to form a coalition government...' (Silber and Little 1995: 232), so to exclude the non-sectarian parties.

a majority of the Slovaks had both said 'yes', then 'yes' it would have been. The biggest disadvantage of this process is that it is still majoritarian: in many instances those involved, both people and politicians, continue to think in terms of just two alternatives: *A* or *B*.

A second defect of consociational voting lies in the fact that it is prone to the use of the veto. In NI, both 'sides' have one, so the future of the Belfast Agreement is dependent on at least the majority of the majority *and* the majority of the minority; in practice, the survival of the Agreement is subject to even smaller groupings (Sect. 1.1.2.2). Meanwhile in Bosnia, it was all the more complicated because of three possible vetoes, and in 'its 18-month-long existence, the [1990-2] Bosnia parliament failed to pass a single law...' (Glenny 1996: 148). Sure enough, where there is the possibility of a veto, sooner or later, it will be exercised.

A third defect relates to the constituencies themselves, for somebody has to know to which constituency each voter belongs. In Czechoslovakia, the constituencies were geographical and therefore separate electoral registers would have been possible, even if the Moravians, located between the two, were just assumed to be Czech.

In NI, where the geographical divisions are both numerous and confused, separate electoral registers based on nationality or religion would be both unacceptable and unworkable. For this reason, the Belfast Agreement stipulates consociational voting for use in the elected chamber only, and not for general use in referendums. To put it into effect, all members of the Legislative Assembly, MLAs, have to designate themselves as "unionist", "nationalist" or "other," and the very sectarianism the Agreement was meant to overcome is thereby perpetuated and entrenched (see also Sect. 5.1.5.4). Nevertheless, consociational voting is still a significant advance on the simple majority vote.

2.3 Multi-Option Decision-Making: Theory

There are several ways of voting on a multi-option ballot, and even more ways of counting those votes. The theory will be considered first, the different counting procedures will be examined towards the end of the chapter.

> *'The truth of an Assembly's decisions depends as much on the form by which they are reached as on the enlightenment of its members.' Le Marquis de Condorcet.* (McLean and Urken 1995: 113)

2.3.1 A Three-Option Continuum

Consider a committee of just three persons – Ms J, Mr K and Ms L again – who have decided to hold a party. Let us buy a barrel, says one, bulk-buying would be

2.3 Multi-Option Decision-Making: Theory

Fig. 2.2 A profile of tastes

	Ms J	Mr K	Ms L
1st preference	*A*	*B*	*C*
2nd preference	*B*	*C*	*A*
3rd preference	*C*	*A*	*B*

cheaper; so they all agree to that as well. Then comes the question: a barrel of what? Ms J suggests ale, option *A*. Mr K likes his bitter, *B*. And Ms L prefers cider, *C*. A debate ensues and it soon becomes clear that each of them has their own preferences, as shown in Fig. 2.2: Ms J likes *A B C*, in that order; Mr K's preferences are *B C A*; and Ms L goes for *C A B*.

Given their differences on these three options, they agree to resolve the matter democratically, and for those who believe in majority voting, this necessitates two majority votes. Ms J suggests a first round vote of *B* versus *C*, with the winner going through to the second round, (*B* or *C*) v *A*. Mr K argues for (*A* or *C*) v *B*. And Ms L proposes a third plan: (*A* or *B*) v *C*. Their motives soon become apparent.

In the first round vote according to Ms J, *B* versus *C*, both J and K prefer *B* to *C*, so the second round is *B* v *A*, where both J and L prefer *A* to *B*, so the winner is *A*.

In Mr K's first round version of *A* versus *C*, both K and L prefer *C* to *A*, and in the second round contest of *C* v *B*, two of them, J and K, prefer *B* to *C*, so the winner is *B*.

And in Ms L's first round contest choice of *A* or *B*, both J and L prefer *A*, while in the *A* v *C* final, a majority of K and L prefer *C*, so the winner is now *C*.

In such circumstances, everything depends upon the order of voting. This is because *A* is preferred by a majority to *B* which is preferred by a majority to *C* which is preferred by a majority to *A* which... and this goes round and round in circles, for ever! In voting terminology, it is called a cycle or the paradox of voting. *A* is more popular than *B* is more popular than *C* is more popular than *A*... which is written as $A > B > C > A$...

So now back to politics. One of the simplest pluralist debates consists of a motion and just one proposed amendment. In this setting, there are in fact three possible outcomes: *A, B* and *C*.

A the motion, unamended
B the motion, amended and
C nothing, the *status quo ante*

If no one group has an absolute majority, the chair can do anything at all: he may just arrange a knock-out competition – a binary decision-making procedure – and he can thus get whatever answer he wants.

As shown in Chap. 1, in two-option majority voting the outcome depends on the wording of the motion (Sect. 1.1.2.8). It is now clear that, in any binary voting procedure, the outcome also depends on the order of business, the agenda. Which proposal comes first? Which amendment takes precedence? The possibilities for fixing the debate in any complex majoritarian scenario are almost limitless.

Even in a two-option setting, the chair has quite a few choices of action. As implied in Sect. 1.1.2.10, she could follow the precedent of M Calonne and "adjust" the majority; or she could resort to the most ancient of all procedures and foment an *A* and *A'* split in the opposing camp – (Sect. 1.1.2.13) – the game of divide and rule. Then, as soon as she has the options on the table and as long as no one option enjoys an absolute majority, she can fix the order of voting to her own advantage and get the outcome she wants.

2.3.2 A Four-Option Conundrum

Just to prove the point, imagine a second scenario in which the same trio – Messrs J, K and L – decide to have another party. Initially, in this example, there are only two options on the table, *A* and *D*, ale and draught. Furthermore, there is to be no argument about the order of voting, for all three are under the strict chairpersonship of no less a democrat than myself.

Now as it happens, Ms J prefers *D* to *A*, Mr K prefers *D* to *A*, and Ms L prefers *D* to *A*. You might think, therefore, that the collective decision of this threesome is in unanimous support of *D*. Ah, but you forget one important consideration: I, the impartial, non-voting but very democratic chairperson, want *A*.

So I proceed as follows. I introduce bitter and cider into the discussion, options *B* and *C*, because I wish to divide and rule. I know that Ms J has preferences *A B C*, so she now has *D A B C*; meanwhile, Mr K (*B C A*) likes *B C D A* and Ms L (*C A B*) opts for *C D A B*. Please note that all three still prefer *D* to *A*, as shown in Fig. 2.3: no-one has changed their mind.

I then ask all to vote in a democratic way, by majority vote of course and, as chair, I insist on the following fair, logical order:

D v *C*, which *C* wins due to K and L
C v *B*, which *B* wins, because J and K prefer *B*; and then

-	Ms J	Mr K	Ms L
1st preference	*D*	*B*	*C*
2nd preference	*A*	*C*	*D*
3rd preference	*B*	*D*	*A*
4th preference	*C*	*A*	*B*

Fig. 2.3 A more complex profile

2.3 Multi-Option Decision-Making: Theory

A v *B*, which with votes from J and L, is a clear victory for *A*. Thus the committee has chosen option *A*, the ale.[6] I might add that this sort of manipulation can take place, not only by a chairperson so structuring the vote, but also in a purely verbal process, by a facilitator "navigating" a group discussion in a direction of his own choosing.

In a vain attempt to bring some semblance of order to the democratic process – assuming, that is, that the only way to vote is via this form of majoritarian or binary decision-making – a number of theorists have long since written certain specific rules and standing orders. 'When the *ekklesia* met... the first day was given over to a presentation of the problem or a statement of the case. The second day was taken up with formulation of motions and with debate. On the third day, the vote was taken... In practice... when the political leaders agreed, they presented their program and had it approved; when they disagreed, the voters chose between the proposals of rival leaders.'(Larsen 1955: 97–8)

This all dates from about 200 BC, by which time the Greeks were well used to notions such as quorums, limited terms of office, extraordinary meetings and so on. So it was utterly reasonable for Pliny the Younger to write in AD 105, 'In ancient times... men learned... the powers of the proposer, the rights of expressing an opinion, the authority of office holders, and the privileges of ordinary members; they learned when to give way and when to stand firm, how long to speak and when to keep silence, how to distinguish between conflicting proposals and how to introduce an amendment, in short the whole of senatorial procedure.'(McLean and Urken 1995: 67)

A modern set of rules and procedures contains little which is new, for it too is based firmly on the old, two-option majority vote (Citrine and Cannell 1982: 53 *et seq.*).

2.3.3 The Wording of Motions

In multi-option voting, the choice of options is still crucial. Accordingly, let us now consider how the options on a multi-option ballot should be expressed. Returning to the earlier topic of dog licenses, we could choose a three-option ballot paper in a number of different ways: Does this House want the cost (in pounds) of a dog license to be option *A*, *B* or *C*, as in Fig. 2.4?

Well, people could get a little suspicious of such a limited choice, so in this and many other debates, perhaps it would be better to go for a few more options, as in Fig. 2.5:

---

[6] This example is an adaptation of one used by (Saari 2001: 13–14). If instead of just three members, the committee consisted of 11 persons who favoured *D A B C*, 10 who preferred *C D A B* and 9 who liked *B C D A*, the three votes would have been passed with comfortable, convincing and compelling majorities of 63%, 67% and 70%.

	Option *A*	Option *B*	Option *C*
One possibility	39 or less	40	41 or more
A variation	34 or less	between 35 and 45	46 or more
Another sort	nothing	between 1 and 79	80 or more

Fig. 2.4 A choice of questions

Option *A*	Option *B*	Option *C*	Option *D*	Option *E*	Option *F*	Option *G*
x = 0	0 < x < 20	20 ≤ x < 40	40 ≤ x < 60	60 ≤ x < 80	80 ≤ x < 100	x = 100

Fig. 2.5 A seven-option ballot

In such a vote, if I wanted a license fee of £45, I could vote: ***D, C, E, B, F, A, G*** if on the other hand I thought £55 would be better, I could say: ***D, E, C, F, B, G, A*** and if I wanted exactly £50, I could vote ***D, E, C, B, F, A, G*** or ***D, C, E, F, B, G, A***

The voting procedure is not perfect, of course, but a seven-option range is obviously better than a three-option choice, and definitely better than any two-option dilemma.

Alas, in adversarial politics, politicians fight their corners. Some want a so-called ideology to prevail, such as communism, socialism, capitalism or whatever (although, in practice, it is sometimes quite difficult to distinguish between these various "philosophies"). Others support unionism or nationalism, and again these two may not be as mutually exclusive as their protagonists pretend.

There are those politicians and members of the electorate who take a more altruistic view and who campaign for the general good. Instead, therefore, of individual Welsh people voting for what each of them would like the Welsh constitution to be, they could vote for what they judge to be the Welsh consensus. Alas, with the introduction of party politics, such idealistic democratic behaviour has to a large extent disappeared. For many people nowadays, it's a case of "I vote for me" (Sect. 3.2.1.8).

At this stage, however, we are considering only the format of the ballot paper and, so far as dog licenses are concerned, seven options should be more than adequate. Then, when everyone has voted, it should be possible to calculate a reasonably accurate answer provided, that is, the number of voters was fairly high, and the options were well balanced over an appropriately wide range.

The range of options would probably be something like Fig. 2.6, especially if the format of the ballot paper were a vital part of the debate.

Option	Option	Option	Option	Option	Option	Option
A	*B*	*C*	*D*	*E*	*F*	*G*
x < 20	20 ≤ x < 30	30 ≤ x < 40	40 ≤ x < 50	50 ≤ x < 60	60 ≤ x < 70	70 ≤ x

Fig. 2.6 Another seven-option ballot

As already stated, the MPs could be asked to give their answer to the nearest pound. (The question would be the equivalent of a 100-option single-preference vote, with a rather unusual count.) This would facilitate a fairly accurate calculation of the consensus opinion (the mathematical mean). With a more practical seven-option preference ballot, especially if the voters list all seven preferences, a similar degree of accuracy is still possible.

If the MPs adopt the more altruistic view of politics, they should be able to submit a complete ballot. If I list *G* as my last preference, I make it pretty clear that I do not like anything more than £70. I am, nevertheless, expressing my opinion to the full. I am also acknowledging the fact that the consensus opinion *may* be over £70, that someone in the debate has actually suggested such an option (for otherwise, presumably, it would not have been included on the ballot paper), and I thus accept both the validity of that option and the right of its proposer to hold such an aspiration.

2.3.4 Single-Peaked Preferences

The above sets of preferences – *D-C-E-B-F-A-G*, *D-E-C-F-B-G-A*, *D-E-C-B-F-A-G* and *D-C-E-F-B-G-A* – are examples of single-peaked preferences. Thus, if the voter thinks £45 is best, option *D* will be her highest preference, and all license fees to either side of option *D* will be on descending scales of lower preferences, with those the furthest away from *D* getting the lowest preferences of all. The example shown overleaf in Fig. 2.7 is for the first set of preferences: *D-C-E-B-F-A-G*.

Alas, when it comes to politics, "there's nowt as queer as folks" as they say, and so too in Wales. Section 1.1.2.8 implied that in a three-option poll, *Plaid Cymru* supporters would probably vote *C B A* (independence, devolution, *status quo*); the unionists would no doubt be their opposites *A B C*; and only those in favour of devolution would be split in their subsequent preferences, *B A C* or *B C A*. In the present scenario, these sets of preferences are all single-peaked. There is, however, another point of view, that of those who are opposed to the introduction of any additional level of government, and these voters might want to give *B* their last preference: *A C B* or *C A B*. In the present scenario, these preferences are not single-peaked.

In debates on relatively simple issues like dog licenses, there may indeed be a single peak in the voters' preferences and therefore a single peak in their collective preferences. On more complex topics, single-peaked preferences are not so common.

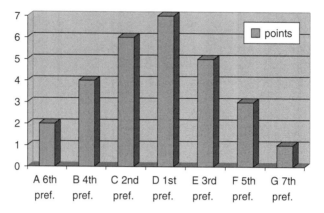

Fig. 2.7 Single-peaked preferences: *D-C-E-B-F-A-G*

2.4 Multi-Option Decision-Making: Practice

Awareness of the paradox of voting (Sect. 2.3.1) is vital to any understanding of the following voting procedures:

Plurality voting
Two-round system of voting, TRS
Approval voting
Serial voting
Alternative vote, AV*
Pairings, Condorcet
Points system, usually a BC
Modified Borda Count, MBC

The relative merits of these procedures will now be considered, both in diagrammatic form in Fig. 2.8 and in written argument. The MBC will then be discussed in rather more detail.

2.4.1 Plurality Voting

In a plurality vote, voters cast only one preference, usually by writing an "×". In a six-option ballot – with options *A, B, C, D, E* and *F* – if the result is *A* 30%, *B* and *C* 20%, *D, E* and *F* just 10%, then *A* wins on 30%, even though a majority of 70% did not vote for *A*. Thus a plurality vote can be a very inaccurate measure of the collective will.

---

*This is actually a single transferable vote, STV, or to give it its American name, instant run-off voting, IRV.

2.4 Multi-Option Decision-Making: Practice

	CLOSED QUESTIONS		SEMI-OPEN QUESTIONS	OPEN QUESTIONS		
	binary			multi-optional		
all preferences	-	-	-	-	-	BC/MBC
						Condorcet
some preferences	-	-	-	approval voting	-	-
				serial voting* Finland, Sweden		AV, IRV, STV
	weighted majority South Africa	consociational Belgium, NI		TRS** Norway		
only first preferences	simple majority$^\infty$	twin majority Switzerland§	plurality Puerto Rico§	-		-
	Voter chooses one of two options		Voter chooses one of several options	Voter chooses one or some of several options		Voter chooses one, some or all of several options
	single preference voting		→	preferential voting		
	VOTERS' CHOICE		→	→		

↑ C O U N T

* a series of majority votes.
** one plurality vote plus, if need be, one majority vote.
$^\infty$ the simple majority vote is used ubiquitously.
§ in referendums.

Fig. 2.8 Decision-making systems

Plurality voting has sometimes been used in multi-option referendums, as summarized in App. D. At the very least, the provision of more than two options suggests to the voters (a) that they do have a real choice, and (b), that if the vote is binding, the executive will execute whatever the people decide. Thus, in theory, plurality voting is a big improvement on a two-option vote. Unfortunately, in practice, the improvement is often marginal, because a multi-option choice is often reduced to two or at best three favourites, often by sections of the media.

2.4.2 The Two-Round System, TRS

The first round is a plurality vote and, if no option gains 50%, a second round majority vote is held between the two leading options from the first round. Norway has provision for TRS in its parliament.

2.4.3 Approval Voting

In a ballot of six options, voters can indicate their "approval" by giving an "×" to either one or many options. The option with the most "approvals" is the winner. They may "approve" of the options as they wish, up to a maximum of one less than the total of six; (in effect, a vote for all six options would be a wasted vote). A major disadvantage of approval voting is that those who are more consensual may vote for up to five options, while the intransigent may vote for only their favourite option. In some scenarios, one of the latter sets of voters might therefore be more likely to enjoy success.

2.4.4 Serial Voting

If, in debate, the six options "on the table" can be listed, in order, let us say from cheap to expensive, then MPS may take a series of two-option votes, initially between the two "extremes." The option which loses is dropped, while the one which wins goes into the second round, another majority vote between the two new extremes; and so it continues. It is a bit like the game of musical chairs: after five votes, there is only one option left, the winner. If everyone has single-peaked preferences (Sect. 2.3.4) and if everyone votes sincerely, the system works fairly well. Furthermore, on those occasions when there is a Condorcet winner (Sect. 2.4.6) – namely, when there is no paradox – the serial winner will be the Condorcet winner.

This methodology is sometimes used in the Finnish and Swedish parliaments, usually when there is a choice of two or more possible amendments (Nurmi 1987: 163).

2.4.5 AV, STV or IRV

In AV, voters are asked to place their options in order of preference, giving a "1" to their first preference, a "2" to their second, and so on, for as many options as they wish; people usually vote for just some options although they may cast all their preferences, if they want to. If one option gets at least 50% of the first preferences, then it wins. If not, the least popular option according to the first stage plurality count is eliminated, and its votes are transferred according to the respective voters' second preferences. The process continues until one option gets 50% of the votes, or until there is only one option left.[7]

One weakness of AV lies in the fact that the system can be capricious and sometimes inaccurate. If option *E* is eliminated first, option *D* may win; but just a few more first preference votes for *E* could mean a different elimination and an altogether different winner.[8]

* * * * *

As mentioned in Sect. 2.4.1, a plurality vote can be inaccurate. We may therefore conclude that any methodology which starts with a plurality vote may also be inaccurate: this applies to TRS and AV.

2.4.6 Pairings, a Condorcet Count

In a Condorcet count, as in AV, voters cast one, some, or all of their preferences. In the count, pairs of options are examined separately. In a six-option ballot, when all the pairings have been examined, if *A* is more popular than *B* and if *A* is more popular than *C*, and more popular than *D*, and *E* and *F*, then *A* wins; i.e. *A* is the Condorcet winner. The trouble is, as we now know, there may be a paradox, and this is especially true if some people do not have single-peaked preferences. Nevertheless, on many occasions, a Condorcet count is an accurate measure of the wishes of the majority, and sometimes too of the overall consensus.

2.4.7 Points System or Borda Count, BC

In a BC, voters express their preferences, as in AV or a Condorcet count. In a six-option ballot, if the voter has submitted a full ballot, a first preference gets 6 points, a second preference 5 points, a third 4 points, and so on. The option with the most points is the winner.

---

[7] It is often said that AV ensures that the winning option enjoys majority support. If, however, many voters cast only a few preferences, many votes might become non-transferable (Chap. 4, note 7).

[8] AV/STV is not monotonic (see glossary and Emerson P 1998: 87–8).

Now if I want option ***A*** to win while at the same time I think option ***D***, my second preference, is a close rival, I might vote tactically and give ***A*** my first preference and ***D*** my last preference, with intermediate preferences going to the other options. There again, if lots of people think and act in this way, they may all finish up with their third preference, or something even less popular.

Guessing the first preferences of everyone can be problematic; guessing *all* of their preferences might be impossible. In practice, then, manipulating a BC is very difficult and the BC is usually an accurate measure of the collective will of those voting; this is even more likely if a modified BC, the MBC, is used (see below). In many instances, the BC gives the same outcome as a Condorcet count, and this is because a *well-measured* majority opinion is often (but not always) the same as the accurately identified consensus opinion. To use a sporting analogy, the winner of the football league is the team which wins the most matches (Condorcet); and in most years, it is this team which also has the best goal difference (a sort of BC) (Emerson P 2007: 86).

2.5 Consensus Voting: The Modified Borda Count, MBC

Consensus voting involves not only a multi-option vote but also a multi-option debate. As will be seen in Chap. 6, this debate should allow for the formation of a (short) list of all proposals aired, (as long as they conform to some agreed norm such as the UN Charter on Human Rights). If in debate a verbal consensus proves to be elusive, this list becomes the basis of the ballot paper, whereupon the participants shall be asked to state their preferences, as in a BC.

Now there may be those who submit only a partial vote. In a BC of *n* options, points may be awarded as follows:

a first preference gets *n* points
a second preference gets *n-1* points
a third preference gets *n-2* points... and so on, until
a last preference gets *1* point.[9]

If a first preference were to get *n* points, even when the voter has cast only one preference, people might be tempted to do just that: cast only a first preference. If everyone did this, the vote would revert to a plurality vote. Accordingly, in consensus voting, the rules are such that, if someone casts *m* preferences – where $1 \leq m \leq n$ – points shall be awarded like this:

a first preference gets *m* points
a second preference gets *m-1* points
a third preference gets *m-2* points... and so on, until
a last preference gets *1* point.

---

[9] Some people prefer a slightly different rule: instead of $(n, n\text{-}1, \ldots, 1)$, they use $(n\text{-}1, n\text{-}2, \ldots, 0)$. If all the voters have submitted full ballots, the outcome will be the same.

2.5 Consensus Voting: The Modified Borda Count, MBC

you may also	Place place	a '1' opposite your 1st preference; a '2' opposite your 2nd preference, a '3' opposite your 3rd preference, a '4' opposite your 4th preference,
	and	a '5' opposite your 5th preference.

Option (or Candidate)	Preference
A	
B	
C	
D	
E	

The modified Borda count (MBC) is a preferential points voting system in which the option(s) {or candidate(s)} with the most points is(are) the winner(s).

The points may vary as follows:

If you cast preferences for:	1 option	2 options	3 options	4 options	5 options
your 1st preference gets	1 pt	2 pts	3 pts	4 pts	5 pts
your 2nd preference gets		1 pt	2 pts	3 pts	4 pts
your 3rd preference gets			1 pt	2 pts	3 pts
your 4th preference gets				1 pt	2 pts
your 5th preference gets					1 pt

Fig. 2.9 An MBC five-option ballot

If, then, a voter casts only a first preference, he will exercise only one point. If another casts two preferences, her first preference gets two points. If someone else casts all *n* preferences, then his first preference gets *n* points. In other words, if in a six-option ballot, someone says something about one option, and nothing at all about any of the other options, he will exercise $1 + 0 + 0 + 0 + 0 + 0$ points. She who casts two preferences will exercise $2 + 1 + 0 + 0 + 0 + 0$ points. While those who submit a full ballot will exercise $6 + 5 + 4 + 3 + 2 + 1$ points.

In summary, a voter's x^{th} preference, if cast, will always get one more point that that voter's $(x + 1)^{th}$ preference, whether or not the latter has been cast. In an MBC, there is no especial weighting. An example of an MBC ballot paper is shown in Fig. 2.9.

2.5.1 The MBC: Theory and Practice

In a majoritarian decision-making process, the protagonist who wants his particular option to win will try to maximize his support from those he considers to be on his side; at the same time, he will care little about those he knows to be of the opposite viewpoint.

In an MBC, it is all very different. When his final total depends not only on those whom he considers to be his supporters, but also on those who in a majoritarian milieu would have been his adversaries, it would pay him both to word his proposal so that it appeals to everybody, and to campaign right across the political spectrum. Success depends not only on getting a large number of high preferences, but also perhaps in gaining lots of middle preferences and a minimal number of low preferences. Thus the system itself encourages greater dialogue – or "polylogue" – amongst all concerned.

In general, the more choice there is in a voting system, the more difficult it is to manipulate. Furthermore, of the systems discussed so far, only one set is not majoritarian: the BC. If, therefore, the word "democracy" implies the identification of the consensus described at the beginning of the chapter (Sect. 2.1.1), this methodology would seem to be the most appropriate.

> *The principle underlying Borda's criterion... is that majorities are of no importance in themselves...* (Dummett 1997: 63)

Its main advantage is of exceptional merit: it is a win-win procedure. In debates of great controversy, it should bring forth the best compromise. In discourses of great sophistication, it may give the collective wisdom. Furthermore, as adapted into the MBC[10] – and this may well have been what Jean-Charles de Borda himself intended (Saari 2008: 197 note 6)[11] – it allows for the participation of everyone.

Another advantage of the MBC lies in the fact that, if a voter wishes to abstain and rely on the consensus of everybody else, he may do so without fear of distorting the outcome. There are no dramatic swings to worry about in consensus voting. Secondly, if the single-minded wish to participate to a certain degree only (i.e., voting only for their own options), then their preferences will be counted but only to a correspondingly limited extent. In this way, the more extreme elements in society may still play their part.

In majoritarian politics, some people are left outside the tent, at least until the next vote. In consensus politics, in contrast, all are inside, and *every* voter influences the average. If one MP changes his mind, the average opinion may change a little. But the consensus of all is not and cannot be drastically altered by the vacillations of just one individual. When decisions are based on majority votes, however, as shown in App. C, the rôle of just one MP can sometimes change the course of history.

---

[10] This procedure is sometimes called a preferendum.

[11] Jean-Charles de Borda proposed that the voter's last preference should get one point, his penultimate two points, and so on. Mathematically, this is the same as the $(m, m\text{-}1, \ldots, 1)$ rule. Unfortunately, many social choice scientists, and in their wake political scientists, have adopted the $(n\text{-}1, n\text{-}2, \ldots, 0)$ rule, which does not cater for partial voting. I think the source of this mistake was Duncan Black. (Black 1958: 59) (See also Emerson forthcoming.)

2.5.2 An Example

In the Oct. 2002 debate in the UN Security Council on Iraq (Sect. 1.1.2.4) France did not like the phrase, 'serious consequences'.[12] Nevertheless, France voted in favour. Now why would any country vote in favour of something that she did not like? Was it because she thought it was better than nothing? Or was it because of the need for international solidarity?

All this begs a further question: why did France go along with the practice of majority voting? If the US/UK option had been called option *A*, France could have drafted its own alternative phrase and put this on the table as well, option *B*, probably with German support. Syria was a member of the Council at that time, and with her specialist knowledge of the Middle East, maybe she would have had another idea: option *C*. Ireland, a neutral country, could have moved a distinctly pacifist alternative, option *D*, and so on.

With all these options, participants could then have engaged in open debate, asking questions, making suggestions, and perhaps having new ideas. In short, the debate could have been allowed to develop in whichever way the delegates wanted it to.

On such a topic, coming to a verbal agreement is bound to be difficult. Let us therefore assume that, when everything has been said but nothing decided, there are indeed five options on the table: *A, B, C, D* and *E*. The chair calls for a vote. Let us also assume that all 15 members cast a full ballot of five preferences.

Consider first a hypothetical situation: if option *D*, say, gets 15 first preferences, then *D* will get $(15 \times 5) = 75$ points, the maximum; if all 15 give option *C* there fifth preference, then *C* will get only $(15 \times 1) = 15$ points; and if all give option *A* their third preference, then *A* will get $(15 \times 3) = 45$ points, which is of course the mean.

In practice, with 15 members casting five preferences on the five options, doubtless some option(s) will be above the mean, and some other option(s) below. 'The Borda count... always gives a definite result.' (Reilly 2002: 358) If the winning option gets more than 70 points, the observer can talk of (near) unanimity; if more than 60, of consensus; and if between 50 and 60, of the best possible compromise. If however the leading option scores less than 50 points, then obviously the other options will also be close to the mean score (45 points), in which case it would be better to accept that there is no agreement and resume the debate, just as they would in Africa.

2.5.3 Other Applications of the MBC

As in the above example, the MBC can be used to identify the participants' social choice – their most popular option – or, in a prioritization, their social ranking –

---

[12] In Article 13, the Security Council '*Recalls*... that the Council has repeatedly warned Iraq that it will face serious consequences as a result of its continued violations of its obligations.'

their collective preferences. While it may be difficult to manipulate an MBC when identifying a social choice, it is definitely problematic when identifying the social ranking. Accordingly, the MBC can also be used in surveys and opinion polls, in focus groups and other forms of deliberative democracy.

To take a simple example, committee members could decide on an agenda by voting on any suggested items, in which case the relative scores would indicate the priority with which those items should be considered; furthermore, the relative strengths of the points totals would indicate whether extended times should be scheduled for the more important items. In like manner, members could agree on a prioritization, a short list of say six from a longer initial list, by asking each to record their top six options in order of preference.

A similar degree of sophistication may be applicable to such complex debates as the budget, where the allocation of more funds to one ministerial department cannot be considered without taking into account the effect such a re-allocation would have on other proposed expenditures. Without such a sophisticated voting procedure, it would be almost impossible for a group of MPs to come to a collective decision on such a topic. It would be even more difficult in an instance of direct democracy, as in participatory budgeting.

2.6 Conclusions

Democratic decision-making could be so much more than divisive debates and majority votes. There are voting procedures by which collective opinions *can* be accurately identified. The Condorcet system can be used to identify a *majority* opinion; the MBC can be used to identify a *consensus* opinion; and the true majority opinion and the consensus opinion will often coincide (Sect. 2.4.7). When they do, all concerned can be reasonably sure the outcome is indeed the will of the voters.[13]

---

[13] Nothing, of course, is perfect. Condorcet might produce a paradox, but not the BC/MBC; the latter, but not Condorcet, is subject to clones and irrelevant alternatives (see glossary).

Imagine three voters are voting on two options, *A* and *B*, with two voters having preferences *A B* and one voter preferring *B A*. In this situation, *A* wins the Borda count with 5 points to *B*'s 4 points. If we now introduce a third option, a clone, *B'*, such that *everyone* prefers *B* to *B'*, the voters' profiles are two of *A B B'* and one of *B B' A*, and the BC scores are now *A* 7, *B* 7 and *B'* 4. Add another clone, option *B''*, such that the profiles are two of *A B B' B''* and one of *B B' B'' A*, and the scores are *A* 9, *B* 10, *B'* 7 and *B''* 4. In other words, the introduction of two clones could turn an *A* Borda victory into an *A* Borda defeat.

An irrelevant alternative, option *D*, may also have this effect. If two people have preferences *A-B-C* and one prefers *B-C-A* then, as above, the scores are *A* 7, *B* 7, *C* 4. If there is an option *D* on the ballot paper as well, such that two prefer *A-B-D-C* and one favours *B-C-D-A*, then the scores will be *A* 9, *B* 10, *C* 5, *D* 6, and again, *A* is no longer the joint winner. In all of these examples, however, *A* remains the Condorcet winner.

Given these two defects of the BC/MBC and the paradox of Condorcet, many experts, often working independently, have come to the conclusion that the best possible methodology is indeed a combined Condorcet/Borda count. (Emerson P 2007: 17 note 6)

2.6 Conclusions

In societies polarized on really divisive issues – constitutional questions in Kosova, for example – the chances of such a Borda/Condorcet coincidence are minimal. There again, in such a society, majority voting would not work well either. The MBC at least offers the best prospects of reaching an agreement via a voting procedure and, in places like NI and Bosnia, consideration should be given to its use. The MBC, after all, is inclusive, in the best sense of the word. In Kosova, on the other hand, it will probably be better to rely on talks under "the big tree."

Of the many voting procedures by which a democratic decision may be taken, the most primitive methodology is the simple majority vote where the government chooses the policy it wants, and then asks parliament or the country to want it too. A better format involves the government, at its own or someone else's behest, asking an independent body – either all-party or even non-party – to study the matter, to facilitate a proper debate on the subject and, if appropriate, to draw up a number of options. These could then be put to the people or the parliament in a multi-option vote. Such a procedure was used in 1992 in New Zealand, where the people were first asked in a non-binding ballot if they wanted to change the electoral system and, if so, to which one of four proposed alternatives. There then followed a binding two option referendum, in which the people chose to ratify that earlier non-binding outcome (see App. D, D.1).

As the reader will now realize, there are even better ways of making decisions, and these could be incorporated into a more sophisticated government structure, which shall be considered in Part III. At this stage, it must be emphasized that multi-option voting procedures should definitely be used whenever there is to be a controversial plebiscite on sovereignty. Consequently, no "people" should be able to determine itself on the basis of only a majority of itself. Instead, all concerned should come to a consensus, both internally within any proposed new borders, and externally with their future neighbours. Such should have been the case in Yugoslavia; and such should now apply to Scotland (Emerson P 2010c) and Quebec, etc., and not just to former conflict zones like Kashmir,[14] Northern Ireland, or islands/regions in Indonesia (Sect. 1.2.3) and districts in Sudan. (Sect. 1.2.4.2) Equally problematic, perhaps, would be a referendum in Tibet (Xīzàng), which has witnessed large-scale Han immigration, as too has Xīnjiāng. Most fragile of all are probably the disputed regions in Iraq such as Kirkuk, where an oft-delayed referendum, originally scheduled for 2007, has still to be held.

> 'A referendum is not the answer. Victor and vanquished cannot be a solution in such an explosive region. The two sides need to sit down and hammer out an arrangement.'
> Abraham Serfaty, a Moroccan leader talking on the future of Western Sahara.
> (The Guardian, 3.2.2000)

---

[14] The 1947 UN resolution on Kashmir called for a referendum but none has yet been held.

2.7 Democratic Decision-Making Defined

With two chapters completed, it is now possible to define democratic decision-making. A democratic decision should represent the will of parliament and therefore, if the parliament is truly representative, the will of the people. Accordingly, decisions may be taken by either the parliament and/or the electorate, although clearly the latter remains sovereign.

As submitted in Sect. 2.1.1, the will of the people is either their unanimous viewpoint, where such exists, or on more controversial issues their average opinion or consensus, or on really contentious matters and especially in any plural society, their best possible compromise.

Accordingly, in a democracy – be it a nation or just an association – all decisions should be taken using an inclusive procedure, so as best to encapsulate that society's consensus. Such a procedure should therefore include some or all of the following features.

1. All votes shall be "free," i.e. without the application of any party whip. Ballot papers may include a blank option. All parliamentary legislation and non-urgent decisions shall be taken in consensus, either verbally or by a consensus vote.
2. On all controversial matters, a team of independent "consensors" (Sect. 6.2.1) or an independent commission shall determine exactly how many options are appropriate and which voting procedure is advisable. In the absence of any verbal consensus, the policy in question shall be put to a preference vote of at least three options.
3. Non-contentious issues may be resolved by a majority/plurality vote, and a minimum weighted majority of 75% will serve to emphasize its uncontroversial nature.

    Contentious matters shall be resolved by an MBC, and the proposal which receives a pre-determined minimum level of support as measured by a consensus coefficient (see Sect. 6.3.2) may be regarded as the best possible approximation to "the will of the people."
4. In the event of no one option attaining the required degree of support, the debate shall be resumed, alternative options shall be considered, and a further vote held. If at the end of, say, three votes, the pre-determined level has still not been achieved, the option with the highest level of consensus, even if it is the *status quo ante*, shall stand in lieu of the consensus, until such time as a consensus *can* be achieved.

References

Black D (1958) The theory of committees and elections. CUP, Cambridge
Citrine N, Cannell M (1982) Citrine's ABC of chairmanship. NCLC Publishing, London
Doyle W (1990) The Oxford history of the French revolution. OUP, Oxford
Dummett M (1997) Principles of electoral reform. OUP, Oxford

References

Emerson P (1998) Beyond the tyranny of the majority. The de Borda Institute, Belfast
Emerson P (ed) (2007) Designing an all-inclusive democracy. Springer, Heildelberg
Emerson P (2010) The next Scottish referendum. Scottish Affairs (73), autumn
Emerson P (forthcoming) The original Borda count and partial voting, SCW, Louvigny, France
Glenny M (1996) The fall of Yugoslavia. Penguin, London
Kobach KW (1994) Switzerland. In: Butler D, Ranney A (eds) Referendums around the world. The AEI Press, Washington
Larsen JAO (1955) Representative government in Greek and Roman history. University of California, Berkeley
Lijphart A (1999) Patterns of democracy. Yale University Press, New Haven and London
McLean I, Urken AB (eds) (1995) Classics of social choice. University of Michigan, Ann Arbor
McRae KD (1997) Contrasting styles of democratic decision-making. Int Polit Sci Rev 18(3): 279–295
Nurmi H (1987) Comparing voting systems. Reidel, Dordecht
Reilly B (2002) Social choice in the South Seas: electoral innovation and the Borda count in the Pacific Island countries. Int Polit Sci Rev 23(4):355–372
Saari DG (2001) Decisions and elections. CUP, Cambridge
Saari DG (2008) *Disposing dictators,* demystifying voting paradoxes. CUP, Cambridge
Sigmund PE (ed) (1966) The ideologies of the developing nations. Frederick A Praeger, New York
Silber L, Little A (1995) The death of Yugoslavia. BBC Penguin, London

Part II
Elections

Chapter 3
Party-ocracies[*]

I've come to be rather skeptical about the very principle of mass political parties.

(Havel 1989: 25)

Abstract When democracy was first devised, there were no political parties. As noted in Chap. 1, the Greeks had quorums, conventions, votes and elections, but no party political structures as such. The latter emerged later on in Europe and the US, partly because the politicians were taking decisions by majority vote, (which admittedly the Greeks also used), and partly because of their chosen electoral systems. Indeed, in large part, the particular system determines the number of effective political parties.

This chapter reviews the historical development of democracy in Europe and America, with particular regard to electoral systems and the emergence of political parties. It also considers the disadvantages of overtly adversarial voting procedures, and refers to some of the tragic consequences.

3.1 The First Elections

In the early days in Greece, the executive was often chosen by lot. Decisions were taken in a public meeting; that was the important part of the democratic process. These decisions were then executed by that executive. Similarly in other cultures, people would meet in some venue like the forum or under a big tree, there to talk and talk until a consensus was found. In theory, both in Greece and elsewhere, those concerned were all equally involved although in practice, it was often the rich old men who did all the talking; some would say that little has changed. There was,

---

[*]From the Italian word, *partitocrazia*, government by political parties.

though, 'nothing resembling a "party system" in sixth/fifth-century Athens or any other Greek state...' (Ste Croix 2005: 198).

In those early days, democracy was more direct than representative. Nowadays, in contrast, with populations measured in millions, some form of representative democracy is clearly desirable. Advances in electronic net-working and so-called e-democracy may mean changes are afoot, but it seems we will continue to have parliaments and elected representatives for a few years yet, at least.

Let us however return to Greece. The forum was the legislature and those present took the decisions, if need be by majority vote. Some functionaries were required to execute these decisions, so a few were chosen, as noted by lot, and such posts were often rotated on a regular basis.

> *At Heraea they changed from holding elections to drawing lots, simply because they found that the successful candidates were those who solicited votes.* (Aristotle V iii, 1303a13)
>
> Interestingly enough, the UK continues to use a lottery for those involved in another area of social responsibility: jury service.

The Greeks elected their generals, but elections for political office only became rather more established in the Roman Republic. The candidate was he – it was always a he – who was *candid,* the one who told the truth, the one who, it might be assumed, would represent his constituents fairly and honestly. Accordingly, he was dressed in white as a symbol of his purity, (while most contemporary politicians prefer to wear grey).

3.1.1 An Old English Tale

In the Middle Ages, certain aspects of democracy were viewed with much suspicion. Elections, it was said, could very easily lead to mob rule. St. Thomas Aquinas, for example, writing in 1270, suggested '*a government is called a democracy when it is iniquitous, and when it is carried on by a large number of people. A democracy is thus a form of popular power in which the common people, by sheer force of numbers, oppress the rich, with the result that the whole populace becomes a kind of tyrant.*' (Skinner 2008: 60)

Progress, then, was slow. In its early years in England, by which time democracy was definitely more representative than direct, the elected member – still male – was supposed to represent only his own constituency. Given the *Zeitgeist,* the democratic structures were not too bad. The franchise still had to be extended; the rotten boroughs still had to be turned into proper constituencies; the excessive influence of the monarch still had to be curtailed; power still had (and has) to be decentralized; a constitution still had (and has) to be written; the church still had (and has) to be disestablished; the second chamber still had (and has) to be replaced by something democratic; the cabinet still had (and has) to be elected rather than appointed; and finally, decision-making still had (and has) to be something more pluralist and non-majoritarian.

Nevertheless, the average MP did his best for his constituents, or at least for all the rich property-owning males who had elected him, if only to get re-elected the next time round. There was however the fatal flaw (Sect. 1.1.1): the House of Commons took its decisions by majority vote. Largely because of this, parliament over time split into two opposing "halves," government and opposition.

The elected representatives of those days were all wealthy landowners, so they split into two types of rich people: some had 'acquired' their estates in the civil war, the Country party, whereas other more established chaps were attached to the Court. In time, they became the Whigs and the Tories respectively. Initially, they were not set in formal parties. Indeed, 'instead of naming themselves, they [nick]named each other'. The word "whig" was slang for a 'money-grabbing Scots Presbyterian' while a "tory" was an 'Irish Papist bandit'. (Churchill 1956: Book II, 294)

As the years went by, these two competing "halves" devised divers means and laid down various rules by which to increase their chances of victory. Thus parties were formed, political patronage came into play, and slowly but surely, they became centralized bastions of power in their own right. On many topics they argued, though there was at least one glaring exception: in 1884, Britain's FPP electoral system 'was shaped throughout by the needs and interests of the party leaders, and settled, symbolically, in a private inter-party conclave.' (Bogdanor 1981: 113)

Today's elected representatives thus have two loyalties: a democratic one to their constituents and a rather less democratic one to the party. If ever there is a clash between the two, it is usually the party which wins.

> *Political parties do not exist to further democracy, but to thwart and distort it: they are, at best, an unavoidable evil.* Sir Michael Dummett, speaking at the 'Majoritarianism or Democracy?' conference in Belfast, April, 1999.

At one stage, the only democracy in the Western world was the one in England where – despite the excellent example set by the good King Arthur at the "head" of his round table – it was decided that the House of Commons should be divided into two, that "these" should face "those" – government versus opposition – and that all questions of substance should be resolved by the two-option, majority vote. Hence, today, when the division bell rings, MPs stand and literally divide, filing through one of two labelled doors, the one marked "Aye," the other "Nay." As discussed in Part I, however, the consensus of a parliament cannot be *identified* by such a process of "long division."

3.1.2 L'état, C'est Quoi?

As suggested earlier, a democratic parliament should represent all the people, and in theory, the consensus of the people should be roughly the same as the consensus of their parliament. Thus it was in the eighteenth century that various members of the French *Académie des Sciences*, who were trying to work out how best to replace their *ancien régime,* looked across *La Manche* to see what the English were doing. As a result, mathematicians like Condorcet and de Borda were highly critical of the simple majority/plurality vote. Something better was required, they insisted, if the democratic process was to be capable of identifying the general will.

They therefore devised new electoral systems and/or decision-making processes, by which the democratic opinion of parliament *could* be more accurately determined. (See chronology 1770 and 1785.) Their emphasis was on elections, but they also considered decision-making and *'the custom which some assemblies have of reducing the subject for debate to the most widely supported opinions about it and, if possible, to just two of them.'* Condorcet. (McLean and Urken 1995: 131)

In 1784, the *Académie* adopted the BC, principally as an electoral system, and it worked. Alas, a few years later, a new member became its president – it was now called *l'Institut de France* – and he decided he did not want any of this consensus nonsense; accordingly he threw out the BC to promote in its place the old and very non-revolutionary majority vote. His name, by the way, is not the first to come to mind when talking of inclusive democratic structures: Napoleon Bonaparte. (Black 1958: 180)

3.1.3 The "New World"

Contemporary revolutionaries in America were also opposed to the *ancien régimes* of Europe, not only the monarchies of England and France, but the two-party political system of Westminster as well. George Washington, for example, in his farewell address of 1796 said that 'the alternate domination of one faction over another… has perpetrated the most horrid enormities [and] is itself a frightful despotism'. Accordingly, when he became the first president of the United States in 1789 he 'ostentatiously stood above factions and parties at a time when the very word "party" had unpleasant and even conspiratorial connotations.' (Jenkins P 1997: 67)

Unlike the French, the new Americans did little to change their decision-making voting procedures. They wrote a constitution, which included the basis of a non-partisan, though still majoritarian, electoral system (see Sect. 3.2.2.1). They had a boundless faith in democracy, (a Greek-style white, male, non-slave democracy), but they did not question the two-option majority vote. Inevitably, therefore, they argued over something. It did not take long: federalism. They argued for-or-against, *A* or *B*. So they too split into two. Thus was born the American two-party system.

They did initially hope to prevent this partisan polarization. Indeed, the first six presidents were determined to stop any factionalism and they tried to establish a non-party democracy instead. Admittedly, Washington's successors used a party label, but theirs were not the party machines we know today. Indeed, Thomas

Jefferson's party was meant to be 'a party to end all parties' (Ketcham 1984: 119), something not unlike the "anti-party party" of Petra Kelly[1] of the German Greens.

Alas, it did not work and by 1829 it was all over. John Quincy Adams' opponents 'made clear their intent to use patronage to punish foes and reward friends', 'the self-righteous [Adams] was swept from office', (*ibid*: 140), and the 'Republican Party (soon renamed Democratic-Republican, D-R, and a generation later Democratic) became the first popularly based *electoral* party in the world'. (Dahl 2000: 88) It was two-party politics from then on, although Adams continued to regret that *'the Presidency has fallen into a joint-stock company.'* (Ketcham 1984: 146) Enter, stage right, George W Bush, whose rise to power was achieved with a few, let us say, donations, from the Enron Corporation (Sect. 3.2.1.9).

> *'If I could not go to heaven but with a [political] party, I would not go there at all.'* Thomas Jefferson, 1801–9, the first of four D-R Party Presidents. (Ketcham 1984: 143)
> *'... the existence [of parties] as the curse of the country...'* President James Monroe, 1817–25. (*Ibid*: 127)
> *... party spirit is 'a prolifick source of misery...'* J Q Adams, 1825–9, the last D-R President. (*Ibid*: 133)

3.1.4 The Collapse of Soviet Communism

Russia also started on the right foot. The USSR, still a communist one-party state, held its first elections in over 70 years in 1989, and the people did what they assumed they should, everyone from Ivan Ivanovich – the Russian equivalent of Mr Average – to those at the top of society like Andrei Sakharov. (Sect. 4.1.1.5) It was all a privilege to witness.

Most constituencies had quite a few candidates. Some were standing on a platform of more *perestroika*, others had a specifically environmental agenda, a few were of the old guard, and so on. Nevertheless, they all came to the public meeting, they all sat on the platform next to each other, they all spoke in turn as directed by the chair, they all respected one another (if only because they thought such obvious respect was a vote-winner, which it was), and they were not all men. There was, then, little which could be called inevitable in what soon became an adversarial and majoritarian two-party and then one-party dominant state (Sects. 3.3.2.3 and 5.1.2.1).

---

[1] Prior to her tragic death in 1992, Petra Kelly was a leading figure in the German GP, *Die Grünen*. This term, "the anti-party party", is not to be confused with Nikita Khrushchev's phrase, "the anti-party group" which was a synonym for opposition. In 1957, the Soviet Presidium split into two, as so often happens, and the General Secretary sent the leaders of this faction off to Siberia. He was sent there himself a few years later, to run a cement factory. In like fashion, another anti-party clique emerged in China in 1976: the Gang of Four.

The newly elected representatives were either overt communists or overt and not-so-overt non-communists, but none wore any specific labels; it was, as it were, a parliament (though not yet a government) of national unity. As happened elsewhere, however, (Sect. 1.1.1) it was decided, or just assumed, that both Congress and the new Supreme Soviet were to be majoritarian.[2]

Decisions were to be resolved – or not, as the case may be – in two-option, yes-or-no votes. (To facilitate this procedure, the authorities had imported some special voting machines from the Netherlands so that the deputies could vote electronically. Unfortunately, however, this sophisticated high-tech technology could only manage the simple, low-tech majority vote.) Therefore the members split into two, just like the Americans in the early 1800s, just like the English of old, but unlike these Anglo-Saxons, it took the Russians only 3 months. The no-party system was transformed into a two-party system, government versus opposition: on one side, the Communist Party of the Soviet Union, CPSU, was represented by Gorbachev, and on the other, the Inter-Regional Group was led by Sakharov; one Nobel peace laureate versus another.

In effect, a parliament confronted by some of the most serious problems which any legislature has ever had to face, had devised for itself a system in which one "half" of the House had a vested interest in the failure of the other "half". It was all because of a belief in a myth.

* * * * *

A party system of politics was perhaps all but inevitable. Suffice to say that, despite the writings of many authors such as Hilaire Belloc and Cecil Chesterton, Jonathan Swift, Lev Tolstoy and others, (Emerson P 1994: 58–9), it has spread to most European countries; only in some other parts of the world have certain politicians spoken with Washingtonian zeal against the two-party structure; more of this in Chap. 5.

I might also add that, to the best of my knowledge, there is nothing to suggest majority rule might be a good thing in the Bhagavadgita, the Bible, the Koran or the Tripitaka. Instead, there is much to say it is not a good thing at all in the practice of the Quakers. (Sheeran 1983: 79 *et seq.*) So where is 'the obligation on the minority to submit to the choice of the majority?' (Rousseau 1975: 173)

3.2 Today's Elections

The two-party structure is now firmly established in many jurisdictions, not least in the Anglo-Saxon democracies – those lands which, because of the influence of the British Empire have adopted and not adapted the simple majority vote and FPP.

---

[2] In the hope that the congress would adopt a more consensual polity, the present author did an interview in *Pravda* (*The Truth*) on 6.2.89. In addition, he co-wrote *Democracy without an Opposition* in *Moscow News*, № 6/89; a more substantial article, *Consensus,* in *Novy Mir*, № 3/90; and a chapter in *Pravo i Vlast (Power and the Law)* (Bazileva and Emerson 1990: 279–93).

3.2 Today's Elections   57

It must be stressed that a political structure depends only in part upon the electoral system, a link which is known as Duverger's Law: '*The simple majority single-ballot system favours the two-party* [structure]'. (Duverger 1955: 217) A second major influence is the decision-making process. But here is a paradox: while electoral systems may vary enormously from one country to another, decision-making processes change hardly at all.

It is at least odd that in the computer based high-tech world of today, people still believe in and operate a political structure which, in some respects, is actually worse than the original models devised by the ancient Greeks. Most of us still believe in majority voting, as they did, but we are not so good on some of the details such as limited terms of office. Admittedly, we place more faith in elections and, quite unlike them, we accept a party structure of politics, but 'The general development of parties tends to emphasize [the parties'] deviation from the democratic regime.' (*Ibid*: 423)

Among the world's many and varied electoral procedures, some allow for the existence of independent candidates: this *could* lead to a non-party system. Other methodologies, such as the closed PR-list (Sect. 4.2.6) entrench the party system, and some jurisdictions, as now in Putin's Russia, actually prohibit the independent candidate from standing. Furthermore, some electoral systems, especially FPP, give the likes of Mugabe far too much power, (Sect. 3.3.1.1), whereas the more proportional systems encourage coalition government. The differences from one country to another are huge, not only in the electoral systems but also in the size of the constituencies, the degree of proportionality (Sect. 4.1.1.2), attempts to ensure gender balance, and the extent of the franchise. These differences are often contentious.

Despite all these variations, many people believe that if the people vote by one electoral system or another, that *ergo*, they live in a democracy; and that as long as their country is democratic, all will be well. If it goes "wrong" (as per a European interpretation), then, rather than question the detail of the voting procedures or the principle of majoritarianism, the West tends to turn its collective blind eye. This happened in the case of Algeria when elections were postponed, because everyone knew the Moslem fundamentalists were about to win an overwhelming majority.[3]

In Guyana, to take another example, the British tried to encourage everyone to be democratic, but the first election in 1953 was won by Cheddi Jagan, who the former rulers suspected was a communist. Accordingly, 'the Governor took the drastic step of suspending the constitution and re-introducing authoritarian colonial rule...' (Emerson R 1966: 317) Lest any other democracies might not make the "correct" decisions, the USA came to a pre-emptive conclusion: in its memorandum

---

[3] On 26.12.1991, in the first round of Algeria's TRS election, the *Front Islamique du Salut,* FIS, took 188 of the 231 seats declared; furthermore, of the 199 constituencies going to a second round, it was pretty obvious that the FIS would take a large number and gain a large majority in the 430 member parliament. The High Council of State therefore cancelled the second round, and the West said hardly a word.

NSC 68, the National Security Council 'outlined "the necessity for just suppression," a crucial feature of "the democratic way"....' (Chomsky 1994: 3)

Human history seems to be a chronicle of mistakes, and the story of democratic development has involved quite a few of them. There is, nevertheless, a ray of hope. While de Borda and other inventors have come to favour points and/or pairings systems for mathematical and psephological reasons, a few have chosen the BC as an electoral system from more pragmatic considerations. Nauru, for example, adopted a version of the BC in 1971, apparently because it was considered to be better, or at least easier to count, than the AV electoral system which they had inherited from Australia.[4] Slovenia is another example, although it uses the BC only for the election of two minority MPs. So may be humankind enjoys an archetypal striving for perfection and eventually majority voting in parliaments and FPP elections may be confined to the history books.

3.2.1 The Politics of Adversarial Electoral Systems

> *The state whose prospective rulers come to their duties with least enthusiasm is bound to have the best and most tranquil government, and the state whose rulers are eager to rule the worst. (Plato Book 7: Ch. 5)*

The belief in majority rule which underlies the world-wide use of the majority vote in decision-making also suggests we could accept the FPP electoral system. Although the latter has many of the faults of the majority vote, it also has a few other flaws, some of which may not even serve a party interest let alone the people's concerns. These additional defects will be highlighted before consideration is given to some other electoral systems.

3.2.1.1 The Swing

As seen in Sect. 1.1.2.13, many political parties use the majority vote for their internal decision-making; furthermore, they sometimes use a majority/plurality vote for their internal elections. As a result, many of these parties have tended to split into two wings. Indeed, such have been the divisions, some parties have at times appeared to consist of a left-wing and a right-wing, with no fuselage at all!

Inevitably, the politicians concerned contradict themselves. Their party, they claim, is a broad church, and thus they hope to expand its membership. According

---

[4] The main instigator, it seems, was an Irishman, Desmond Dowdall, at the time Nauru's Secretary for Justice. Alas, according to the Nauruan State Secretary, all the old cabinet records on this subject were destroyed a few years ago in a fire.

3.2 Today's Elections   59

to Robert Dole, a presidential hopeful in 1996, the Republican Party is *'broad and inclusive. It represents many streams of opinion and many points of view.'* (Hillygus and Shields 2008: 27) The country itself, in contrast, is *not* a broad church. Indeed, it is the very opposite, apparently, because it has to be divided into two not quite so broad churches.

Section 1.1.2.2 implied that a tiny faction, perhaps a couple of vacillating MPs or maybe a few members well bribed, can turn a majority into a minority. Similarly, in elections, especially in any FPP contest, a shift of public opinion of just 1 or 2% can sometimes turn a massive victory into a humiliating defeat. In the USA, it all depends upon the "swing states," which is why both US parties tend to woo "middle America." Their British equivalents meanwhile chat up "middle England," and in many UK general elections, such as that of 1997 between Blair and John Major, there is little to separate these "opponents"; indeed, that particular campaign was often referred to as a beauty contest. The upshot appears to be somewhat anomalous: the two-party structure is actually a form of one-party state. 'To-day the Republicans stand at the helm in the US, to-morrow it will be the Democrats or the Republicans once again. There is no particular difference.' (Gorbachev 1987: 216)[5]

3.2.1.2 Minority of the Majority

There is also the case of the Russian dolls to think about (Sect. 1.2.5). If somebody wants to lead a party he probably has to go through a majority vote hurdle first. If he loses, he becomes quite a small fish in quite a big pond. On the other hand, if his minority breaks away and sets up its own (different or similar) party, he may become a big fish again, albeit in a rather small pond.[6]

3.2.1.3 Another Murphy's Law

Because the outcome of an FPP election may sometimes depend on a tiny swing, the system itself tends to encourage the unscrupulous candidate to use what might be called uncivilized tactics. All too often, electoral campaigns deteriorate into a

---

[5] In the wake of Gorbachev's *perestroika* revolution, lots of Western politicians and their political scientists rushed over to Moscow to tell Mikhail Sergeyevich of all the delights and benefits of our two-party democracy, without realizing that the Russian word for "majoritarianism" is "bolshevism", (App. C, C.1.2)

[6] This happened in Ireland in 1985 when, after failing to secure the leadership of *Fianna Fáil*, FF, Des O'Malley set up a new party, the Progressive Democrats.

mud-slinging contest, and he who slings the most often gains the prize: the Zinoviev letter is a case in point.[7]

3.2.1.4 Democratic Leaders

The phrase "democratic leaders" is in part an oxymoron. If ultimate sovereignty lies with the people, those chosen (by lot or election) to execute the people's wishes should be the electorate's servants, not their overlords. In theory, the elected representative is meant to represent the people. However, whenever it comes to an election, the populace is often asked to choose from a range of candidates, each of whom has shown how they intend to represent themselves, each in pursuit of their own "-ism" (or schism).

Most political parties claim to be democratic, as do many other organizations. For reasons unclear, only the latter have AGMs where they elect or re-elect their "leaders" every 12 months or so. Many political parties have annual conferences instead, and their party constitutions often mean their leaders do not have to put themselves up for re-election.[8]

> Elected leaders are sometimes chosen by a plurality vote and yet, as instanced in Sect. 2.2.1.1, there may be one majority in favour of candidate **A**, another majority which likes **B**, and so on.
>
> When the College of Cardinals chooses a new pope, every member is a candidate. Therefore the result depends on whoever sets the agenda: who do they vote for first? Weighted majority voting was introduced in 1179, but that still gave an awful lot of power to those who organised the programme. So a points system was suggested by Cardinal Nicholas Cusanus in 1435, albeit in relation to the choice of Holy Roman Emperor. This would mean that no-one could profit from the order of votes, for only one ballot would be needed. Alas, today, the cardinals have reverted to simple majority voting.
>
> ---
>
> In the British Labour Party leadership election in 1994, two of the candidates were Blair and Gordon Brown. Rather than trust their own voters, these two drew up a pact, so the latter did not stand. Blair was thus elected, but no-one knows for sure whether he would have won the contest if it had not been so "fixed."

3.2.1.5 The Mandate

In FPP, the voter can write only the letter "x." By an extraordinary process of extrapolation, the elected politicians then assume that (a plurality of) their voters have approved *all* of their party's manifesto pledges.

---

[7] In 1924, just before the UK Oct. elections, a forged letter was published in the press suggesting that the Labour Party was being directed by the bolsheviks, not least by one Grigory Yevseyevich Zinoviev. Come polling day, Labour lost.

[8] The English and Welsh GP is one notable exception: the leader has to stand for re-election at least every 2 years. Likewise, the Irish Greens use a 5-year term.

3.2.1.6 Donkeys

There is an old saying in Belfast which suggests that if you tie a union jack or a tricolour onto the tail of an ass, the poor beast will get elected. In 1958, Cacareco the rhino actually won an election for the mayor in Sao Paulo, although it was the human runner-up who took the seat. And in Sweden's elections of 1991, the Donald Duck Party was the ninth most popular.

In many party structures, there is little to prevent ambitious people, sometimes of dubious talent, from joining the party and becoming a candidate.[9] Without a party label, the young man concerned, or occasionally the young woman, would probably have no chance at all. But with it, if he does what the whip demands, he could become an MP or even PM.

> ...in representative government not only is it possible that power will be seized by cunning, immoral and artful mediocrities, such as various prime ministers and presidents have been, but the construction of those governments is such that only that kind of people can obtain power. (Tolstoy 1906: 329)

Politicians, after all, are not trained. If you want to be a bricklayer, you have to do a course. If you want to become a doctor, you have to go to university and put yourself into debt. But to become an MP? You just join a party – a big party mind you, find the one nearest to your own philosophy if you have one – then vote as you are told, push yourself forward and/or wait for a colleague to die.

Few involved in the business of decision-making – the science of social choice – have studied this specialization. Some are there to fight for their corner, their "-ism" of whatever hue. Granted, many are motivated by a strong sense of public duty, but a few are there to promote themselves. It does seem a pity that those who are the more altruistic should continue to participate in a system which also encourages the unscrupulous.

3.2.1.7 Votes of Confidence

As often as not, votes of confidence take on the character of an election rather than that of a decision and, unless they are like a Germanic "constructive vote of no confidence" (Sect. 1.1.2.3), they usually fall into the "*A*, yes-or-no?" category rather than "*A* versus *B*." As in decision-making, it is just not a good methodology.

3.2.1.8 Vote for Me

Whoever they are, most politicians are a little egocentric. Vote for me, they demand, as they knock on your door, thump the lectern or get in a little

---
[9] With a view to being its candidate, the author has been approached over the years by three separate NI political parties.

sound-bite; and do not vote for that other so-and-so of that other party. Sadly, it is often easier to criticize the opponent, and we have all seen election campaigns descend into personality clashes and the rather silly beauty contest we mentioned (Sect. 3.2.1.1). This is most definitely true in any two-party setting, but it also applies to any electoral system where the threshold is high, of which more in a moment (Sect. 4.1.1.3).

Unfortunately, all too many of us like to be wooed. It comes as no surprise, therefore, to see a pre-election budget full of nice little goodies, designed to persuade the electorate to vote from a selfish motivation, and lots of us, I'm afraid, vote in our own self-interest: we too "vote for me."

Fear is an even more dangerous emotion, yet this sometimes plays a part in a pre-election campaign as well. In the US, for example, 'in the 1950s [and subsequently], eager politicians on the electoral hustings... [exploited] the mythical "bomber gap" and "missile gap" for their own purposes.' (Aldrich 2001: 640) Indeed, throughout the Cold War, with the exception of Jimmy Carter in 1976 when the United States was in a post-Vietnam phase, every successful US presidential candidate was the one who was the more anti-Soviet. It mattered not if he were a Democrat (John F Kennedy and his "missile gap") or a Republican (Ronald Reagan's "empire of evil"); all he needed to do was to whip up those emotions of fear. In this respect too, the US two-party system was, and still is, a sort of one-party system. The parties emphasize their differences. In 1960, Kennedy said, *'his campaign should "make clear that the two parties are wholly different in goals..."'* (Hillygus and Shields 2008: 44) As often as not, however, there was indeed – Gorbachev again – 'no particular difference'. (Sect. 3.2.1.1.)

Carter's mantra of human rights did not last very long, I'm afraid. By the time he came up for re-election in 1980, some American hostages had been incarcerated in Teheran; he was tempted and he succumbed to military adventurism. His rescue attempt failed, and he lost the election. If he had succeeded in the former, doubtless he would have also won the latter. Margaret Thatcher was rather more successful in her 1982 war in the Falklands/Malvinas: she did win her subsequent "khaki election."

One notable exception to the rule took place in Kosova where the Kosova Liberation Army, KLA, won its war in 1999, admittedly with the help of NATO, but lost the subsequent elections of October 2000 and November 2001 to Ibrahim Rugova, a declared pacifist.[10]

3.2.1.9 A Threat to the Planet

All of the above defects of overtly adversarial electoral systems apply to any country plagued with FPP, even in peacetime. India's *Bharatiya Janata* Party, BJP,

---

[10] A second exception is Winston Churchill's defeat in the post WWII British general election of 1945; but maybe that was because he was already contemplating another war in Operation Unthinkable. (Aldrich 2001: 58–9)

for instance, carried out a nuclear bomb test in 1998; it helped them to win the next election. (App. C, C.1.4)

With the advent of Gorbachev's *perestroika*, the US debate changed, but not necessarily the tactics, and during his pre-election campaign of 2000, Bush promised the oil companies certain privileges in return for a dollar or two. In this way, via these emotions of greed and/or fear, a two-party democracy (especially when it is in the most powerful country in the world) should be seen for what it is or can become: a threat to the survival of the species.

During the Cold War, the US democracy was actually an exacerbating factor in the arms race. Today, in times of relative peace (or of smaller, hotter wars), the political structures play a part in global warming. Oil and other companies do what they do, with in many instances little regard for the needs of future generations. It sometimes pays them, therefore, to cosy up to those in power, who are also obsessed with the short term. Given the American two-party system, it should come as no surprise to know that some donors give to *both* parties.[11] It is true in Ireland too, for what was done by Mr Dunne was nobody's business in fact, but everybody's in effect.[12]

So why is it all as bad as it is? The answer is partly because of the party political structure. It is a structure which the politicians themselves perpetuate, for it is they who choose the electoral system which all but guarantees the structure's longevity. It is now time, therefore, to have a look at the more common electoral systems, just to see how undemocratic some of them can be, and the party system of government will be further examined in Chap. 5.

3.2.2 The Mathematics of Adversarial Electoral Systems

Apart from the block vote, the most divisive electoral system is FPP, a majority vote when there are just two candidates, a plurality vote when there are three or more. It is called first-past-the-post and the obvious weakness is this: 'There is no post...' (Dummett 1997: 39) The candidate with a majority or, failing that, the biggest minority wins. If there are only two candidates, she will need at least 50% + 1. If there are three candidates, he could do it with only 33⅓% + 1. If 4, 25% + 1. If 10, 10 % + 1. In PNG in 1992, the winner passed the non-existent post with a

---

[11] In early 2002, in what became the biggest corporate collapse in history, it was revealed that Enron Corporation not only subsidized both the US Democrats and Republicans, they also funded both the UK Labour and Tory Parties. (The *Guardian*, 30.1.2002)

[12] In 1997, the McCracken Report revealed that the Irish businessman, Ben Dunne, gave £1.3 million to the then *Taoiseach*, (PM), Charlie Haughey of FF, as well as some financial assistance to Michael Lowry of *Fine Gael*, FG.

non-majority of only 6.3%, (IDEA 1997: 42), and in 2002, 'several candidates... won seats [with] only 5%'.[13]

Even if there were only two parties, the system could still be very unfair. If party *W* has 49% support in every constituency in the land, and party *X* has 51% support, then *X* will win every single seat. There again, if party support varies and if some constituencies are big in terms of the size of their electorates while others are small then, depending on the draw, *W* with less than a majority of votes can nevertheless win a majority of seats. The difficult work of a boundary commisssion, which tries to keep all the constituencies roughly the same numerical size, is therefore crucial.

Without some form of impartial arbitration on this matter, there would be much gerrymandering – the unsubtle art of drawing constituency boundaries, as doubtless M Calonne would have done, (Sect. 1.1.2.10) – so that one particular party gains the most seats. The word, by the way, comes from a certain Governor Eldridge Gerry who, in 1812, designed a new electoral district for Massachusetts and while it benefited his own party enormously, it had the unfortunate appearance on the map of a salamander. (Fishkin 1995: 117)

The biggest inaccuracy comes from the fact that a single-preference electoral system, like FPP and most of the PR-list systems, cannot accurately reflect the views of the voter. We are all sophisticated creatures and doubtless, most of us have preferences. To restrict the choice of the voter to an Orwellian selection – this one candidate "good," all those other candidates "not good" – is bound to lead to inaccuracies in the way many voters express their individual will. And if the expression of the individual will is inaccurate, then no mathematical formula can interpret such dodgy information to identify society's collective or general will with any degree of precision.

So let us now consider the theory of using a single preference system in the simplest of plural worlds, in an election involving three candidates: *A*, *B* and *C*. Accordingly, let us imagine a constituency, as in Fig. 3.1, where an electorate of 100 persons has the preferences shown (even if the electoral system allows the voter to express only a first preference):

In FPP the winner is *A*, even though an absolute majority of 60% think *A* is the worst. An objective assessment of these preferences would surely suggest that *B* should be the winner.

Number of voters:	40	29	31
1st preferences	*A*	*B*	*C*
2nd preferences	*B*	*C*	*B*
3rd preferences	*C*	*A*	*A*

Fig. 3.1 A voters' profile

---

[13] The Administration and Cost of Elections, ACE, electoral knowledge network. http://aceproject.org/ace-en/topics/es/esy/esy_pg (Accessed 28 May 2010).

> *'Nothing can be more absurd and unfair than... elections carried out by simple majority rule.'* Joseph Morales writing in 1797 (McLean and Urken 1995: 214)

It is a bit like the Welsh referendum, really. If only the first preferences are taken into account, one simply does not know and one cannot know who (or what) is the most popular. In such a procedure, the only way to be really sure that the winner has won is to devise a "post" of 50%.

When there is a plurality of candidates, many votes are cast tactically and, in consequence, many multi-candidate elections under FPP amount to a two-horse race. As Duverger said, FPP leads to a two-party system. (Sect. 3.2) Moreover, if some of the more pluralist countries were to change from FPP to a simple multi-party electoral system, the two "broad churches" could easily splinter, not necessarily along ideological cleavages but on ethno-religious lines. In the US for instance, there could all too quickly emerge a black party, an Hispanic party, an American-Irish party, and so on. Likewise, 'Were India to switch to PR, it is a safe conjecture that it would quickly become one of the most fragmented, if not atomized, of all known party systems.' (Sartori 1986: 68) The argument is certainly sound if the electoral system is a single-preference form of PR.

3.2.2.1 The US System

As was said in Sect. 3.1.3, the US founding fathers did nothing to change the "Old World" decision-making process. They did, however, change the electoral system or rather, the way the votes were counted. 'The person having the greatest number of votes shall be the president... [and] after the choice of President, the person having the greatest number of votes... shall be the Vice-President.' (US Constitution 1787: Art II, Section I, para 3.) Initially the system was fine but with the introduction of parties, it was no longer candidates versus other candidates, it was parties versus other parties. This meant, in practice, one big party versus the other big party, with each putting forward two names on their respective tickets. What was an adversarial electoral system had thus degenerated further.

3.2.3 The Application of Adversarial Electoral Systems

In some electoral systems, the voter is entitled to express one preference only; other systems are preferential. Now it is said that people get the politicians they deserve. This would perhaps be true if the electoral system itself were accurate but, as just shown, many electoral systems give an imprecise representation of the people's wishes. It should come as no surprise, therefore, if on certain occasions, the elected politicians appear to be at odds with their electorate. The existence of such a disparity can be inferred, perhaps, from opinion polls, and confirmed, again only perhaps, by the results of referendums.

> ...*Maastricht, which enjoyed the support of parties with 80% of the seats in [the Danish parliament], was rejected by the voters in 1992.* (Bogdanov 1994: 72)
> ...*in New Zealand and Italy where referendums have exposed the unpopularity of politicians and helped to transform the governing system.* (Butler and Ranney 1994: ix)

3.2.3.1 Multi-Preference Electoral Systems

In most multi-preference voting procedures, voters are free to cast their preferences as they wish. The greater the degree of choice enjoyed by the electorate, the less the degree of control in the hands of the political parties. The latter sometimes seek to regain their dominant influence by other means.

In NI under PR-STV, for instance, voters are allowed to express any number of preferences; furthermore, they are free to vote across party, gender and even sectarian divides. Unfortunately, in practice, a party with two candidates, *A* and *B*, will sometimes issue "instructions" to its voters to vote *A*-1 *B*-2 or *B*-1 *A*-2 only, so to ensure both *A* and *B* get reasonable first preference scores; this means in the count that neither gets eliminated too quickly. As a tactic, it works: such "instructions" are often obeyed to a large extent, and when they are not, there is talk of a lack of voter discipline and other "democratic" phrases.

Thankfully, despite the attentions of the parties, many voters still think independently. In a 1980 by-election in Australia, 'Over 99% of Labour supporters did not follow the party's how-to-vote instructions.' (Wright 1986: 136) Likewise in Switzerland, 'Those who usually support one of the large established parties seem to follow the advice of their parties more consistently... [whereas] voters attracted by minor, peripheral parties seem to have a rather independent voting behaviour...' (Trechsel and Kriesi 1996: 200)

3.2.3.2 Electoral Systems for Use in the Legislature

In various countries and for countless reasons, a wide variety of electoral systems is in use. There are, after all, over 300 to choose from. Accordingly, if the elected representatives wanted to elect their government and/or the prime minister, they could do so. Parliaments, however, seldom use internal elections for the appointment of their executives. In the British House of Commons for example, if and when one party wins (not necessarily a majority of the votes but) a majority of the seats, the leader of that party then becomes PM – the 'elected dictator' to quote Lord Hailsham's apt description of Thatcher, (Hailsham 1978: he uses the phrase frequently) – and she then appoints the cabinet without any election at all.

Admittedly, the British parliament elects its speaker, a tradition which dates back to the fourteenth century. Furthermore, there are many committees on which all major parties are represented and these committees are not without considerable clout. Nevertheless, the present structure of government allows far too much power to be placed into the hands of a minority of, sometimes, just one person.

In the NI Assembly, members do not have elections either but at least ministers in Stormont are appointed by a d'Hondt interpretation of party strengths, (Sect. 5.1.5.4), rather than by fiat of the First and Deputy First Ministers.

3.2.3.3 Electoral Systems Used in Committees

We have probably all participated in an AGM in which proceedings are conducted along lines first written, many years ago, before the days of Pliny the Younger. (Sect. 2.3.2) Lord Citrine and others have written modern versions of the same with just a few embellishments, so current "democratic" practice sometimes proceeds along the following lines.

Mr J, the outgoing chair, stands down, and asks someone else to conduct the elections. A neutral individual steps forward. "Nominations for chair?" she asks. "I nominate Mr J," says one, quickly. "Seconded," adds another, and both names are recorded in the minutes. (Their vote, therefore, is hardly secret.) Then silence. "Any other nominations?" Someone in the back of the hall desperately wants Ms K to be chair but, when everyone is so fond of Mr J, well, maybe next year, which is what he thought last year. "No other nominations? Thank you ladies and gentlemen; I therefore declare Mr J elected, unopposed, to serve another year." So he returns to the chair and thanks all concerned for this quite unexpected honour.

Some committees go further and prefer all their officers to be "elected" unopposed. On those occasions when there are two or even more nominees, however, they still practice majority or plurality voting, and such procedures are invariably enshrined in their constitutions.

At one extreme, some groups suffer from an "all-nice-candidates" syndrome so that everything is best sorted out during the nomination process. At the other, the nomination-cum-election procedure is often rather time-consuming until at last it is finished, whereupon people praise the likes of Mr J with almost Stalinist enthusiasm.

3.3 Today's Elections: Practice

> *Ethnic parties developed, majorities took power, and minorities took shelter.*
> *(Horowitz 2000: 629)*

In many societies, political campaigning prior to an election has often led to increased tensions in society, if not indeed violence. This is not always the case, of course. Sierra Leone, for example, suffered a civil war in 2002 and yet, in the subsequent elections in 2007 in which FPP replaced the previous system of PR, everything went reasonably smoothly. Nevertheless, in those instances where violence does occur, perhaps the use of a less adversarial electoral system might have been the wiser course.

Consideration will now be given to how single-preference electoral systems – FPP, TRS, simple PR-list and the single non-transferable vote, SNTV – have sometimes made matters worse.

3.3.1 FPP

FPP is sometimes called plurality voting. (Sects. 2.4.1 and 4.2.1) Reference has already been made to its frailties, not least in the UK and USA, but also in India for example. (Sect. 3.2.1.9) Mention is now made of two other case studies, Zimbabwe and Kenya.

3.3.1.1 Zimbabwe

After several years of struggle, Zimbabwe gained its independence in 1979. The subsequent elections of 1980 were held to contest a parliament of 100 seats split into two rolls: 80 seats for the black population, 20 for the white. On the first roll, Mugabe won 63% of the vote and 71% of the seats; Joshua Nkomo won 24% of the vote and 25% of the seats. In Matebeleland, however, the picture was reversed: of the 16 seats contested, Mugabe gained just 1; Nkomo won all the other 15.

There followed the Matabeleland Massacres, when Mugabe crushed any resistance. Thousands died. In the subsequent elections of 1990, his party gained 81% of the vote and 98% of the seats, 117 of the 120 contested. There followed years of misrule.

3.3.1.2 Kenya

Partly in response to international pressure, Kenya reverted from Mzee Kenyatta's one-party state to a multi-party democracy in 1991. His equally corrupt successor, Arap Moi, lost the presidency in 2002 in what were, to the happy relief of many, largely peaceful elections. The former Vice-President, Mwai Kibaki, a Kikuyu, took over the presidency and the government. Five years later, Kibaki stood again, this time against Raila Odinga, a Luo, the son of Oginga Odinga, Kenyatta's old colleague before independence and rival afterwards. Officially, Kibaki and Odinga won 4,584,721 and 4,352,993 votes respectively, but the exit polls gave victory, not to the former by this 3%, but to the latter by a 6% margin. At the same time, Odinga's Orange Democratic Movement won 99 seats in the new parliament, compared with the 43 seats of Kibaki's Party of National Unity. Allegations of

3.3 Today's Elections: Practice   69

massive fraud in the count in Kibaki's tribal areas, where international observers had been refused access, led to widespread, inter-tribal violence.

Kenya now has a form of power-sharing, with Kibaki, the loser, still the President and Odinga in the new post of Prime Minister. A win-win electoral system allowing for this sort of outcome would have been more appropriate.

3.3.2 TRS

While FPP was adopted by many countries of the former British Empire, those with a French legacy tended to opt for TRS. (Sects. 2.4.2 and 4.2.2) One such was Algeria (Sect. 1.1.2.8) and another Côte d'Ivoire. Other states which have adopted this system include the former Belgian colony of DRC, Russia and Ukraine.

3.3.2.1 Democratic Republic of the Congo, DRC

The 1994 genocide in Rwanda (Sect. 1.2.1) and the subsequent victory of Paul Kigame's Rwanda Patriotic Front, RPF, led to a mass exodus of *Interahamwe* forces into Eastern Zaire. The RPF followed 2 years later and, under Laurent-Désiré Kabila, marched all the way to Kinshasa, thus sweeping the incumbent President, Mobutu Sese Seko, into exile. The latter had ruled the DRC, which he had renamed Zaire, since 1965, having taken power in 1960 in a *coup d'état*. Kabila, however, was unable to hold the country together. Jean-Pierre Bemba led an armed up-rising, other countries joined in, and Kabila was then assassinated. The latter's son Joseph took over and soon helped to broker a peace deal. In the first round of the subsequent presidential elections, scheduled for 2006, 33 candidates were whittled down to a win-or-lose second round between the above two antagonists of the earlier violence: Kabila and Bemba. So there was yet more violence.

Thankfully, Bemba went into exile. An electoral system more suited to power-sharing, however, even just the simple winner and runner-up election devised in the US (Sect. 3.2.2.1), might have led to a more peaceful outcome. Meanwhile, 54 different political parties, albeit with 28 of them gaining only 1 seat each along with 63 independent candidates, were elected to parliament under FPP.

3.3.2.2 Côte d'Ivoire

Côte d'Ivoire is another African country that has suffered the horrors of war. The bloodshed lasted from Sept. 2002 to late 2004 and, partially as a consequence, the elections originally scheduled for 2005 did not take place until Oct. 2010. All but inevitably, the TRS electoral system led to a final run-off, a win-or-lose battle, between the incumbent, Laurent Gbagbo, and his old rival, Alassane Ouattara.

The election was followed by claim and counter-claim, and then violence. The matter is still unresolved, but the intervention of outsiders, not least those of the same continent, may help to resolve the conflict. It is to be hoped that they might use a less adversarial electoral system next time.

3.3.2.3 Russia

The first round of Russia's first post-*perestroika* election was very civilized (Sect. 3.1.4) In those constituencies where a second-round was held, however, the politicians' good natured behaviour quickly dissipated. A TRS second round, a straight majority vote between only two candidates, is a most adversarial electoral system. Hence the candidates and their supporters became aggressive, and the atmosphere deteriorated considerably.

3.3.2.4 Ukraine

People from the western side of Ukraine tend to be more Ukrainian-speaking in their language, more Catholic or Uniate in their religion, and more western-oriented in their politics. In the East, in contrast, people are often Russian-speaking Orthodox and more inclined to Moscow's ways. The two languages, of course, are both Slav and therefore very similar, while the religions are both conservative forms of Christianity. To suggest or imply, therefore, that there is a dividing line which splits Ukraine into two would be quite wrong if not even dangerous. That is what the current electoral system does.

In 2010, Julia Timoshenko and Viktor Yanukovich competed in the first and then second round of a presidential contest. Much of the language of their respective election campaigns was of the mud-slinging variety but fortunately, just as Ukraine did not descend into violence at the time of the 2004 Orange Revolution, so too this country seems to survive every divisive provocation.

Because the election went to a second round, the OSCE (and other international observer missions) spent a financial and ecological fortune to return hundreds of personnel to observe the second round as well. Regrettably, while the OSCE criticizes everything from the colour of the ballot box to the dreadful shenanigans that took place in some counting centres in 2004, it does not comment, one way or the other, on the choice of electoral system.[14]

---

[14] The author was in Ukraine as an OSCE short-term observer twice in 2010, once in 2007, thrice in 2004, and as a long-term observer in 2006. In addition, he gave a lecture to the OSCE on inclusive voting procedures in Warsaw in 2009.

3.3 Today's Elections: Practice 71

3.3.3 FPP and PR-List

One example of a country which uses a combination of FPP and PR-list is Tunisia. Most PR-list elections allow the voter only one preference. (Sect. 4.2.6) Ratios of seats to be won under the two parts may vary, but this single vote combination is a form of the additional member system, AMS.

3.3.3.1 Tunisia

In the 2009 elections, 152 MPs were elected under FPP, with the voter voting only for a party list; the other 37 seats were awarded on the basis of a PR-count of those votes. The Constitutional Democratic Rally of President Zine El Abidine Ben Ali won 75% of the seats, while he himself won the TRS presidential contest with 90%. Given his Jan. 2011 overthrow, the fairness and accuracy of the electoral system should now be scrutinized.

3.3.4 TRS or PR-List

The electoral system chosen for Bosnia after the 1992–5 war was very much the product of international opinion but likewise the earlier pre-war poll was also heavily influenced by outsiders. In 1990, the chosen methodology was TRS, just as it was in Croatia, Macedonia and Serbia. (Emerson and Šedo 2010: 8)[15] It was a terrible system. 'Driving across Bosnia in 1990 just prior to the elections afforded me a brief glimpse into the republic's miserable future. One village drowning in a sea of green crescents, (Moslem)... would give way to another... where the HDZ, [Croatian Democratic Party], was sovereign, or where every wall was covered with the acronym SDS [Serbian Democratic Party]. In some villages, the western half was green while the eastern half was red, white and blue (Serbian)... Many doomed settlements were a jumble of all three.' (Glenny 1996: 147) The vote was little more than a sectarian head-count: from a total of 240 seats, the Bosniak Party of Democratic Action, SDA, won 87 seats, the SDS 72 and the HDZ 44. It was, in effect, a cause of war (Emerson P 1999: 37) for by 'organizing parties along national lines, all three communities bear responsibility for [Bosnia's] appalling fate.' (Glenny 1996: 147)

Post Dayton, the chosen system was closed PR-list. The voter was allowed only one preference, so this contest, too, was another terrible system, another sectarian

---

[15] Montenegro used closed PR-list, while the electorate in Slovenia opted for the Swiss model: voters 'had as many votes as there were seats in their constituency and could vote either for a party list or cast preference votes for individual cndidates of one or more parties.' (Rose and Munro 2003: 294) Sadly, this was changed in 1991 to closed list-PR, but revised to open list-PR in 2000.

head-count. A National Working Group was then set up to consider the matter, but it consisted of representatives of the three main ethno-religious parties and, despite the sterling efforts of an impartial chair, each did their very best for their own "community." Thus all agreed to a system designed to perpetuate the three main parties: PR-list, although at least it is now an open system.[16]

3.3.5 PR-List

Many former communist countries have adopted either a version of the system used in France, TRS, or one based on the German system, a double vote combination of FPP and a PR top-up called multi-member proportional, MMP. (Sect. 4.2.10) Other countries have chosen a form of PR-list, (Sect. 4.2.6) a methodology which is also widely used in South America.

3.3.5.1 Kosova

The system selected for the post-war elections of 2000 onwards in Kosova was the result of discussions held abroad, not least by the OSCE[17] and the International Foundation for Electoral Systems, IFES. The net result was a form of closed PR-list with set-aside seats for any ethnic minorities, not only the Serbs but also the Roma and Gorani for example. (Emerson and Šedo 2010: 21) The consequence was an effect similar to that seen in Bosnia: the election was yet again little more than a sectarian headcount, albeit with some variation in the large ethnic Albanian vote which, like so many other societies elsewhere (Sect. 1.1.2.13) had already split into two.

3.3.5.2 Iraq

In post-war Iraq, many would argue that the most important task is to keep the diverse groups together: Sunnis, Shias and Kurds. Despite this goal, the 2010 parliamentary elections were held under a single-preference system, open PR- list. In attempting to form a *cohesive* parliament, they used a *divisive* electoral system.

As it happened, of the 325 seats contested, the two biggest winners were 91 seats for al-Iaqiyya under Ayad Allawi and 89 for Nouri al-Maliki's State of Law Coalition. This led to a record-breaking impasse in forming a government. Initially

---

[16] In January 1999, the author made a verbal submission to the National Working Group on QBS.

[17] In a written submission to the OSCE, the author again suggested QBS, having first visited Kosovo in July 1999.

In 2001, the author was an international trainer for the OSCE based in Prizren.

they argued over who was to form a majority administration but eventually, in Dec. 2010, parliament chose a power-sharing government. The negotiations had taken 249 days. (See chronology, 2010)

3.3.6 SNTV

In SNTV, the voter casts a single preference, as in FPP, but in a multi-member constituency. (Sect. 4.2.5)

3.3.6.1 Afghanistan

Afghanistan is another multi-ethnic, post-conflict society. As an absolute minimum, therefore, a preferential form of voting should be used. At the moment, presidential elections are held under TRS and parliament is elected under SNTV. The election thus is little more than yet another sectarian head-count, with Pashtuns voting for Pashtuns, Tajiks for Tajiks, etc., against a backdrop of warlords and widespread corruption let alone war.

Not solely for these reasons, both of the most recent contests – the 2009 presidential and the 2010 parliamentary elections – have been dogged by countless accusations of fraud, vote buying, ballot stuffing and so on. The win-or-lose nature of the electoral system is an exacerbating factor.

3.4 Conclusions

While many politicians seldom question decision-making processes, they do at least discuss the merits or otherwise of various electoral systems. Unfortunately, they usually choose the system which, first and foremost, benefits themselves. Even or especially in such delicate situations as persist in NI and Bosnia, most political parties, it seems, act first and foremost in their own interests.

The main conclusion is that there are good, not so good, and downright bad electoral systems, just as with decision-making processes. Given (a) that for any electorate with its own voters' profile, a change in the electoral system could lead to a change of the persons elected; (b) that the nature of the electoral system in part determines the nature of government; it follows that the choice of electoral system is a very important question. It should not be left to the politicians. If democracy is sacrosanct, the choice of electoral system should really be a matter of human rights.

It must also be said that we the people can hardly complain about the quirks of our politicians if we ourselves use very primitive electoral systems and decision-making processes in our own committees. Parliaments do what parliaments do, but partly because we do too.

References

Aldrich RJ (2001) The hidden hand. John Murray, London
Aristotle (1992) The Politics. Penguin Classics, London
Bazileva I, Emerson P (1990) *Vlast, psikhologiya i politika konsensusa* (The power, psychology and politics of consensus). In: Vyshinsky MP (ed) Pravo i vlast (power and the law). Progress, Moscow
Black D (1958) The theory of committees and elections. CUP, Cambridge
Bogdanor V (1981) The people and the party system. CUP, Cambridge
Bogdanor V (1994) Western Europe. In: Butler D, Ranney A (eds) Referendums around the world. The AEI Press, Washington
Butler D, Ranney A (eds) (1994) Referendums around the world. The AEI Press, Washington
Chomsky N (1994) World orders, old and new. Pluto, London
Churchill WS (1956) A history of the english-speaking peoples. Cassell, London
Dahl RA (2000) On democracy. Yale University Press, New Haven
de Ste Croix GEM (2005) Athenian democratic origins. OUP, Oxford
Dummett M (1997) Principles of electoral reform. OUP, Oxford
Duverger M (1955) Political parties. Methuen & Co., London
Emerson P (1994) The politics of consensus. Samizdat, Belfast
Emerson P (1999) From Belfast to the Balkans. The de Borda Institute, Belfast
Emerson P, Šedo J et al (2010) Electoral systems and the link to the party systems. In: Stojarová V, Emerson P (eds) Party politics in the Western Balkans. Routledge, Abingdon
Emerson R (1966) From empire to nation. Beacon, Boston
Fishkin JS (1995) The voice of the people. Yale University Press, New Haven
Glenny M (1996) The fall of Yugoslavia. Penguin, London
Gorbachev M (1987) Perestroika. Collins, London
Hailsham Lord (1978) The dilemma of democracy. Collins, London
Havel V (1989) Open letters. Faber and Faber, London
Hillygus DS, Shields TS (2008) The persuadable voter. Princeton University, New Jersey
Horowitz DL (2000) Ethnic groups in conflict. University of California, Berkeley
IDEA (1997) The international IDEA handbook of electoral system design. IDEA, Stockholm
Jenkins P (1997) A history of the United States. Macmillan, London
Ketcham R (1984) Presidents above party. University of North Carolina, Chapel Hill
McLean I, Urken AB (eds) (1995) Classics of social choice. University of Michigan, Ann Arbor
Plato (1888) The works of Plato – the Republic, Timaeus and Critias (trans: Henry Davis). George Bell and Sons, London
Rose R, Munro N (2003) Elections and parties in new European democracies. CQ Press, Washington
Rousseau J-J (1975) The social contract and discourses. JM Dent and Sons, London
Sartori G (1986) Influence of electoral systems. In: Grofman B, Lijphart A (eds) Electoral laws and their political consequences. Agathon Press, New York
Sheeran MJ (1983) Beyond majority rule. Regis College, Philadelphia
Skinner Q (2008) The Italian city-republics. In: Dunn (ed) Democracy, the unfinished journey, 508 BC to AD 1993. OUP, Oxford
Tolstoy LN (1978) The meaning of the Russian revolution in Russian intellectual history. In: Raeff M (ed) Russian intellectual history. Humanities Press, New Jersey
Trechsel A, Kriesi H (1996) Switzerland: the referendum and initiative as a centrepiece of the political system. In: Gallagher M, Uleri PV (eds) The referendum experience in Europe. Macmillan Press, London
Wright JFH (1986) Australian experience with majority-preferential and quota-preferential systems. In: Grofman B, Lijphart A (eds) Electoral laws and their political consequences. Agathon Press, New York

Chapter 4
The Candid Candidate

> *Political power means capacity to regulate national life through national representatives. If national life becomes so perfect as to become self-regulated, no representation becomes necessary.*
>
> Mahatma Gandhi (Bose 1968: 40)

Abstract This chapter first considers the principles upon which an electoral system should be based. Next it compares most of the better-known existing systems. Then it examines the methodology of consensus voting, not only for elections to parliament, but also for contests in parliament for the appointment of a government. Finally, it adds a draft definition of a democratic election.

4.1 Free and Fair Elections

If an electoral system is to be "free and fair", the phrase used by international observation missions, not only should the election be conducted in a neutral environment, but the system itself should also be equitable. Unfortunately, at the moment, this phrase usually refers to everything except the choice of electoral system: to the registration of voters and the formation of the electoral register; to the eligibility of citizens to stand as candidates; to the freedom to campaign via public meetings and so forth; to the role of the media in providing a balanced coverage; and to the conduct of the election and the transparency of the count. In a nutshell, the voter must be able to go to the polling station and vote in secret, without fear of intimidation or worse. In Bosnia in 1996, for example, such a free and *almost* fair election did indeed take place, and all credit to the OSCE.[1] But the system itself – closed PR-list – "forced" the voters to make a decision for one candidate only. (Sect. 3.3.4) That was neither free nor fair.

---

[1] The author was a short term observer in Republika Srpska.

4.1.1 Electoral Principles

> *If a form of election is to be just, the voters must be able to rank each candidate according to his merits, compared successively to the merits of each of the others.* J-C de Borda. (McLean and Urken 1995: 84)
>
> *... I define a just election... as one in which each elector has assigned to each candidate the level of support which in his judgment he deserves in comparison to the rest.* Joseph Morales. (*Ibid*: 225–6)

For an electoral system to be fair, it should comply with a certain number of principles, and these shall now be examined. Some of them may appear to be mutually exclusive.

4.1.1.1 Constituency Size

In theory, the elected representative should be a local person, known to and acquainted with the particular constituency. This would suggest (a) that in terms of numbers of voters, the constituency should be reasonably small, and (b) that all candidates should have a qualification of residency.

At present, some societies suffer from what is called a "chicken run", in which various candidates scoot around the country looking for a "safe" seat, i.e., a seat which their particular party always, or nearly always, wins. Meanwhile other seats are subject to gerrymanders. (Sect. 3.2.2) So much for the practice. The theoretical argument for reasonably small constituencies, however, is sound.

4.1.1.2 Proportionality

For a plural society, proportionality is essential. Indeed, for multi-ethnic societies (if that is the appropriate term) such as exist in Northern Ireland, in many Balkan countries, in most African countries and, in fact, in almost every country, proportionality should be seen as an obvious requirement of the chosen electoral system.

There are, however, two types of proportionality. In most PR-list systems, proportionality is based on party labels. In other systems – PR-STV and the quota Borda system, QBS, of which more in a moment – voters are able to express multiple preferences, and proportionality is based on whatever the voters decide is important. If, for example, in a land where most of the parties are ethno-religious, a number of voters is concerned about the specific issue of nuclear power, and if each of them gives their first and subsequent preferences to anti-nuke candidates from all of their various parties, then, in the count, if the group is sufficiently large, at least one anti-nuke candidate is bound to get elected.

Similarly on gender, the more sophisticated PR systems tend to encourage a better gender balance than would otherwise be the case. Admittedly, this is

4.1 Free and Fair Elections

sometimes achieved a little artificially by a rule which insists that parties are obliged to include a minimum number of female candidates. In Bosnia for example the electoral law stipulates that in its PR-list system, every third name *must* be female. In general, though, 'Evidence across the world suggests that women are less likely to be elected under plurality-majority systems than under PR ones. The Inter-Parliamentary Union... found that on average women made up 11% of the parliamentarians in established democracies using FPP, but the figure almost doubled to 20% in those countries using some form of PR.' (IDEA 1997: 30)

Another possible advantage of a preferential form of voting is that it sometimes means any independent candidates may also have a fair chance. In a two-party system under FPP, they have an equal chance only in theory; as we know from US presidential elections, to use the most glaring example, they have next to no chance in practice. In a PR-list system, if they are allowed to stand, they might have a chance, depending on the list system used and the threshold, (see the next section). Accordingly, if the system is both preferential and proportional, as long as that threshold is not too high, the independent candidate may well enjoy an almost equal prospect of success.

Before moving on, attention should be drawn to an anomaly. Many protagonists of PR-STV agree that any electoral system which works on first preferences only, like FPP, might give hopelessly inaccurate answers; and yet, in many elections, these same people then analyze the robustness of the PR-STV electoral system on the basis of first preferences only. (Baker 1996: 733–7)

4.1.1.3 Quota and Effective Threshold

In any election, the quota is the specific number of votes which, if attained, ensures the election of the representative concerned. In a proportional system, it varies according to the number of elected representatives to be elected, as shown in Table 4.1.

The effective threshold of an electoral system, though largely dependent upon the quota, depends on a number of other factors as well: the comparative strength of other parties, and so on, (Lijphart 1994: 25 *et seq.*) and on balance, maybe a suitable size is a five-seater, with a corresponding threshold of about 17%.

For any specific number of MPs in a parliament, the constituencies will clearly be smaller if they are all single-seaters, and vice versa, but the proportionality principle tends to clash with the constituency principle. The obvious answer to this

Table 4.1 The quota

№ of representatives to be elected	Quota
1	50% + 1
2	33⅓% + 1
3	25% + 1
4	20% + 1

dilemma is to incorporate a top-up (Sect. 4.2.10), for thus both the constituency and the proportionality principles could be combined to get the best of both worlds.

4.1.1.4 Voters' Choice

To be fair, a vote should be free. That is, the voters should be able to choose whomsoever they wish, whether party candidates and/or independents, and vote for them in their own order of preference. Moreover, a fair electoral system should enable the voters to vote *sincerely,* without their having to take tactical concerns into consideration. Any unnecessary restriction on the voters' choice should be regarded as unfair.

For example, the voter who chooses to vote for a particular party should have the choice of a pro-nuke and an anti-nuke candidate if (a) the subject is topical and (b) that particular party is itself divided on such an important matter. Perhaps the voter should also have the choice of both a male and a female candidate.

It is interesting to note that in the US, where there was originally considerable antipathy towards the idea of party politics (Sect. 3.1.3) there has been a fairly strong trend towards non-partisan elections. 'In a majority of US municipal elections (probably about two thirds), candidates run for office on tickets without party labels. Such non-partisan elections are a product of the municipal reform of the early twentieth century which attempted to limit the power of corrupt party machines, insulate local elections from the influence of state and national party politics, facilitate more efficient and businesslike administration of local government, and encourage recruitment of superior candidates for local office who might be reluctant to associate themselves with party organizations.' (Cassel 1986: 226)

Admittedly, in some instances, the candidates concerned were not true independents: they just ran, as quoted, 'without party labels'. In other parts of the world, too, the sound practice of having independent candidates has sometimes succumbed to the pressures or temptations of the party system. In West Africa, for instance, 'In the days when elections were still free it was common for a rural district to elect a local man as an "independent" representative, on the understanding that after the election he would join whichever party had won, and so protect the interests of his constituents...' (Lewis 1965: 22)

The conclusion is similar to that on decision-making. Any system which tempts or even "forces" the voter to vote for either *A* or *B* only, when other candidates should also be able to stand, is unfair, for it restricts the voters' freedom of choice.

4.1.1.5 Candid Candidates

In Sect. 4.1.1.1 it was recommended that any candidates should be resident in the constituency; that would cut down on the "chicken run" type of politician. Is it also possible to reduce the number of representatives of the "vote for me" egocentric kind? After all, there are lots of people in every constituency who would never dream of standing for election but who, if persuaded to do so, might prove to be excellent representatives.

4.1 Free and Fair Elections

> *In the summer and fall of 1988, I refused a number of nominations to the Supreme Soviet... Later, in January, after my candidacy for the Congress was supported by large majorities in many Academy institutes, I decided I couldn't refuse...* (Sakharov 1991: 96)

Perhaps, therefore, it would be better if every adult resident in the constituency were eligible. Every local community or constituency has its rather better known personalities, who might or might not be attached to a particular political party. Accordingly, in any election, voters could cast their preferences for a fixed number of local persons.

With such an open ballot, although politicians from various parties would no doubt be making their presence felt, even the modest might get elected. Certainly, with computers, the theoretical existence of scores or even hundreds of candidates need not create any insurmountable administrative problems. And such a ruling would be more realizable if politics were to be regarded, rather like jury service, as a civic duty.

The other methodology, the chosen instrument of the ancient Greeks, is the lottery. Given the advances in modern technology, a truly random sample could easily be found on this principle. Disadvantages there might be, but at least this system would be balanced between male and female, young and old, urban and rural, etc.

> In a 1999 public meeting of community activists in NI, the author suggested such a random sample might be appropriate for the proposed Civic Forum, an advisory body designed to work in parallel with the Assembly. If accepted, such a suggestion would have reduced the chances of any of these activists of serving on this Forum from about one in a thousand to one in a million, the size of the NI electorate. The suggestion was rejected.

An open ballot, one in which all adult residents who have not yet served a term or two would be eligible candidates, would be very inclusive. At the very least, the ballot paper could allow for the possibility of another name, just as some multi-option referendums allow the voter to add their own option. (App. D, Guam) If, therefore, some people wanted to vote for a particular resident who was not included on the official list of any of the parties, they could still do so. A variation of this methodology has been used in local elections in Norway,[2] and thus were rather more women elected.

4.1.1.6 Win-or-Lose or Win-Win

As in decision-making, so too in elections, an important feature of any electoral system relates to whether it is less adversarial and, *ipso facto*, more consensual. Obviously, if the system is used in single-seat constituencies – majority, plurality, TRS or AV/STV – it will be of the win-or-lose variety. Furthermore, if the subsequent parliament is also to be adversarial, the contest in the constituency could become

---

[2] 'Voters in municipal elections can also add candidates from other lists to their preferred party's list.' (Dalbakk 2003: 5) Not only did so many women add female names, they were also able to cross out lots of males. (Lakeman 1974: 107)

bitter and polarized: of the above four systems, only AV encourages a certain degree of cross-party co-operation.

So what should a consensual electoral system look like? To have more than one winner per constituency would seem to be sensible; PR should therefore be on the menu. Secondly, to guarantee a fair degree of freedom of choice, a preferential system would be advisable. Thirdly, in view of what has already been said, a top-up would be a sensible way of combining the constituency principle with a low threshold.

The question, then, is this: can an electoral system be inclusive and, if so, to what extent? For many people the only time they actually play an active part in the democratic process is every few years when they vote in an election. If the democratic process is the supposedly peaceful means by which all political disputes are to be resolved; if in addition the democratic process is to be an intrinsic part of any peace process, in conflict zones like NI and the Balkans, then surely the act of voting should itself be "peace-ful".

In many instances, it is the very opposite. Candidates *fight* elections, in the hope of *beating* their opponents; it is indeed win or lose, victory or defeat; it is all the language of war. The voters, too, are often in adversarial mood, voting not so much *for A* as *against B*, and hoping that they and theirs will outnumber you and yours. It is not the force of arms, perhaps, but it is the force of numbers. And this adversarial feature applies as well to some forms of PR, especially those with a high threshold.

4.1.1.7 Inclusivity

In theory, a more "peaceful" electoral system is possible. In an intriguing variation of FPP used in Lebanon, every constituency elects a set number of representatives, n, in order to reflect not only the size of the electorate therein but also its multi-confessional make-up. To take a hypothetical example, if the latter consists, say, of 50% Druze, 25% Maronite and 25% Shia, then n, the number of representatives to be elected, would be 4 or a multiple of 4: 2 Druze, 1 Maronite and 1 Shia. If a party wishes to stand, it must nominate the same number of candidates, n, 2 + 1 +1, each demarcated by their faith. Furthermore, when someone wishes to vote, they must do so in a similarly non-sectarian way, voting for persons of each religious denomination, 2 + 1 +1; the easiest way to do that is to just vote for the party ticket. In effect, then, voters are asked to vote across the ethnic or religious divide, and in strict proportion, so to ensure a predetermined cross-community proportional result.[3]

---

[3] Elections are preceded by much bargaining to see who is going to share a list with whom. Sometimes 'influential leaders from various constituencies [will stand together] on one list,' (Khazen 1998: 34), so as to form what is called locally a 'bulldozer list', in which case, 'if you [also] put a donkey on, it will get elected'. (Correspondence from the Centre for Lebanese Studies and shades of the Belfast ass. Sect. 3.2.1.6)

In the 2009 contest, 128 MPs were elected: 2 Alawites, 5 Armenian Orthodox, 8 Druze, 8 Greek Catholic, 14 Greek Orthodox, 34 Maronite, 1 Protestant, 27 Shia, 27 Sunni and 2 others.

Other attempts at making the chosen electoral system more peaceful include the variation devised in Dagestan: constituencies right across the country are divided ethnically, so many for this group, so many for that, roughly in line with the national demographics. In the election, in any one constituency, all the candidates of whatever party will all be of the one nominated ethnicity. (Matveeva 1999: 18)[4] Bulgaria takes a different approach: its 'constitution explicitly bars ethnic parties,' (Rose and Munro 2003: 46)

Some electoral systems are not quite so prescriptive but perhaps no less "peaceful". Under PR-STV, voters *may* vote for others but they do not have to; unfortunately, some parties campaign for their supporters to vote for only their own. (Sect. 3.2.3.2) In QBS, the Lebanese/Dagestani idea is developed further, so that not only the electorate but also the parties have a vested electoral interest in crossing the divide. (Sect. 4.3)

4.2 A Comparison of Various Electoral Systems

> *'It's not the people who vote that count, it's the people who count the votes.'*
> Joseph Stalin.

To compare the merits of various electoral systems, for which a schema is shown in Fig. 4.2, reference will be made to the voters' profile shown in Fig. 3.1 and here repeated overleaf as Fig. 4.1.

This comparison concerns the following systems, arranged not so much in alphabetical order, but rather according to their sophistication. Some of these voting procedures can be used in decision-making and were examined in Chap. 2; proportional methodologies are confined to elections only.

plurality vote or FPP (Sect. 2.4.1)
TRS (Sect. 2.4.2)
approval voting (Sect. 2.4.3)
AV, IRV or STV (Sect. 2.4.5)
SNTV
PR-list
PR-STV
Condorcet (Sect. 2.4.6)
BC/MBC (Sect. 2.4.7)
top-up systems
QBS

---

[4] For the 2007 elections, Dagestan changed to a form of PR-list. See the Institute for War and Peace Reporting report № 384 of 22 Mar 2007: http://iwpr.net/report-news/dagestans-dirty-election (Accessed 3 Dec 2010).

Fig. 4.1 A voters' profile

Number of voters:	40	29	31
1st preference	*A*	*B*	*C*
2nd preference	*B*	*C*	*B*
3rd preference	*C*	*A*	*A*

4.2.1 Plurality Vote or FPP

As seen in Sect. 3.2.2, a plurality analysis of the above voters' profile would mean that *A* would win on a score of 40, the largest minority. The UK, which still uses FPP (although a referendum on AV is planned for May, 2011), is a two-big-plus-one-smaller-party system. It is therefore difficult for a third let alone a fourth party to flourish in the context of an FPP election. This was exemplified in the emergence of the Labour Party in the nineteenth century, which resulted in the almost inevitable demise of the Liberals.

4.2.2 TRS

If no candidate gets 50% in first round, then, as in a French presidential election, a second round is held[5]. In the above example of Fig. 4.1, this would mean a second round contest between *A* and *C*, which (if everyone voted according to the preferences shown) *C* would win by 60 to 40. Some people might think TRS is better than FPP but the former also descends into what is usually a two-horse race or at best a three-horse contest; in other words, it is still a two-party or, at most, a three-party electoral system. Thus France, for example, has a two-party system, admittedly with the addition of a number of very small parties.

Section 2.4.5 suggested that a TRS system could be inaccurate, if for no other reason that the initial plurality vote might itself be erroneous. The first round French presidential elections of 2002 implied that Jacques Chirac with 20% of the vote was most popular, and that Jean-Marie Le Pen of the National Front with 17% was second. In fact, Lionel Jospin of the *Parti Socialiste*, on 16%, should have been second, for he would have gained numerous second preferences, had the voters been able to cast them. In the second round, Chirac gained 82%, a result which highly inflated his popularity, while Le Pen stayed at 18%. A more accurate assessment of their relative strengths came in the TRS parliamentary elections in

---

[5] In France, any candidate gaining more than 12.5% is allowed to stand in the second round, which then becomes a straight plurality vote.

4.2 A Comparison of Various Electoral Systems

June: in the first round, Chirac's *Union pour un Mouvement Populaire,* UMP, won 33%, Jospin's Socialists won 24, and Le Pen's National Front gained only 11%.

4.2.3 Approval Voting

As in decision-making, this election methodology is not the best way of encouraging an inclusive polity. It is not used for any parliamentary elections.

4.2.4 AV or STV or IRV

In STV elections, as in AV decision-making, voters cast their preferences, 1, 2, 3... as they wish. In the count, with no candidate (in Fig. 4.1) gaining the quota of 50% + 1 first preferences, candidate *B* is eliminated because she has the smallest total of first preferences, and all 29 of her votes are transferred to *C*, in accordance with *B*'s voters' second preferences. Thus this system, which is used in Australia, also boils down to a two-and-a-bit party system. It does however encourage some parties to co-operate with each other and is less adversarial than FPP (Fig. 4.2)[6].

4.2.5 SNTV

SNTV is like FPP except that the election is conducted in multi-member constituencies. The voter has only one preference. If two representatives were to be chosen in the example given in Fig. 4.1, they would be candidates *A* and *C*.

4.2.6 PR-List

In a closed PR-list election, voters vote for a single party only. In most open PR-list systems, they can vote either for one party only or for one candidate of one party only; in a few instances, as in Belgium, voters can vote for more than one candidate

---

[6] As stated in Chap. 2 note 7, AV cannot guarantee that the winning candidate has gained majority support. The 2010 contest for the UK's Labour Party leadership was an internal party election and therefore the number of full ballots was probably higher than it would have been in a parliamentary election. Nevertheless, Ed Miliband won only 49.1%, his brother David gained 47.9% and 3.0% of the votes were non-transferable. In Australia's 2010 AV elections, for instance, only 50% of the ballots cast included a second preference.

	CLOSED		SEMI-OPEN		OPEN		OPEN	
	THRESHOLD		THRESHOLD		THRESHOLD		THRESHOLD	
	High	Low	High	Low	High	Low	High	Low
all prefs.	-	-	-	-	-	PR-listopen Switzerland 1891-	QBS+ top-up QBS BC Nauru§ 1971- Slovenia# 1992- Condorcet	-
many some prefs.	-	-	-	-	PR-STV* Ireland 1921- approval voting** AV* Australia 1948-	-	-	-
few	TRS France 1831- Russia 1989 Bosnia 1990	-	PR-list,two-tier Denmark, Sweden mixed FPP + PR Russia 1993-2007	-	MMP Germany 1949- New Zealand 1993-	-	-	-
first pref. only	FPP UK 1884- Kenya 1964-	PR-list closed Iraq, Israel, Bosnia 1996 SA1994- Russia 2007-	SNTV Afghanistan 2004- AMS	PR-list open Netherlands Bosnia 2000-	multiple FPP Lebanon 1989-	-	-	-
	Voter chooses one party only		Voter chooses one candidate of one party, once or twice		Voter chooses one or some candidates of one or some parties		Voter chooses one, some or all candidates of any or all parties	
	single preference voting		VOTERS' CHOICE →		→ preferential voting →			

§ Nauru's particular form of the BC is described in Chap. 4, note 8.
# A BC is used for the election of two ethnic minority representatives only; the other 88 MPs are elected by open list-PR.
* In AV and PR-STV, voters may cast all of their preferences, but many of the lower preferences sometimes remain uncounted.
** In approval voting, all preferences cast have the same value.

Fig. 4.2 Electoral systems

but only from the one party; while in Luxembourg and Switzerland, they can vote for more than one candidate of more than one party, voting in each constituency for as many candidates as there are representatives to be elected. From the elections in 2009 and 2007 respectively, the Luxembourg and Swiss parliament both have five large or medium-sized parties.

Whether or not a PR-list system leads to the state concerned having three, four or five established parties depends largely upon the size of the constituency and the number of candidates therein to be elected. As shown in Sect. 4.1.1.3, if two representatives are to be elected, a party will need 33⅓ % support to be guaranteed a victory; if three candidates, the threshold is 25%; if twelve (as in Belgium), it is about six per cent; and if the number of MPs is 150, as in The Netherlands where the whole country is treated as one constituency, the threshold is 0.67%. (Lijphart 1994: 29)[7] The Dutch thus have a six/seven party system while Israel, another single-constituency country, currently has two large, three medium and several small parties.

As shown in the glossary, there are several ways by which a PR-list election can be counted: by a divisor like d'Hondt or St. Laguë, or by using a quota such as Hare or Droop. If electing two representatives in the example of Fig. 4.1, the outcome would be candidates *A* and *C*, no matter which methodology is used. In general, d'Hondt and Droop favour the larger parties, while Hare and St. Laguë are fairer to all. (Emerson 1998: 54)

4.2.7 PR-STV

A PR form of STV is used in Ireland, Malta and Tasmania. The voters vote as they would under STV, casting as many preferences as they wish, in multi-member constituencies. In the count, any candidate gaining the (Droop) quota is elected. If she has a surplus over the quota, this surplus is transferred in proportion to all of her voters' second preferences. In the given voters' profile, Fig. 4.1, with two candidates to be elected, the quota is 33 + 1 = 34. Candidate *A* is elected with a surplus of 6 votes. These are transferred to *B* who thus gains a score of 35, so she will also be elected.

Given that PR-STV has a rather complicated counting procedure, the maximum number of elected representatives per constituency is seldom more than six. PR-STV usually prompts something between a two-party and a five-party system. In Ireland, with an average of 3.75 seats per constituency, there are 2.76 'effective parliamentary parties'. (Lijphart 1994: 31 and 1999: 312)

---

[7] Guyana, Montenegro, South Africa and Ukraine also treat the entire country as one constituency.

4.2.8 Condorcet

The voters cast their preferences as in PR-STV. Taking the first of the three pairings from Fig. 4.1, *A:B*, it is seen that 40 prefer *A* to *B* while 29 + 31 prefer *B* to *A*. So *A:B* = 40:60. The three pairing scores are as follows:

$A : B = 40 : 60$, so $B > A$; ($B > A$ reads "*B* is more popular than *A*");
$B : C = 69 : 31$, so $B > C$, and
$C : A = 60 : 40$, so $C > A$.

The most popular candidate is *B*, and the second most popular is *C*. Condorcet pairings are rarely used in elections: there are, after all, three pairings in a three-candidate contest, six pairings with four candidates, 45 with 10, and it soon gets rather cumbersome.

4.2.9 BC/MBC

In a BC/MBC election, the voters will usually be asked to cast as many preferences as they might wish, but only up to a certain maximum: when the number of candidates is small, 6 or less, that maximum will be the same number; when more than 10 candidates are standing, the maximum will usually be of the order of 6.

Referring to Fig. 4.1 again, with three points for a first preference, two points for a second preference and one point for a third preference, the scores are calculated as follows:

$A = 40 \times 3 + 29 \times 1 + 31 \times 1 = 120 + 29 + 31 = 180$
$B = 40 \times 2 + 29 \times 3 + 31 \times 2 = 80 + 87 + 62 = 229$
$C = 40 \times 1 + 29 \times 2 + 31 \times 3 = 40 + 58 + 93 = 191$

So *B* wins and *C* is second. This is a simple example of how a Condorcet count may often give the same outcome as a BC. (Sect. 2.4.7) A particular form of BC is used in Nauru as an electoral system[8] (Sect. 3.2), while in Slovenia, as was also noted, an ordinary BC is used for the election of representatives from their two ethnic minorities. It should be pointed out, however, that the BC/MBC is not proportional.

---

[8] The Nauru variation of the Borda count is such that, instead of casting points in the range *n, n-1, ... 1*, they use the following scale: *1, 1/2, ... 1/n*. (Reilly 2001: 13–14) The system has been used 'apparently without difficulty, for some 12 national elections.' (*Ibid*: 15) (See also Chap. 3, note 4.) Unfortunately, however, on decision-making, the Nauruan parliament is still majoritarian and has witnessed a number of votes of no-confidence.

4.2.10 Top-Up

An electoral system may have a two-tier structure. In Germany, for example, in a system called multi-member proportional, MMP, every voter has two votes: some seats are awarded by FPP in relatively small constituencies on the basis of the first ballot paper and, to ensure overall proportionality, a PR-list count is conducted in large regional constituencies on the basis of the second ballot papers.[9] The FPP part gives the Germans two big parties; the PR top-up allows for some smaller ones as well. Germany therefore tends to have a two-big-plus-three-small-party system. For the same purpose, Sweden uses two versions of PR-list, the first in small constituencies, the second in larger ones, and thus has a two-large-plus-five-small-party system.

Malta uses PR-STV but somewhat incongruously adds a "disproportional" top-up in order to give the party with a majority of first preference votes a majority of seats in parliament. (Katz 2001: 143) Italy introduced a similar provision for its new PR-list system in 2005. (Fig. 6.1, note *j*)

4.3 Consensus Voting for a Parliament: QBS

The Quota Borda System, as the name implies, consists of two elements: the quota and the MBC score. Unlike the MBC, therefore, QBS is proportional.

In both PR-STV and QBS, the voters may cast preferences, although in QBS, the voters may be restricted to a fixed maximum number of preferences. A typical QBS ballot paper is shown in Fig. 4.3, and is similar to an MBC ballot such as the one in Fig. 2.9.

4.3.1 QBS: Theory and Practice

As with the MBC, so too in any QBS election, every preference cast is counted. It therefore pays the candidate to campaign right across the constituency. If the voters are being asked to cast six preferences, the party activist may well expect his own supporters to give his nominee a first or at least a second preference, so spending time and energy in an effort to get these voters to increase their support may be rather pointless. In contrast, it could well pay handsome dividends to persuade any erstwhile opponents that his candidate is not as bad as they had thought, and to

---

[9] This two-ballot system, MMP, is sometimes confusingly called AMS, but the latter is a single-ballot system.

	Place	a '1' opposite your 1st preference;
you may also	place	a '2' opposite your 2nd preference,
		a '3' opposite your 3rd preference,
		a '4' opposite your 4th preference,
	and	a '5' opposite your 5th preference.

NB only five preferences shall be considered valid.

Candidate	Party	Preference
A	W	
B	X	
C	W	
D	independent	
E	Z	
F	Z	
G	Y	
H	independent	
I	W	
J	X	

The quota Borda system (QBS) is a preferential electoral system in which candidates are deemed elected if they receive a high number of top preferences and/or a high score in an MBC count. Preferences do not change in the count; in the MBC part of the count, however, points awarded to preferences may vary, as per the table below.

If you cast preferences for:	Number of candidates				
	1	2	3	4	5
your 1st preference gets	1 pt	2 pts	3 pts	4 pts	5 pts
your 2nd preference gets		1 pt	2 pts	3 pts	4 pts
your 3rd preference gets			1 pt	2 pts	3 pts
your 4th preference gets				1 pt	2 pts
your 5th preference gets					1 pt

Fig. 4.3 A QBS five-candidate ballot paper

persuade them to give her a fourth or even a third preference instead of a fifth or sixth. Thus in QBS elections, an altogether different atmosphere prevails.

A QBS count of up to four representatives consists of two Parts with two stages in each; (for more complex counts, see Emerson 2007: 41). Progress to the next stage is undertaken only if there are still seats to be filled. The count takes into consideration (a) the number of first preferences gained by single candidates, (b) the number of first/second preferences gained by pairs of candidates,[10] and (c) the individual candidates' MBC scores.

---

[10] If x voters give candidate *D* a first preference and *F* a second preference, while y voters give *F* a first and *D* a second; and if $x + y \geq$ a quota, then the *D-F* pair is said to have gained one quota. (Emerson 2007: 41)

4.3 Consensus Voting for a Parliament: QBS

In an election of just two representatives, in Part I stage (i), all single candidates gaining a quota of first preferences are elected. In Part I stage (ii), all pairs of candidates gaining two quotas of first/second preferences get both candidates elected.

In Part II, any candidate elected in Part I is no longer taken into consideration. In Part II stage (iii), any pair of unelected candidates gaining just one quota leads to the election of whoever of the two candidates has the greater MBC score. Finally, in Part II stage (iv), only the MBC scores are considered.

4.3.1.1 Full Ballots

In a three-candidate election, a voter may express up to three preferences. In the MBC part of the count, points are therefore awarded on the following basis: a first preference gets three points, a second preference two, and a third preference one point.

To show how QBS works, reference is again made to Fig. 4.1, repeated here below as Fig. 4.4:

In this case, *A* gets 40 first preferences,

B gets 29 first preferences,

and *C* gets 31 first preferences.

In electing two representatives, the quota is again 33% + 1, which is 34. Candidate *A* is therefore elected in Part I stage (i). We then look for a pair of candidates with two quotas, i.e., a total of 68 first/s preferences – Part I stage (ii) – but the solid coalition of *B* and *C* shown here in tint has only 60 votes, that is, they only have one full quota between them. In Part II stage (iii) of the count, this *B-C* pair does qualify, so we now look at the MBC scores to see which of *B* or *C* actually gets the better score and therefore the seat. These scores are as they were in Sect. 4.2.9.

$$(A = 180) \quad B = 229 \quad C = 191$$

So *B* is the second person to be elected.

4.3.1.2 Partial Ballots

What would have happened if, while *C*'s supporters were very consensual and submitted full ballot papers, *B*'s supporters voted for *B* only, while *A*'s supporters

Number of voters:	40	29	31
1st preference	A	B	C
2nd preference	B	C	B
3rd preference	C	A	A

Fig. 4.4 A QBS analysis

Fig. 4.5 A partial vote

Number of voters:	40	29	31
1st preference	*A*	*B*	*C*
2nd preference	*C*	-	*B*
3rd preference	-	-	*A*

gave some points to the consensual *C* candidate but none to *B*. In other words, suppose they voted as in Fig. 4.5.

If a voter votes for only two candidates, then his first preference gets only two points, and his second preference one point; and if another casts only a first preference, then that candidate gets only 1 point.

In this example, the first preference scores remain exactly the same at 40, 29 and 31 respectively, and again, in Part I stage (i), only one candidate gets the quota, *A*. In stage (ii), there is again no pair which has got two quotas. In Part II stage (iii), there is no pair with even one quota either. So we go to Part II stage (iv) and look for the points totals instead, which are now, very different:

$$A = 40 \times 2 + 29 \times 0 + 31 \times 1 = 80 + 31 = 111$$
$$B = 40 \times 0 + 29 \times 1 + 31 \times 2 = 29 + 64 = 93$$
$$C = 40 \times 2 + 29 \times 0 + 31 \times 3 = 80 + 93 = 173$$

so in this instance, *C* would win the second seat.

It must be emphasized that partial voting does not affect the totals of first preferences. A first preference is a first preference, regardless of how many other preferences that particular voter casts or does not cast. The MBC scores, however, may be affected considerably. The effect is benign. If certain voters want their candidate *B* to be successful, it would be better for them to give *B* their first preferences *and* to give all other candidates at least something. In other words, to help your favourite to win, it would be advisable to vote for the Catholic *and* the Protestant; for the Maronite, the Druze *and* the Shia; for the Bosniak, the Croat *and* the Serb. A voter would be more likely to do that if first he were at peace with his neighbour.

4.3.2 Inclusive Counting Procedures

Some electoral systems allow the voter to be "peaceful" in the way just described. They include approval voting, AV, PR-STV and QBS, with or without a top-up, along with the unique Lebanese and Dagestani systems. (Sect. 4.1.1.7) These inclusive systems sometimes encourage the candidates and the parties to work together. If candidate *B* wants *A*'s second preferences and vice versa, and if such MBC totals mean that both candidates might win together, candidates may enter an electoral contest *with* rather than *against* each other. Furthermore, if the chamber uses a consensual decision-making process, those elected can take decisions *with* each other as well.

The big difference between PR-STV and QBS lies in the count. In QBS, every preference cast by every voter is taken into account, while in PR-STV some preferences cast may remain uncounted: all the second preferences of ***B*** and ***C***, for example, in the election quoted in Sect. 4.2.6.

Furthermore, while the PR-STV voter may *think* she is voting for a Catholic *and* a Protestant, her vote may be transferred, literally, from one to the other – hence the name, single *transferable* vote. Thus in many PR-STV elections, her vote is counted for a Catholic *or* a Protestant candidate. With QBS, the word is *and*.[11]

To summarize, the fairest system is probably QBS with a top-up, the former in, say, five-seater constituencies; the latter based on a regional/national count of, say, the top three preferences.[12] As noted earlier, there are hundreds of different electoral systems in the world; some are good and some not so good, some are more democratic and some less so. Unfortunately they are nearly all designated as democratic, no matter how good or bad they are.

4.4 Consensus Voting in Parliament, Electing a Government: The Matrix Vote

It really is odd that many parliaments, though full of democrats, do not have democratic governmental elections at all. (Sect. 3.2.3.2) Instead, as in the old days, an autocratic ruler (PM) hires and fires at will or whim.

4.4.1 The Matrix Vote: Theory

If parliament were to elect a government, it would be choosing a team of supposed specialists, each of whom would be required to have appropriate talents. Someone might make a good minister of finance, another perhaps could specialize in law and home affairs, a third might understand the industrial portfolio, and so on. The last thing needed in a cabinet is a team consisting of, say, only economists.

The problem is this: how can a parliament elect an executive, every member of which has a different job description, while still retaining overall proportionality? One answer is to use a matrix vote, which works as follows. Imagine a parliament

---

[11] A more detailed comparison of PR-STV and QBS is published in Emerson (2010b: 197–209).
[12] In Russia, in 'the 1993 single-member district Duma election, the [blank] vote... 14.8%, was greater than for any named party.' (Rose and Munro 2003: 56).

	preferences		
Posts	1st	2nd	3rd
minister of "this"	-	-	-
minister of "that"	-	-	-
minister of "the other"	-	-	-

Fig. 4.6 A matrix ballot

wishes to elect a three-person executive: a minister of "this", a minister of "that" and a minister of "the other". The appropriate ballot paper would be as shown in Fig. 4.6.

Every MP would be a candidate for any ministerial post, (or at least every member who has not already served a term or two, or who has not opted out for some reason or other); and every MP would have a vote. Each could choose three of their fellow MPs, one for each position, and then, in order of preference, assign each to a slot on the matrix ballot paper. Furthermore, voting could be done electronically, with every MP having their own little "zapper". A valid full ballot would consist of three different names, one in each column, and one in each row.

4.4.2 The Matrix Vote Count

A matrix vote count consists of a QBS election followed by an MBC election, both based on the same voters' profile. The first is the QBS election: in the given instance, this would be a two-Part, two-stage election, as in Sect. 4.3.1. Once the three successful candidates have been thus identified, the MBC election decides which of the three elected representatives would be appointed to which position. Each serves in the position for which they get the most points. In other words, they serve in those ministries for which, in the consensus of all voting, they are most suited.

In effect, a matrix vote would allow every MP to choose a full cabinet: to cast their preferences not only for those whom they wished to be in cabinet, but also for the particular portfolio in which they wanted each of these nominees to serve. The outcome, the consensus of the entire parliament, would be inclusive, proportional and fair; that is, it would constitute a sound basis for any power-sharing administration. (Emerson 2007: 61–85)

4.4.3 The Matrix Vote: Practice

In a parliament in which parties *W*, *X*, *Y* and *Z* had 40, 30, 20 and 10% of the seats, each could expect to get roughly the same percentage of seats in cabinet. If a parliament were to elect a 20-member cabinet in this way, the ballot paper would be a table of 20 ministerial posts on one axis, and 20 preferences on the other.

In such a scenario, party **W** could expect to win 8 ministerial posts. Now, as has been shown, an MBC intrinsically encourages the voters to cast all their preferences. Any party **W** MP, therefore, would probably want to use their top 8 preferences for party colleagues (or maybe 9 or 10, just in case); and any other lower preferences for those whom they regard as the best of the other parties. Thus the very nature of the voting procedure would encourage the sort of cross-party behaviour which should be an intrinsic part of any inclusive form of governance.

The matrix vote is a win-win system. If, to take the example of the UK, all 651 MPs were to choose a cabinet of 22 ministers, every member would be able to choose any one of the 651 for any one of 22 ministerial posts; next, any one of 650 for any one of 21 posts, and so on. In effect, every MP would have a choice of over 6.2×10^{82} different ways of voting: it is called pluralism. The chances of any one MP winning everything, with each of her chosen 22 ministers in cabinet, and each in the ministerial post she has chosen for them, would be just about nil. Furthermore the chances of any party whip being able to dominate proceedings would again be minimal. But *ipso facto* the chances of nearly every MP winning something would be all but guaranteed. An example of a five-member government matrix vote ballot paper is shown overleaf in Fig. 4.7.

In Westminster, a member of the government must be a member of parliament. In France, this requirement is waived, and membership in the cabinet is not restricted to the National Assembly. Before a vote could take place in the *Palais Bourbon*, therefore, a list of potential candidates would have to be agreed and published.

* * * * *

In most parliaments, all might feel that the post of PM is particularly important. So maybe that particular post should not be included in the matrix and perhaps a separate election should be held. In consensus politics, however, we seldom vote for only one position. At the very least, it would be better to have a PR election for both a PM and a deputy PM. Such a scenario could consist of a QBS election based on a ballot for which every MP is a candidate – except for those who opt out – and in which every MP is asked to cast up to ten preferences.

4.4.4 *The Matrix Vote for Use in Committees*

When an association is having its AGM, there are invariably a number of posts to be filled – chairperson, secretary, treasurer and so on – with again, different talents required for each. The obvious thing to do is to run a similar matrix vote. If some people want Mr J to be the deputy chair (Sect. 3.2.3.3) they can vote accordingly; if they want Ms K to be on the committee as well, they can vote for her too, at the same time, with no hard feelings between the two.

In this situation, it is advisable to suggest that every voting member of the group be a candidate. Anyone who wants to opt out, for personal reasons or because they have already served a term or two, may do so; but no-one should feel the

Place the name of your first preference in the first column, opposite the ministerial post in which you wish this nominee to serve;
you may also place the name of your second preference in the second column, opposite the ministerial post in which you wish this nominee to serve;
you may also place the name of your third preference in the third column, opposite the ministerial post in which you wish this nominee to serve; and so on.

	Preferences				
	1st	2nd	3rd	4th	5th
Prime Minister					
Minister of A					
Minister of B					
Minister of C					
Minister of D					

A valid full ballot will contain five different names, one in each column, and one in each row.

The matrix vote is an electoral system in which candidates are elected on the basis of their overall popularity as measured in a QBS count. Successful candidates are appointed to that ministry to which, in the consensus of those voting, they are most suited, as measured by the individual candidates' MBC scores for each ministry.

For the calculations of the quota, a first preference is always a first preference, regardless of how many other preferences you cast.

The points, however, may vary as follows:

If you cast preferences for:	Number of candidates				
	1	2	3	4	5
your 1st preference gets	1 pt	2 pts	3 pts	4 pts	5 pts
your 2nd preference gets		1 pt	2 pts	3 pts	4 pts
your 3rd preference gets			1 pt	2 pts	3 pts
your 4th preference gets				1 pt	2 pts
your 5th preference gets					1 pt

Fig. 4.7 A matrix vote ballot paper for a five-person executive

need to promote themselves, thereby falling into that "vote for me" version of egocentricity.

4.5 Conclusions

A major defect of current electoral practice is that the choice of electoral system is made by the politicians themselves. Admittedly, in some countries, electoral systems were imposed by some outside power: Ireland, for example, was given

PR-STV as part of the 1920 settlement and, in the Republic, this was bound into the constitution. When de Valera of FF tried to replace this British imposition with another British institution, FPP, the people said "no". (Sect. 1.1.2.8) FF did not like that very much so it tried again, and the people said a bigger "NO". Other jurisdictions – including Andorra, Italy (Fig. 6.1, note *j*), Slovenia and New Zealand – have changed their electoral systems by referendum; the last two votes were multi-option ballots. (See App. D, D.1 for the unsuccessful Balkan story and Sect. 2.6 for the more positive antipodean experience.)

In most countries, though, the choice of electoral system depends only upon the powers that be which, needless to say, wish to continue to be. It would therefore be better if, as suggested in Sect. 3.4, certain basic democratic rights were enshrined into human rights declarations and international law.

Alas, electoral systems themselves are seldom scrutinized, not even by international observers (Sects. 3.3.2.3 and 4.1) not least for the following reason. The UN was established by three old men sitting in Yalta: Churchill, Theodore Roosevelt and Stalin. Two of them liked first-past-the-(no)-post and one liked first-but-no-contest. Accordingly, all three agreed that any international charters would not interfere in the internal affairs of any other state. *Inter alia,* electoral systems were off limits.

So how can democracy evolve further? I suppose a group of people is needed to campaign for such democratic procedures as will remove those elements of control which so many political parties have acquired for themselves. Condorcet suggested in 1792 that parties will probably continue to exist,'. . .*for although we can suppress political parties, we cannot prevent the formation of groups of people with the same opinions.'* (McLean and Urken 1995: 148) It is not political parties as such which are harmful; it is the excessive powers of patronage which they have accumulated for themselves. They have achieved this not least by advocating and using improper voting procedures, both in decision-making and in elections. To use Petra Kelly's phrase again, it is not so much an "anti-party party" (Sect. 3.1.3) that is required, just a more inclusive polity.

Some more sophisticated democratic rights would also be helpful and, like all human rights, they should be universal. Certain principles should be laid down: principles of proportionality and voters' choice upon which electoral systems should be based, principles of inclusiveness as the foundation of any decision-making, and principles of power-sharing which will be discussed in Part III.

4.6 Democratic Elections Defined

Democratic decision-making was defined in Sect. 2.7; democratic elections for use in both parliaments and local committees can now be defined as well.

In a representative democracy:

1. The legislature and/or the executive shall be elected; the former shall be elected directly, the latter either directly or indirectly.

2. Elections shall be under a preferential system of PR so that all elections shall lead to the appointment of at least two persons, the chair *and* a deputy, for example, or the premier *and* the vice-premier; consequently, in every election, there will be a minimum choice of three candidates or parties.
3. As with decision-making, the ballot paper may include a "blank" option.
4. The conduct of the elections shall be free and fair, with voting undertaken in secret. Votes taken by the elected representatives in parliament, however, shall be open to public scrutiny.
5. The electoral system shall enable every voter to vote sincerely, i.e. to express their preferences on a fixed number of some if not all of the candidatures.
6. The degree of proportionality shall ensure the fair representation of all sections in society. Accordingly, the threshold shall be suitably low and, if need be, the electoral system shall be two-tier or a top-up.[13]
7. In every election, all preferences cast by all voters shall be taken into account.

References

Baker J (1996) Fair representation and the concept of proportionality. Irish Political Studies 44(4): 733–737
Bose NK (1968) Selections from [Mahatma] Gandhi. Navajivan Publishing House, Ahmedabad
Cassel CA (1986) The nonpartisan ballot in the United States. In: Grofman B, Lijphart A (eds) Electoral laws and their political consequences. Agathon Press, New York
Dalbakk S (2003) Norway's political parties and the Norwegian electoral system. University of Oslo, Norway
Emerson P (1998) Beyond the tyranny of the majority. The de Borda Institute, Belfast
Emerson P (ed) (2007) Designing an all-inclusive democracy. Springer, Heildelberg
Emerson P (2010b) Proportionality without transference: the merits of the quota Borda system, (QBS). Representation 46(2):197–209
Idea (1997) The international IDEA handbook of electoral system design. Idea, Stockholm
Katz R (2001) The 2000 presidential election: a perverse outcome? Representation 38(2):141–149
Khazen el F (1998) Prospects for Lebanon. Centre for Lebanese Studies, Oxford
Lakeman E (1974) How democracies vote. Faber and Faber, London
Lewis Sir A (1965) Politics in West Africa. George Allen and Unwin, London
Lijphart A (1994) Electoral systems and party systems. OUP, Oxford
Lijphart A (1999) Patterns of democracy. Yale University Press, New Haven and London
McLean I, Urken AB (eds) (1995) Classics of social choice. University of Michigan, Ann Arbor
Matveeva A (1999) The North Caucasus. Royal Institute of International Affairs, London

---

[13] Just as there are many electoral systems, so too there are many ways to configure a top-up. In an undated Green Party/*Comhaontas Glas* Discussion Document published in 1996 for the Dublin Forum for Peace and Reconciliation, the writer co-authored a proposal for a top-up based on a party's MBC scores. The top-up count, it was argued on page 7, should consider only one preference per party, the top one. Thus, in a 6-candidate election, if someone voted Y–1, Y–2, Y–3, Ind.–4, W–5, W–6, top-up points would be awarded to the parties on the basis of Y's first preference and W's fifth preference: Y 6 W 2 points.

References

Reilly B (2001) The Borda count in the real world. Macmillan Brown Centre for Pacific Studies, Christchurch

Rose R, Munro N (2003) Elections and parties in new European democracies. CQ Press, Washington

Sakharov A (1991) Moscow and Beyond. Alfred A Knopf, New York

Part III
The Art of Governance

Chapter 5
The Elected Dictator

>   ... the will of the people[1] is a will-o'-the-wisp.   (McLean and Urken 1995: 7)
>
>   The voice of the people... in the things of their knowledge is said to be as the voice of God.
>   From *The Apology,* presented by the Commons to King James I of
>   England, after his coronation in 1603. (Churchill 1974: Bk. II, 116)

Abstract Having looked at both decision-making and electoral systems, it is time to consider forms of governance. The world has devised one-, two-, multi- and all-party states, as well as the oldest form of all, the non-party state. In many of these jurisdictions, parliaments do indeed represent the people, but many governments represent only a faction.

This chapter considers the bases of these forms of rule, before next examining the structure of government, whether that be presidential or parliamentary. Then, crucially, the manner in which debates are conducted is scrutinized, and so too the mechanisms by which people are consulted.

5.1 Party Structures of Governance

Some of the terminology gets a little confusing: for example, there may be little difference between a one-party state, a power-sharing executive, an all-party coalition and a government of national unity, GNU. In many circles, however, the first is often regarded as an anathema, the second as a concoction suitable only for conflict zones, the third as something which could only work in Switzerland, and

---

[1] The Will of the People was also the name of a very small terrorist organization in Russia in the latter part of the nineteenth century; their most infamous deed, after many unsuccessful attempts, was the assassination of the Tzar, Alexander II, in 1881.

P. Emerson, *Defining Democracy,*
DOI 10.1007/978-3-642-20904-8_5, © Springer-Verlag Berlin Heidelberg 2012

the fourth as the sort of extraordinary measure that might be needed when a country is in a state of war.

5.1.1 The One-Party or No-Party State

Some associate the phrase "one-party state" with Soviet communism and the horrific deeds of the bolsheviks. Other one-party states have emerged in Africa where the likes of Gen. Idi Amin in Uganda and Mobutu in the DRC/Zaire have also shown what evils can be perpetrated in such jurisdictions. Nevertheless, 'Single parties are not homogenous. From the philosophical standpoint, one must make at least two distinctions: between totalitarian and limited parties and between ideological and open parties' (Lewis 1965: 56).

5.1.1.1 The Soviet Union

Without a shadow of doubt, the USSR's one-party state under Lenin and then Stalin was appalling, while under Khrushchev and Leonid Brezhnev, it was perhaps tolerable. It has all changed now of course: life improved enormously under Gorbachev, (Sect. 3.1.4) lapsed under Boris Yeltsin, and is currently (2011) very uncertain under Putin and Dmitry Medvedev (Sect. 5.1.2.1). The particularly bad example of the USSR and the CPSU, however, does not mean to say that a one-party state cannot be 'ideological and open'.

5.1.1.2 Tanzania

Perhaps the best example is Tanzania where, in stark contrast to its immediate neighbours to the North (Kenya) and West (Rwanda and Burundi), tribal divisions have been largely overcome.[2] 'In Western democracies, it is an accepted practice in times of emergency for opposition parties to sink their differences and join together in forming a national government. *This is our time of emergency*, and until our war against poverty, ignorance and disease has been won, we should not let our unity be destroyed by a desire to follow somebody else's "book of rules."' President Nyerere (Sigmund 1966: 199).

---

[2] In the 2005 elections, the largest party, *Chama Cha Mapinduzi*, the Revolutionary Party, won 70% of the votes and 93% of the seats. In Tanzania today decision-making tends to be majoritarian. Interestingly enough, however, the word *baraza* (Sect. 1.1) is still in use: many a political party has a council of elders, *baraza ya wazee*, while the House of Representatives in Zanzibar is called *Baraza la Wawakilishi*.

5.1.1.3 Uganda

After years of sectarian strife under Milton Obote and then Amin, Museveni came to a similar conclusion in Uganda: 'As soon as political parties were introduced, they became sectarian, based on ethnicity and religion' (Museveni 1997: 200). No wonder he changed to a one-party or no-party state under the National Resistance Movement, NRM.

To a large extent, he managed to bring his country back from the brink of disaster, yet there are those abroad who are convinced that, by definition, one-party states must be wrong and that multi-party (or even two-party) states are right. 'Many people do not understand our aversion to political parties, but it is because of the history of sectarianism which these parties have fostered in our society, mainly on the basis of religion' (*Ibid*: 190).

Some of those who 'do not understand' are the well-respected members of Human Rights Watch. In a lengthy report, they called on the Ugandan government to respect the right of its citizens 'to form political parties without undue government interference, and to engage in political party activities such as, for example, the holding of delegate conferences and political rallies, the sponsoring of candidates for public office, and issuing of party membership cards' (Human Rights Watch 1999: 9).

The debate led to a referendum in July 2000 in which 92% of a 51% turnout voted to continue under Museveni's version of a one-party state. In Mar. 2001, in a mainly fair election, he was re-elected for his fifth and (what should have been his) last term by a margin of 69%. Then, in an example of a "donor democracy" (see Sect. 5.1.2), 91% of a 47% turnout voted in July 2005 for a multi-party system. In the subsequent elections of 2006, Museveni competed against four other candidates and won on 59%, while his NRM won 205 of the 319 seats in parliament.

5.1.1.4 Kenya and Rwanda

Even if the rhetoric of the politicians refers to a more pluralist, multi-party régime, many countries have long since put into practice a dualist two-party state. The colonial powers should have known, however, that a two-party administration would not work well in Kenya, a land where two major peoples – the Bantu and the Nilotic – with a major tribe in each – the Kikuyu and the Luo – share one artificial state (Sect. 3.3.1.2). It certainly would not work in Rwanda where, just before those appalling massacres of 1994, it was said that 'Democracy means that the Hutus must rule because they are in the majority, and the Tutsis must be suppressed because they are the minority'[3] (Sect. 1.2.1).

---

[3] This was in a statement from the National Republican Movement for Development and Democracy and its more extreme offshoot, the Coalition for Defence of the Republic (The *Guardian*, 11.9.1994).

5.1.1.5 The Non-Partisan State

Despite evidence of its inappropriate nature, the West persisted and still does persist in promoting majoritarianism. Perhaps we do not even realize that, '...the Western assumption of the majority's right to overrule a dissident minority after a period of debate does violence to conceptions basic to non-Western peoples. Although the Asian and African societies differ vastly among themselves in their patterns of customary action, their native inclination is generally towards extensive and unhurried deliberation aimed at an ultimate consensus' (Emerson R 1966: 284). Not only do we not understand, we dismiss: '...the Confucian ethos [in] many Asian societies stressed... the importance of consensus... [in contrast] with the primacy in American beliefs of... democracy' (Huntington 1997: 225).

Many traditional societies believed in the village meeting – the *baraza* or *gacaca* (Sect. 1.1), – which was, if you like, a no-party system. If today a state is run in an open manner, with decisions taken in consensus, and with each district electing its representatives in an open electoral system (or if, in the UK for example, every elected member were to be an independent), then that would surely be getting close to the democratic ideal.

> *Our ultimate aim is to provide Egypt with a truly democratic and representative government... [in which the] deputies will serve all the Egyptians rather than a few.* President Gamal Abdel Nasser (Emerson R 1966: 270). The events of Jan. 2011 demonstrate, however, that the above aim was not pursued by his successors.

As described in Sect. 3.1.3, inclusivity was also an ideal in some other countries when they too were young. In the US, 'Political "factions" and partisan organizations were generally viewed as dangerous, divisive, subversive of political order and stability, and injurious to the public good' (Dahl 1998: 87).

Some small nations have managed to retain this ideal. In Kiribati and the Cayman Islands, every member of their first parliaments was an independent, although today political parties have been established there as well. Those which still maintain a non-party polity include Falklands (Malvinas), Guernsey, Jersey, Micronesia, Nauru where 15 of the 18 MPs are non-partisan, Norfolk, Palau, Tokelau, Tuvalu and a recent addition, the Nunavut Territory: its Legislative Assembly, first elected in February 1999, still 'consists of 19 independent members without formal party affiliation' (Maher et al. 2009: Vol 1, 1124).

As is well known, a one-party state can all too easily go wrong. A clue lies in the nature of rule: if the party sets up its own administration which then runs alongside the state structures, the party often becomes a class of its own and tends to act like an oligarchy. If, on the other hand, the two are as one, if the one-party state becomes a GNU, with only one set of administrative structures in the country, the prospects for an open, inclusive democracy are strong, in which case '...the single-party is really a grand free-for-all political seminar' (Lewis 1965: 58).

5.1.1.6 Other One-Party States

The world still has many regimes which operate a form of one-party state, some of which have definitely gone wrong. The worst example is probably North Korea, currently under a hereditary dictatorship. Another instance is Libya, where Mu'ammar al-Gaddafi has been in power since deposing the monarchy in 1969. His ideas on democracy are confined more to the local level, where people do have a choice of sorts; his own post, apparently, is not subject to change... yet.

The largest of all one-party states is, of course, China which, since 1949, has been ruled by the Communist Party of China, CPC. Initially, not least during the so-called Cultural Revolution, millions died. Today though, while maintaining the one-party status with often excessive use of state power, Běijīng has opted to pursue a path of development quite unlike that chosen by post-*perestroika* Moscow, where a multi-party form of majoritarianism has now degenerated into a one-party dominant state (Sect. 5.1.2.1). Whether or not the CPC under Hú Jīntāo or his successors will eventually adopt a more western-form of democracy is open to speculation. Certainly, at the moment, the ever wider use of the internet and other aspects of the information revolution suggest that change is inevitable. Western adversarial structures, however, may not fit too easily into what is, after all, the oldest civilization on earth (Sect. 1.1).

5.1.2 One-Party Dominant States

The term "donor democracy" relates to those democratic structures which are funded from abroad and which otherwise would not be introduced (Matlosa et al. 2007, 332). In Africa especially, the West has sought to promote its own ideas, if need be by paying for them. As a result, many states have changed from what was a one-party to a multi-party state, although the consequences have not always been to the liking of the donors. Some countries are what is now called a one-party dominant state. Tanzania is one good example (Sect. 5.1.1.2); Zimbabwe a very bad one (Sect. 3.3.1.1). Sudan and Ethiopia, to quote two 2010 election results, are two more,[4] while Tunisia is, or was, a further instance (Sect. 3.3.3.1). Further examples are found in the former USSR.

---

[4] The incumbent Sudanese president, Omar al-Bashir, though convicted by the International Criminal Court, ICC, for war crimes in Darfur, won 68% of the vote, while the candidate from South Sudan, Yasir Arman, won a high percentage in his own balliwick and thus a fair amount of the total: 22%.

In Ethiopia, the Ethiopian People's Revolutionary Democratic Front, and its allies won 545 out of 547 seats in the House of People's Representatives (The *Guardian*, 22.6.2010).

5.1.2.1 The Commonwealth of Independent States, CIS

Today's Russia is an instance of one-party, if not one person, dominance. Under current structures, Putin's United Russia Party, EP, wins and is almost bound to win (Fig. 6.1 note *m*); in 2007, for example, EP won 64% of the vote. Belarus is another instance of dominance: in its 2010 presidential election, Alexander Lukashenko, sometimes referred to as Europe's last dictator, not only took 80% of the vote compared with 2% by the nearest of nine rivals, but his security forces also arrested and sometimes injured his opponents (The *Guardian*, 23.12.2010). Similarly, in some of the former Soviet Republics in Central Asia, there are a number of "democratic dynasties". In Turkmenistan, to name the worst of them, the presidential elections saw Gurbanguly Berdimuhamedow win 90% of the vote, despite all the other five candidates being fellow members of his own party.

5.1.3 The Two-Party State

> *The idea that democracy is effective only when there are two parties, one in government and the other in opposition, is an Anglo-American myth.* (Lewis 1965: 70)

As M Duverger said, FPP often leads to a two-party state. There might be some other little parties in parliament to add some colour to the proceedings but, as often as not, when it comes to decision-making, it is "option *A*, yes or no?" or at best "*A* versus *B*", government versus opposition.

> *What is necessary for democracy is not an organized opposition, which, in order to offer itself as an alternative government, adopts every obstructive and even at times destructive measure and maneuver to overthrow [the] government...* Kofi Baako, Minister of State for Parliamentary Affairs in Ghana (Sigmund 1966: 193).

It must be emphasized that the adversarial nature of the two-party system is not just a consequence of the electoral system, it is also the result of the majoritarian decision-making process. Majority voting in parliament and FPP in elections is a combination which ill befits a modern, plural, high-tech society. Yet this two-party state structure is practiced in 68 countries of the world (IDEA 1997: 21) with, sometimes, the most ghastly consequences. A recent example is the violence in Kenya which followed the December 2007 elections, an explosion of inter-tribal hatred that was caused not only by the abuses which took place at the count but also by the adversarial two-party system itself (Sect. 3.3.1.2).

In Britain, the US and elsewhere, two-party systems function. That is true. Likewise monarchies functioned, dictatorships like that of Ben-Ali in Tunisia functioned until, in the latter instance, it was overthrown in Jan. 2011. The capacity to function does not mean, *ipso facto*, that majoritarian structures are right. Indeed, '...majority rule and the government-versus-opposition pattern of politics that it implies may be interpreted as undemocratic...' (Lijphart 1999: 31).

5.1 Party Structures of Governance   107

A further aspect of the two-party system in either its parliamentary (UK) or presidential (US) form is that, because it is based on winners and losers, it often gives the winner too much power. Britain has 'an elected dictatorship' and the rules of the UK parliament give the PM almost unlimited power in the selection (rather than election) of the cabinet (Sect. 3.2.3.2). Under his (or occasionally her) guidance if not control, the executive then decides what to do. And because, as often as not, the party of government has a majority in the House, parliament does what it is told to do and provides the rubber stamp. It should not be forgotten that it was via such a majoritarian system that Hitler came to power (App. A, A.1.3).

> *The so-called modern state of Cameroon, and elsewhere in Africa, is built on the colonial model, and the new leaders – like their colonial masters – do not wish to share their power with traditional leaders...* (Menang et al. 2007: 135)

5.1.4 Multi-Party States

Change the electoral system and you change the make-up of parliament. The voters remain exactly the same, with the same opinions, the same outlooks, the same preferences, the same cares and concerns. It is the electoral system that counts, literally.

If the composition of parliament is changed, the *nature* of that parliament may also change, if not indeed the very future of the state. The most obvious consequence of switching from a two-party electoral system to a genuinely multi-party form is that, almost certainly, no one party will have a parliamentary majority of MPs. Unfortunately, as far as decision-making is concerned, most of these elected chambers still practice majority voting. Hence, in many multi-party democracies, elections are often followed by an interim period, as various parties meet to see who will form a majority coalition with whom. Let us first consider the theory.

If four parties – *W, X, Y* and *Z* – share a parliament with 39%, 29%, 19% and 13% of the seats respectively, *W* could go into majority coalition with *X* and/or *Y* and/or *Z*; alternatively, *X, Y* and *Z* could go into coalition against *W*. So who gets into bed with whom? If *W* joins *Z*, their overall majority at just 2% would be rather fragile. If *W* teams up with *X*, then *X*, being a relatively large partner, would want quite a large share of the ministerial seats and other perks of office. Probably the best thing to do, from *W*'s point of view, is to seek an alliance with *Y*.

Political factors might come into play as well. If *W, X, Y* and *Z* are on the political left-right spectrum, *W* will find it relatively easy to agree with *X* and quite difficult to do so with *Z*. Politics, however, the art of the possible, allows for the impossible. There was a *W/Z* alliance in the UK in 1977–1978 when the supposedly left-wing Labour Party teamed up with the definitely right wing Ulster Unionists (App. C, C.1.3).

In theory, of course, three parties could form a broad-based coalition – *W, X* and *Y* – or even all four could choose an all-party coalition – *W, X, Y* and *Z*. In practice, parties usually prefer the majoritarian option, and a narrow one at that, something like $W + Y$. These two parties then meet in cabinet to formulate their joint policy, but how do these majoritarian ministers make their collective decisions? Needless to say, it is not by majority vote. Consideration will now be given to the practice in a number of multi-party states.

5.1.4.1 Germany

Germany currently has a two-big-plus-a-three-small party system (Sect. 4.2.10). In the wake of the 2005 general election, the results were as follow. The two big parties – the Christian Democrats, CDU, (with their allies in Bavaria) and the SPD – won 226 and 222 seats respectively. The three little parties, the liberal Free Democrats, FDP, The Left (*Die Linke*) and the GP won 61, 54 and 51 seats. A majority in the 614-seat Bundestag required at least 308. There were thus seven possible minimum coalitions: either the two big parties in what is called a grand coalition, or one of the big plus any two of the small in a majority coalition. All of these possibilities were different. For those who believe in majoritarianism, every single one of them was seen as *totally* democratic.

5.1.4.2 Pakistan

In countries which have even more parties in government, the mathematical permutations and combinations become almost too numerous to count. Apart from 18 independent members, the 2008 election gave Pakistan ten parties in parliament, although three of these had only one member. The largest, the Pakistan People's Party, PPP, held 124 seats out of 340. The second and third largest were the Pakistan Muslim League, PML, which had divided into two blocks, (N) and (Q): (N) is the block led by the former prime minister, Nawaz Sharif, while (Q) or Quaid supports the former President, Pervez Musharraf. The PPP, however, teamed up with the fourth and fifth parties, the Muttahida Qaumi Movement, MQM, and the Awami National Party, ANP. In Jan. 2011, the MQM opted out of government, whereupon the PPP lost its overall majority, but the immediate crisis was averted when the MQM was persuaded to reverse its decision.

5.1.4.3 India

An even more complex scenario exists in India (Sect. 3.2.1.9 and App. C, C.1.4). In the 2009 elections, a parliament of 543 seats was shared by 44 parties. Admittedly, many of these were already in coalitions, the largest of which combined 15 parties, but coalitions (not only) in India can be fickle, with changes taking place not only pre-election, but also afterwards and sometimes even during the electoral campaign.

On this occasion, the incumbent prime minister, Manmohan Singh of the Indian National Congress, INC, led his United Progressive Alliance, UPA, a coalition of 11 parties, back into power with the support of four other smaller parties plus some tinier ones, so to command a majority of 322 seats of the 543 total. This left the BJP and partners, plus the communist Third Front and their cohorts, in opposition.

* * * * *

There is little which is logical in the theory which insists that a multi-party parliament must have a majoritarian government. Many multi-party administrations differ from their two-party counterparts, and coalition governments differ from any single-party majority rule, because the former tend to operate in a much more consensual manner. In Denmark, for example, '...one finds a far-reaching search for compromise... in the legislature,' and 'Plural societies may enjoy stable democratic government if the political leaders engage in coalescent rather than adversarial decision-making' (Lijphart 1977: 111 and 99–100).

5.1.5 All-Party States

There are quite a few all-party states. The Swiss version came about as a result of democratic development and appears to be permanent. In some instances, a second form, the GNU, tends to be of a temporary nature. A third variety is called power-sharing, and attempts to use such a structure are usually made in what were or still are conflict zones. And the fourth is often a part of such a power-sharing arrangement: a consociational government.

In recent years, various forms of power-sharing have been tried in a number of settings: Lebanon, Northern Ireland, Bosnia, and South Africa, to name but four, while consociational democracy has been used in some other pluralist countries as well. In Belgium and Canada, for example, it has proved to be fairly successful although at the time of writing, the former is under some strain; (see chronology 2010). Furthermore, one form or another of power-sharing has often been considered advisable in other lands in crisis; in recent years, such has been advocated if not used in countries such as Afghanistan, Honduras, Iraq, Kenya, Tunisia and Zimbabwe.

5.1.5.1 Switzerland

Switzerland has now enjoyed a form of all-party coalition government for over 50 years: a collective presidency called the Swiss Federal Council. Having had some power-sharing throughout the first half of the twentieth century, the four main parties agreed to a 2:2:2:1 *Zauberformel* or magic formula in 1959: four parties in government with the same four and a few other smaller ones in parliament. With the growth of the SVP, People's Party, they have had to fine-tune this formula, but Switzerland continues to have one of the most stable democracies in the world.[5]

5.1.5.2 The UK

The UK had a GNU or all-party coalition during World War II and some years earlier during the slump. As soon as the war was over, the country returned to majority rule. In recent years, as the percentage of those voting for other than the two main parties has steadily increased, the two-party system has shown itself to be more and more inappropriate, and in the wake of the 2010 elections, the UK is ruled by a two-party coalition (App. C, C.3, 2010), so maybe further change is afoot.

5.1.5.3 Lebanon

Since the Taif Agreement of 1943, Lebanon has enjoyed a form of power-sharing in which '...the president was a Maronite, the prime minister a Sunni [and] the speaker... a Shia; even in parliament, there had to be six Christians for every five Muslims' (Fisk 2001, 67). The ratio was later changed to 50:50. Decision-making, however, was and is still based on the majority vote.

Taif survived until the 1975–1990 civil war – a conflict in which the 1978 Israeli invasion was a major factor – but was then resuscitated, not least by Rafik Hariri, a Sunni, Prime Minister from 1992 to 1998 and again 2000–2004. In Feb. 2005, he was assassinated. Fingers were pointed both at Syria and Hezbollah, and the mass demonstrations which followed soon became known as the Cedar Revolution. Then, in 2006, fighting broke out between Israel and Hezbollah. One year later, when Émile Lahoud's term of office expired in Oct. 2007, more violence occurred. A further period of power-sharing was negotiated but without any form of consociationalism; instead, the opposition was given the power of veto. With the Jan. 2011 collapse of the premiership of Saad Hariri, the late premier's son, the post passed to Hezbollah (see also Sect. 4.1.1.7).

5.1.5.4 Northern Ireland

The basic idea underlying the Belfast Agreement was that, instead of the unionists ruling over the nationalists, power would now be exercised by the "nice" parties, the UUP and SDLP, which could out-vote the "not so nice" DUP and SF, albeit within an

---

[5] In 1959, the Christian Democrats, CVP, the FDP, and the Social Democrats, SPS, all got two seats, while the People's Party, SVP, got one. The latest formula is two each for the FDP and SPS, plus one each for the CVP, the SVP and a splinter group of the SVP set up in 2008, the Conservative Democrats, CDP.

all-party structure. The Agreement involved (a) a system of appointments based on a d'Hondt interpretation of the Assembly elections; (b) a system of decision-making on "key" matters of policy which was a form of consociationalism (Sect. 2.2.1.5); and (c) another form of decision-making, majoritarianism, for any referendums. The d'Hondt procedure is based on party labels and consociationalism on designations (Sect. 2.2.1.5). Majoritarianism is also adversarial. In a nutshell, the Belfast Agreement '…remains grounded in the very structures it aspires to transcend,' because it 'reinforces and perpetuates sectarian division…' (Taylor 2009: 320).

The fact that the politicians have agreed to share power is to be applauded, of course, but it is at least unfortunate that they should have chosen this d'Hondt methodology in which the last person selected is almost bound to be unsuitable for the post concerned.[6] It also seems strange that a person can be appointed to a ministerial post on the basis of an election in which, in any one constituency, the electorate has no definite knowledge of whether or not any of its candidates is standing for any one or more of the ministerial posts. Indeed, at the time of the first NI Assembly elections in 1998, no-one knew exactly how many ministerial posts there were going to be: there was just a ball-park figure of somewhere between six and ten.

While it is a huge advance on simple majority rule, consociationalism nevertheless suffers from at least three basic drawbacks: the concept is still majoritarian; secondly, decisions are therefore still taken by majority vote; and thirdly, questions of policy are still viewed as dichotomies.

5.1.5.5 Bosnia

A similar picture was painted in Dayton Ohio, when Bill Clinton, Franjo Tudjman, Alija Izetbegović and Milošević sat down to impose a peace agreement on the Bosnians. The result[7] was another consociational form of government (Sect. 2.2.1.5), but this one came with a three-way veto. In fact, in at least one respect, this Agreement was actually more sectarian than the accord the local parties had devised for themselves in 1990.[8] For various reasons, not least the excessive use of the veto and then the holding of the 1992 two-option referendum, the 1990 agreement did not hold. The post-war treaty, in contrast, has survived, but mainly because the international community has kept it in place.

---

[6] By all accounts, Brid Rodgers MLA, who was chosen to serve in the first 1998 executive, turned out to be an excellent Minister of Agriculture. That, however, is not the point. Under the d'Hondt arrangement, the ten ministerial posts were to be awarded in order, to the four big parties: UUP, SDLP, DUP, SF, UUP, SDLP, DUP, SF, UUP, SDLP. So the SDLP knew who their third minister was going to be, long before they knew which post she was going to get.

[7] The 1995 Dayton Accord is otherwise known as the General Framework Agreement.

[8] Before the war, the presidency was based on a 2:2:2:1 ratio of Bosniak:Croat:Serb:Yugoslav respectively. Dayton stipulates only 1:1:1, with no Yugoslavs.

5.1.5.6 South Africa

When South Africa first broke away from the shackles of apartheid, Nelson Mandela and others rejected any majoritarian form of governance and instead opted for a power-sharing transition government which, until FW de Klerk withdrew, seemed to work quite well. Sadly, they now appear to be reverting to a majoritarian structure, and it was particularly disappointing to see that Mandela, in his autobiography, first dismissed the very thought of majority voting as being distinctly unAfrican, but later adopted this methodology without so much as a word of explanation.[9]

* * * * *

In summary, many current power-sharing arrangements institutionalize the very sectarianism they were supposed to obviate: these include the Taif Agreement in Lebanon with its emphasis on confessional beliefs, the Belfast Agreement which uses party labels and designations, and the Dayton Agreement which relies on ethno-nationalist demarcations.

One form of rule which could replace the dualist, consociational democracy is a more pluralist, consensual polity. Some writers regard consociationalism as virtually the same as a consensual democracy but a more inclusive definition of the latter would allow the final decision-making process on matters of contention to be multi-optional. An agreement or a compromise, with a minimum consensus coefficient should be sought (see Sect. 6.3.2), and where no such option is immediately identifiable, the matter should be deferred, if need be with the assistance of an impartial third party, until such time as an accommodation *can* be found.

Mention should be made of one other possible state structure: a multi-party lower chamber plus an upper house in which only non-partisans or independents may serve (See also Sect. 5.1.1.5). Having endured a troubled post-WWII history, Thailand introduced such an arrangement in 1997: a multi-party House of Representatives and a directly elected non-partisan Senate to replace the previously appointed second chamber. Improvements were marginal, the constitution was annulled in the bloodless coup of 2006, and a new Senate was formed in 2008. 76 non-partisans were elected; the remaining 74 of the 150-seat upper house were all appointed.

Bhutan's constitutional monarchy was replaced by a similar mixed structure in 2007: a National Assembly of 47 members was to be a multi-party parliament, while a National Council consisting of 20 non-partisans and five royal appointees would serve as the second chamber. Alas, only two parties managed to be registered, and in the first elections of 2008, one of them won 45 of the 47 seats. Meanwhile, the non-partisan candidates for Council had to be university graduates, and five elections were postponed because there were not enough contestants.

---

[9] 'Democracy meant all men were to be heard,' he said. 'A minority was not to be crushed by a majority.' Later on, however, he changed his mind and stated that, 'After 5 years, the government of national unity would become a simple majority-rule government' (Mandela 1994: 25 and 727).

A similar non-partisan chamber was envisaged in the Belfast Agreement in the Civic Forum, but it did not survive (Sect. 4.1.1.5).

5.2 Governments and their *Modus Operandi*

Having discussed the various party-structures of government, it is time to examine the way they function.

> ... the difference between a government consisting of one party and a government consisting of a [majority] coalition... is that in the former [people] of different opinions and interests form a coalition before going to the polls; while in the latter the coalition is not formed until after the voting has taken place. (Lewis 1965: 70)

In most Anglo-Saxon democracies, when one party has an absolute majority in parliament, that party then forms a single-party government. If that party wins *every* election, its two-party state is little better than a one-party state. Such was the story in NI where, on coming to power in the 1920s, the unionists threw out the PR-STV electoral system because it did not serve their purposes. They then had a permanent majority for the next 50 years.

Please note, they did not change the decision-making process. As far as they were concerned, the two-option majority vote was the perfect tool. By our own definition, NI was a bad one-party state because the party continued to have its own party structures alongside the state structures. Indeed, it was an oligarchy run by the Orange Order, albeit in the guise of a multi-party democracy.

In contrast, in jurisdictions which enjoy PR and in which no one party has an absolute majority of the seats, there are usually two forms of government. First, the party with a plurality (largest minority) of the seats can form a minority administration, as sometimes happens in Canada and Spain for example, and is currently (2011) the arrangement in Scotland. Secondly, there can be a coalition, either narrow $(W + Y)$, broad $(W + Y + Z)$ or grand $(W + X)$ (Sect. 5.1.4) which is usually the case in Germany, the Netherlands and elsewhere.

As already noted, in a single-party majority government, the cabinet can and often does dictate policy, and parliaments become little more than talking shops. In minority and coalition governments, in contrast, parliaments tend to be more powerful because, if only a few members abstain or vote against, the government might lose its policy. Such a government, some say, is unstable. Yet in the long term, many single-party majority governments are also unstable, creating as they do "the politics of the pendulum" – huge swings in government and huge changes of policy, which are then reversed at a subsequent election (by perhaps just a tiny swing of the electorate).

The instability of some coalition governments is to some extent due to the continued emphasis on the majority vote. Reference was made to the German style of no-confidence motion in Sect. 1.1.2.3. The same principle applies in consensus politics: anyone disagreeing with a policy proposal *A* would normally be obliged to put forward an alternative proposal *B*, and this would often turn what was a two-option debate – *A*, yes-or-no – into a three-option discussion: *A*, *B* or *status quo ante*. Such is the basis of a pluralist approach and such is equivalent in outline to a process of conflict resolution (Sect. 1.1.2.1).

It is as if the root cause of so many of our ills is indeed a belief in the majority vote. Without it, there would be little or no justification for a single-party-majority government or even a majority coalition, and democracy might have evolved into something in between the 'ideological and open' one-party state, the no-party state and/or the all-party coalition, all three of which could qualify as a GNU.

It is worth recalling the evolution of democratic practice: the early practitioners realized that everybody should work together, that somehow or other, everybody should come to a collective decision. That was the founding principle of democracy. Initially, in ancient Greece, this was achieved by means of a majority vote. Later on, despite many advances in social choice theory, the Europeans resorted to the same methodology, while others relied on the shade of the big tree. As will be seen shortly, a structure which combines the principle of inclusivity with the pragmatics of efficiency is certainly possible.

5.3 Government Structures

The two principal forms of representative democracy are the presidential and the parliamentary. In the former a president is directly elected by the people, in the latter a PM is elected or selected indirectly by parliament, and some countries – France, Russia and now Kenya – have both a president and a PM.

The theory behind the presidential form is based on the principle of the separation of powers: the legislature, the executive and the judiciary. According to the early US constitutionalists, the president was to be the executive, independent of the legislature in Congress. The judiciary, once appointed, would also be independent. In the intervening two centuries, the presidency has alas increased in size such that nowadays it can propose its own legislation, and the lines of separation have become somewhat blurred.

When the premier and the president belong to two different parties, as can happen in France, there has to be a form of power-sharing or co-habitation as it is called; (see Fig. 6.1, note *g*). Elsewhere, in Ireland for example, the president though directly elected has only one main responsibility, to safeguard the constitution: so the *Taoiseach* or Premier in Dublin is as powerful, relatively speaking, as many of his equivalents abroad.

Further variations on the democratic theme may be seen in the legislature, for parliament can be single or twin chamber – uni- or bi-cameral – and in some countries, the second chamber serves to represent the federal nature of the state. What's more, some decentralized administrations allow several functions of government to be devolved to regional assemblies and/or local councils.

5.4 The Debate

The most important procedure of all is that of the debate. This applies to every forum, whether it be a local council, a sub-committee, parliament or an international gathering.

> *Once your fall-back positions are published, you have already fallen back to them* (Eban 1998: 81).

In many forums, political debates are conducted in a majoritarian context, that is, they culminate in a binary decision-making process, a majority vote. In contemporary practice, the political discourse often starts with a motion or policy proposal. Various parties may then move amendments to this clause or that, (as long as they are not wrecking amendments) but the fate of each amendment, along with the final decision on the substantive motion, are all determined by a binary, for-or-against, majority vote.

Someone proposes the motion. Others oppose. Amendments are taken one at a time and people are called in turn, the speaker or chair doing their best to ensure that those called are roughly equal in number, for or against. Fairness, however, operates only within this adversarial context.

In parliaments under single-party majority rule, the majority party will win unless a few rebels defect (and thus risk their ministerial prospects or even their seats; rebels they may be when a government has a large majority, but they tend to disappear in a hung parliament or when an election is due). For those in the minority, there are few possible courses of action. Indeed, virtually the only weapon available is the filibuster, the "art" of talking for as long as the bladder permits in the hope that the debate runs out of time. If need be, the government can then retaliate with a guillotine, so to curtail the debate.

All aspects of the debate are set in an adversarial mode. Much good work is done in all-party committees, where every piece of proposed legislation is put under scrutiny. There was also a very constructive atmosphere in the Dublin Forum for Peace and Reconciliation[10] which for obvious reasons tried to operate within a consensual milieu. Furthermore in many non-party-political gatherings these days – sometimes in the UN and always in the OSCE, etc. – decisions are taken as it were "under the big tree", i.e. when there is a (verbal) consensus. In parliamentary chambers, however, especially when in plenary session, the image of Westminster-style parliamentary democracy is often a disgraceful performance of almost childlike squabbling. Governments propose because, mistakenly, they think

---

[10] This Irish Government response to the 1994 Irish Republican Army, IRA, cease-fire brought together representatives of all Irish political parties, North and South, but not all of the former attended. One of the specific purposes of the Forum was to produce a consensus document on the nature of the Northern problem and the current author voted against; it was a majoritarian document, with nearly everyone acting inclusively to agree on exclusivity.

that is their job; for similar reasons, the others oppose, in a supposedly *loyal* way, not least because their long-term interest so demands.

One of the worst aspects of many a political debate is the fact that it is often not allowed to proceed in a positive direction, even if the participants want it to. This is because the final vote is invariably on the *original* motion. Admittedly, the latter might now be amended, but much of it will retain its initial imprint. Any new idea or any compromise which the debate itself might have inspired, any collective wisdom which could have resulted from the meeting of so many active minds, proceeds no further. It is not on the order paper. Too often, the debate has one and only one purpose: the PM wants the House to want what he wants, so that is what the House will want too.

Not only MPs in parliament but also numerous other committee members in society at large appear to undergo a metamorphosis in debate. In the tearooms beforehand, in the bar afterwards, there is often a pleasant camaraderie. In the chamber itself, though, it is a gladiatorial contest, a battle of numbers, a win-or-lose argument in which even the losers may shine a little; if the latter put on a good performance and gratify the press gallery, their prospects at the next election might benefit.

It is worth recalling that we human beings are often able to determine the conditions which then determine us (Sect. 1.1.2.6). If we go to a football field, we play against each other. If we are deployed to the trenches of Flanders, we fight against each other. Likewise if we enter the majoritarian debating chamber, we often turn what should be a pluralist discussion into a sometimes dangerous dualist argument.

To summarize, reform of both our debating structures and our decision-making voting procedures is crucial to any civilized form of human interaction; the dual nature of numerous debates is little better than the duel nature of many other disputes. The necessary reform is set out in Chap. 6.

5.4.1 People Power

There are lots of ways in which the electorate can participate in government. Representative democracy, after all, is meant to be something which involves more than marking an "x" or a "1, 2, 3…" every 4 years or so. For some specific issues, government may sometimes call a public enquiry or an independent commission (Sect. 1.3). In addition, it may seek to determine public opinion via focus groups, social surveys and opinion polls, though the results of these have only an advisory function[11] and do not necessarily influence policy. These forms of deliberative democracy can be done either *in situ* or on the web (Emerson P 2010: 83–101).

---

[11] Interestingly enough, many forms of fact finding involve academics with the most up-to-date computers and other associated technologies, not least to ensure the sample chosen is as random as possible. When it comes to decision-making, however, the chosen methodology is often a majority vote.

The advisory nature of some enquiries and commissions suggests that the government has already decided what the outcomes of these consultations are going to be. Accordingly, if government is to be accountable and transparent, the commission itself should use a form of multi-option decision-making, so that all concerned may know which options exist and, *inter alia,* what are the government's priorities or preferences.

Another prime instrument of people power is the citizens' initiative, especially if it takes the form of a multi-option poll. These can be an excellent counter to what is often too great a concentration of power in central government.

> *Politicians usually dislike referendums – although there are occasions... when party leaders turn to them as last-ditch devices for resolving issues so contentious that, if left to the ordinary ways of party government, they might shatter the established parties altogether.* (Butler and Ranney 1994: 259)
>
> *Far from being an instrument of majority rule, the referendum has helped to establish a political system in which the very notions of majority and minority have ceased to have much meaning.*
>   *For Switzerland has used the referendum, together with federalism and a coalition government embracing all the main political parties, precisely to* defuse *the conflicts that might otherwise arise in a divided society.* (Bogdanor 1994: 88)

Direct democracy can also involve other forms of campaigning in which members of the public lobby their MPs or try to affect public opinion, either to support a single issue campaign or with a view to standing in an election; this theme will be revisited in Chap. 6.

5.4.2 International Government

Another factor of increasing significance relates to international government. In world organizations like the UN or regional gatherings like the EU and the OSCE, umpteen delegations from many countries come together to make decisions. Sometimes, as in the UN Security Council, decisions are still taken by a majority vote (Sects. 1.1.2.4 and 2.5.2). In many instances, as in the December 2009 UN Copenhagen conference on climate change, reliance is placed on reaching a (verbal) consensus, if need be via discussions which continue into and maybe throughout the night. As at Copenhagen, such a methodology is not always successful; nevertheless, given the diversity of our species, the dominance of the majority vote may well be obsolescent, at last.[12] After all, as an OSCE official once explained to the

---

[12] The EU uses qualified majority voting, where each country has a certain number of votes, depending on their populations, and where a resolution is considered passed if it gains a predetermined number of these votes.

The IMF is also majoritarian. In the wake of *perestroika,* Yugoslavia no longer held a strategic position in the world. The Federation began to fall apart, mainly through internal arguments over

author, it is very difficult to get a consensus in a meeting of representatives from 54 nations if, just before the final document is to be agreed, Liechtenstein exercises its veto.

5.5 Conclusions

> *Beneath its "idealistic" appearance, every political party actually represents a definite class or definite economic interest which it must defend in parliament. The result of this is a squabbling among selfish oppositions that has nothing in common with the true and exclusive interest of the nation... they stop at nothing: lies, demagogy, compromise, corruption...We have nothing to do with these poisons.* Alexandre Adande of Dahomey. (Emerson R 1966: 287)

Just as there are both good and bad decision-making processes and electoral systems, so too there are good and bad structures of government. Experience suggests that the more consociational or consensual governments are, the better they are suited to the modern "multi-multi" pluralist society. The required reforms are firstly, that decision-making in parliaments has to be more inclusive; secondly, where appropriate, electoral systems *to* parliament need to be improved; and thirdly, more electoral systems *within* parliaments should be introduced.

Even without such reforms, the multi-party or all-party coalition would appear to be the optimal form of governance. If everything is 'ideological and open' (Sect. 5.1.1) and if government itself is federal and decentralized, there might indeed be very little difference between the no-party or one-party state, the all-party state, the power-sharing administration and the GNU. Furthermore, with power-sharing and job-rotations, the question of whether or not the head of state is directly or indirectly elected is rather less crucial.

> *But as we reach the end of the twentieth century, signs indicate that the mass party as we have known it since the beginning of the century, far from being inherent to any democratic system of government, may represent merely a phase of democratic development that is passing away.* (Bogdanor 1994: 97)

As it happens, there are many signs of change, and one of the most encouraging is the advent of the computer. Multi-option voting might have been difficult in days when people expressed their opinions on what they thought was right by raising the right hand. Today, however, the deployment of modern technology in the elected chamber must lead, sooner or later, to the following:

---

money – which Republic was to pay how much to, and which was to receive how much from, Central Government – but Yugoslavia was heavily in debt. Sadly, '...the IMF began to tie conditions for new credits to political reform. Its first demand for re-strengthening the governing capacity of the federal administration... was to change the voting rules in the National Bank from consensus to majority decision.' (Woodward 1995: 74)

(a) the introduction of multi-option preference voting, and
(b) the end of the whip system.
   If that happens, we can then expect
(c) the end of the present rigid party structure of politics.

Parties will still exist, of course, possibly as 'small groups of seven or eight. We [Irish] will not have parties on definite lines of political cleavage,' suggested Kevin O'Higgins (Lyons 1986: 474–5) and such parties as do exist will not be run on such authoritarian lines as they are at present.

> *I'm not opposed to the solidarity of various interest groups of like-minded people. It's just that I'm against anything that serves to cloud personal responsibility, or rewards anyone with privileges for devotion to a particular power-orientated group.* (Havel 1989: 25)

References

Bogdanor V (1994) Western Europe. In: Butler D, Ranney A (eds) Referendums around the world. The AEI Press, Washington
Butler D, Ranney A (eds) (1994) Referendums around the world. The AEI Press, Washington
Churchill WS (1974) A history of the English-speaking peoples. Cassell, London
Dahl RA (1998) On democracy. Yale University Press, New Haven
Eban A (1998) Diplomacy for the next century. Yale University Press, New Haven
Emerson P (2010) Consensus voting and party funding: a web-based experiment. European Political Science 9(1):83–101
Emerson R (1966) From empire to nation. Beacon, Boston
Fisk R (2001) Pity the nation. Oxford University Press, Oxford
Havel V (1989) Open letters. Faber and Faber, London
Human Rights Watch (1999) Hostile to democracy. Human Rights Watch, New York. http://www.hrw.org/legacy/reports/1999/uganda/Uganweb-03.htm#P323_33670. Accessed 13 Jan 2011
Huntington SP (1997) The clash of civilizations. Simon and Schuster, New York
IDEA (1997) The international IDEA handbook of electoral system design. IDEA, Stockholm
Lewis Sir A (1965) Politics in West Africa. George Allen and Unwin, London
Lijphart A (1977) Democracy in plural societies. Yale University Press, New Haven and London
Lijphart A (1999) Patterns of democracy. Yale University Press, New Haven
Lyons FSL (1986) Ireland since the famine. Fontana, London
McLean I, Urken AB (1995) Classics of social choice. University of Michigan, Ann Arbor
Maher J et al (eds) (2009) The Europa world year book, 2009. Routledge, Abingdon
Mandela N (1994) Long walk to freedom. Little Brown and Company, London
Matlosa K et al (2007) Challenges of conflict, democracy and development in Africa. EISA, Johannesburg
Menang T et al (2007) Traditional leadership and democracy in Cameroon. In: Matlosa K (ed) Challenges of conflict, democracy and development in Africa. EISA, Johannesburg
Museveni YK (1997) Sowing the mustard seed. Macmillan, London
Sigmund PE (ed) (1966) The ideologies of the developing nations. Frederick A. Praeger, New York
Taylor R (ed) (2009) Consociational theory. Routledge, Abingdon
Woodward SL (1995) Balkan tragedy. The Brookings Institution, Washington

Chapter 6
Governance

> *In a plural society the approach to politics as a zero-sum game is immoral and impracticable. Words like "winning" and "losing" have to be banished from the political vocabulary of a plural society.*
> (Lewis 1965: 66–7)

Abstract The MBC for decision-making along with QBS and the matrix vote for elections are three of the tools required for creating a consensual polity. In this chapter, consideration is given to the way these tools can be used in such a democratic structure. The procedures for the conduct of debates are examined in some detail and various forms of power-sharing are analysed.

The current state of democratic development will then be reviewed, all 2,500 years since democracy was first devised; needless to say, some countries are doing rather better than others. Finally, the text concludes with a complete draft definition of a democratic structure, embracing decision-making, elections and governance.

6.1 First Principles

Three of the defining principles upon which any form of representative democracy should be based can be outlined as follows:

- The democratically elected parliament should represent *all* the people. Accordingly, the electoral system must be free and fair – not just the process in the polling station, but the system itself and the count as well.
- Secondly, just as parliament must represent the people, all of them, so too any democratic government should represent that parliament in its entirety. Assuming that two or more parties are represented in parliament, this means '...not

only that some parties ought to form a coalition, but that all the major parties ought to...' (Lewis 1965: 81)
- Thirdly, matters of controversy should be resolved by an inclusive decision-making process and not by majority vote.

In brief, majority rule is unsatisfactory while majority voting is both divisive and often imprecise. Therefore any form of single-party majority government or even majority coalition is also far from the democratic ideal. A minimum requirement for an elected chamber to qualify for the adjective "democratic" is that it should be an inclusive, power-sharing coalition of regional or national unity, either no-party or all-party.

To achieve such inclusivity both in government and in parliament, decisions on controversial matters should be resolved via a non-majoritarian decision-making process, and every effort should be made to do this in consensus, either verbally and/or with a consensus vote. In addition, parliament should reclaim its right to be superior to the executive.

At the same time, on a broad range of policies, the people should have the right to move a citizens' initiative, a two-option or ideally a multi-option poll, either to propose new legislation or to repeal an existing law. If need be, the formulation of the appropriate question(s) should be the responsibility of an independent commission, and only those options which do not infringe existing human rights legislation should be considered eligible.

6.2 The Debate

It is now time to consider the nature of decision-making, not so much the vote itself (if vote there is to be), rather the process which precedes the vote. This may be a debate in chamber or the public hearing of an independent commission, but what follows also applies to a meeting of a company board, an open gathering of a local community group, or any other committee or general meeting, although in some of the less formal settings, a few relaxations can be tolerated.

If a controversy arises and an urgent but not immediate decision is required, then in a democratic body there must first be a debate. Several conditions are necessary. There should be an impartial chair to facilitate proceedings. Sometimes, as in the UK's House of Commons, this is the speaker, an MP of one party or another who then assumes a neutral role. In other instances, as for example in a Dutch city council, it is a supposedly unbiased mayor who, after due consultation with the relevant political parties, is not elected but 'appointed by the province's Queen's Commissioner', ((Dutch) Ministry of Foreign Affairs 2000: 44). A third possibility would be for the forum concerned to elect someone who is absolutely impartial – if such there be – by choosing a member of the judiciary to undertake this function.

6.2 The Debate

6.2.1 The Consensors

In addition, there should be a team of, say, three "consensors", independent and non-voting persons also elected from amongst the judiciary. Their function is threefold: the first two tasks are (a) to ensure that every policy proposal conforms to certain laid-down norms of human rights, and (b) to identify, collate, and as necessary up-date a list of all the valid proposals emerging during the course of the debate. These proposals may be displayed *in situ* in their original, edited or composited form, as appropriate, either via a data projector onto a computer screen and/or a dedicated web-page. (The third task is in Sect. 6.2.2.)

During the course of the debate, all members shall be asked to restrict their contributions to a fixed time limit, as was done nearly 2000 years ago for Pliny the Younger. (Sect. 2.3.2) One very persuasive way to apply this rule is by using a set of "traffic lights": when the chair gives a speaker the floor, the light is green; when, say, 30 seconds remain, it goes to amber; and when time is up, it turns red.

As the debate proceeds, members may seek points of clarification, move amendments to any of the proposals, make new suggestions and/or, if all agree, remove certain clauses. In some discussions, after perhaps an initial period during which many diverse opinions have been expressed, it may become obvious that all concerned are moving to a consensus. This may happen slowly as changes to various options are accepted and/or as composites are proposed and adopted: in other words, the debate may *proceed*, just as many a good conversation proceeds, often in a direction which none of the participants could have predicted. Sometimes, therefore, the process of examining all the various options will lead to a verbal consensus and there will be no need to vote. Even in these circumstances, however, and especially when the subject matter is not so much contentious as complex, participants may wish to know just what are the relevant levels of support, in which case they may vote as well.

There will be other debates in which there is no apparent agreement and in which, when everyone has aired their views, several options remain "on the table", computer screen and/or web-page. If this happens, the chair will ask all concerned whether they agree that the list of options includes their particular aspiration, either verbatim or perhaps included in a composite. Next, if all do agree, members may proceed to the vote; the most appropriate decision-making process will usually be an MBC and, in any modern setting, MPS would use a system of electronic voting. Thus, at the click of a mouse, both the voters' profile and the results of their vote could then be displayed.

If the voting system to be used is indeed an MBC, protagonists will know that their particular option will have a greater chance of being adopted if it receives support from right across the spectrum of participants. Success depends upon the opinions of *every* voter: it is worth repeating that the winning option will need not only a good number of high preferences, but perhaps too a fair number of middle preferences and very few low preferences. (Sect. 2.5.1) In this way, the very prospect of such a decision-making process will help to ensure the atmosphere in debate is constructive. In short, the decision-making process used at the end of the debate determines the nature of that debate (Sect. 1.1.2.6). We determine us. And in the context of an MBC, people will have a vested interest in drafting their policy proposals in inclusive language and arguing their case in a similar vein.

6.2.2 Composite Resolutions

The consensors' third task relates to the analysis of the vote. If the dispute in question is a minor altercation over dog licenses and if, say, option D comes a close second to the winner, option C, then, if the consensus coefficient (see Sect. 6.3.2) has been surpassed and if the social ranking is single-peaked (Sect. 2.3.4), the consensors may rule that the collective opinion of the House is for a dog license of £x, a compromise between the two, C and D. They should also be able to calculate the accuracy of this outcome – assuming, that is, that the corresponding voters' profile is accurate and that all MPs have voted sincerely – to within plus or minus £y and, when it is a vote of some hundreds of MPs, "y" may well be equal to or even less than one.

Whenever the debate is more complex, such calculations may be impossible. Nevertheless, if a second and maybe even a third option are close to the most popular option, and if certain aspects of these well-placed options can be incorporated into the leading one, the consensors may well decide to form a final composite.

6.2.3 The Art of Compromise

In any consensus debate, the participants will compromise. All are allowed to speak but they speak not so much *against* but *with* each other. In the vote, they may cast a preference not only for their favourite option, but also for those other options on which they would be prepared to compromise. Thus in an MBC, given that all the points are totalled together, they not only talk *with* each other, they also vote *with* each other. And nobody votes "no". Nobody votes "against" anything or anyone.

If the consensors do choose to combine the winner and the runner-up into a composite, the process becomes even more win-win and 'The final result is not a compromise of conflicting views but a synthesis of the best thoughts of all...' (quoted in Sheeran 1983: 53.)[1] The outcome may not have been one of the original proposals. The debate started with the latter but because it *proceeded*, because it was *allowed* to proceed, it may well have come to an unexpected conclusion.

The legislature, having thus decided upon a policy, informs the executive. The executive then executes that policy. That is their job. If for whatever reason, any member of the executive feels they cannot execute the policy, they should resign.

---

[1] Said in reference to a verbal consensus.

That is what politics is meant to be, what it was in some of the forums of old, and what it still is in many committees in society at large. If the principle of the separation of powers were to be properly enforced, and if parliament were to be truly sovereign over its government, this procedure could also be the case in parliament: the executive would do what the legislature told it to do.

6.3 Inclusive Government

The sovereignty of parliament over the executive can best be facilitated in a pluralist democracy, i.e. when parliament's debates are themselves pluralist. This will not happen until the final decision-making process is also pluralist and therefore multi-optional.

With the executive properly subject to the will of an inclusive parliament, the operation of an all-party, power-sharing system of coalition government becomes not only desirable but feasible. It should first be affirmed (a) that no majority has the right to dominate but everyone has the reponsibility to co-operate, and (b) that the enactment of the collective consensus is a democratic right. There remain just a few small details to facilitate this ancient, archetypal, new-found ideal.

6.3.1 Power-Sharing

In coalition governments, the principle of power-sharing should relate, not only to the way decisions are taken, but also to the appointment of representatives to positions of power or influence. As described in Chap. 4, a parliament can elect its government democratically by using the matrix vote, which can also be used for the appointment of other smaller groups, sub-committees and so on. Furthermore, power-sharing can be more readily effected if such appointments are of a limited tenure and regularly rotated. There 'is advantage in having many of the democratic rules such as tenure of office for only 6 months, so as to give all, being similar, a share in it; their similarity makes them, as it were, into a demos...' (Aristotle V, viii 1308a3.)

> ...*infinite precautions were taken lest any Senator should seize excessive power and attempt dictatorship. The Rector wore a superb toga of red silk with a stole of black velvet over the left shoulder, and was preceded in his comings and goings by musicians and twenty palace guards; but he held his office for just 1 month... this brevity of tenure was the result of ever anxious revision, for the term had originally been 3 months, had been reduced to 2, and was finally brought down to the single month.** (West 1967: 250–1)
>
> *This tale comes from the city-state of what is now Dubrovnik, the original name of which was Ragusa. It was incorporated into Croatia in the twentieth century.

A term of just 1 month may be too short for today's complicated world, but to suggest a time-scale of 1 year (as is the case for presidents in Switzerland) or two terms (for occupants of the White House) is certainly a good starting point. Whenever 'authority in the *state* is constituted on a basis of equality... between citizens, they expect to take turns in exercising it. This principle is very old...' (Aristotle III, vi 1279a8)

Even with relatively short time scales, there is always the possibility that the individual concerned may fail to be as *candid* as first promised. The voters, therefore, should be able to '...recall any deputy before his term is up, if he fails to justify their trust,' (Latov 1974: 14), to quote one of the rules of the Soviet electoral system, although how the good comrades were to decide on this course of action was not made clear.

Power-sharing is a very necessary element of many post-conflict settlements: Taif, Belfast, Dayton etc. (Sects. 5.1.5.3/4/5) It must be emphasized, however, that these peace processes should include not only post rotations and power-sharing; they should also cater for (a) decision-making processes which are preferential and subject to a minimum cross-community consensus coefficient (see below) for use in both the elected chamber and any national polls; and (b) an electoral system which is both preferential and proportional, the latter subject to a maximum threshold.

6.3.2 Consensus Coefficient

The level of consensus under which any one parliament may choose to function may be varied. The measure of this degree of consensus is called the "consensus coefficient". For any one option, it is defined as that option's MBC score divided by the maximum possible score.

Consider, for example, a parliament of 100 members voting on a five-option ballot in which every member submits a full ballot. If every member gives option *C* a first preference, option *C* will gain 100 × 5 = 500 points, the maximum score, and a consensus coefficient of 500/500 = 1.0. If at the same time everyone gives option *D* a fifth preference, then *D* will gain a score of 100 × 1 = 100 points and a consensus coefficient of 100/500 = 0.2. Only in a ballot where nobody gives a certain option any preferences at all will that option get a consensus coefficient of zero.

The consensus coefficient is therefore a measure, not only of the level of support for a particular option, but also of the degree of participation with which everyone has embraced the democratic process on this matter. In a highly hypothetical scenario, if everyone gave option *C* a first preference without casting any preferences at all for any of the other options listed, then option *C* would get an MBC score of 100 × 1 = 100 points and a consensus coefficient of 0.2. (Such a

6.3 Inclusive Government

scenario is of course highly unlikely because doubtless the consensors would not have allowed other options to be on the ballot paper if these options had not been proposed during the course of the debate.)

If in a different setting on another five-option ballot, everyone submits a full ballot and they all give option *A* their third preference, then, as shown in Sect. 2.5.2, option *A* will get the mean score, a total of $100 \times 3 = 300$ points which relates to a consensus coefficient of $300/500 = 0.6$. In like manner, if 50% give a first preference to option *C*, while 50% give it a last preference, it will gain $50 \times 5 + 50 \times 1 = 250 + 50 = 300$ which again equates to a coefficient of the order of 0.6. In a polarized vote where 50% + 1 totally oppose 50% − 1, the consensus coefficient of the leading option will still be very mean.

Now a parliament or assembly may wish to state in its standing orders that only those policies which receive a consensus coefficient sufficiently above the mean will then be enacted into law. Furthermore, if the chamber is in a conflict zone like NI, it may wish to set a slightly higher threshold, if only to guarantee that the adopted policy will have the support of the representatives of both or all "sides". Once set, this threshold can be put into operation, without anyone having to know which MPs or MLAs have which, if any, designations or even party affiliations. (Sect. 5.1.5.4)

6.3.3 Collective Responsibility

In majoritarian governance, no matter whether the government be single-party or a multi-party coalition, the cabinet operates under the principle of collective responsibility. In consensus politics, that principle applies to the entire parliament. Individual members may have their different preferences on various matters, and these differences will be shown in *Hansard* just as soon as the relevant vote is taken. On those occasions when a member of parliament fundamentally disagrees with a particular decision then, as noted above, the appropriate course of action is to resign.

Differences of opinion there will always be. If the preferences cast by all the MPs are indeed on public record, then society can know how one member of the government/parliament differs from the others. Come the next election, all the sitting MPs will be able to stand on their record, accepting the decisions of their parliament, but pointing out that, if the electorate were now to choose a different parliament, future decisions would perhaps be rather different. Furthermore, if the electoral system were a good one, a countrywide swing of 2% towards, say, a greener politics, would see a similar 2% swing in parliament and in government.

6.3.4 *Direct Democracy*

A society of millions will never get to the stage where everybody can be an MP, albeit just for a limited period. At the same time, there must be better ways by which the electorate can exercise its democratic rights beyond marking the occasional ballot paper. In recent years, and most especially in the US, there has been a considerable growth in the field of direct democracy, where single-issue groups campaign for, and often succeed in getting, a particular law enacted. This, I would argue, is far from ideal, even if such developments are accompanied by lots of modern software to help inform those concerned of the issues involved. Given the US two-party system, however, one can well understand why committed environmentalists, for example, might reject the party political approach and seek instead to hold local referendums[2] on subjects of their choice.

The thought of a majority of bicycle-riding vegetarians imposing a ban on both fishing and cars fills me with dread, however, even though I am a vegetarian cyclist. A recent poll in California in which an English-speaking majority tried to ban dual-language schools is an example, I would suggest, of "the tyranny of the majority". Furthermore, any prospect of a moral majority, be it Christians from the bible belt, Moslem fundamentalists in Algeria (Sect. 3.2) or the Taliban in Afghanistan does not bode well.[3]

This is why, of course, all politics should be conducted within a human rights framework. Accordingly, if a proposal does not conform to certain laid down norms, the consensors will not allow that proposal to get onto the agenda and the computer screen, let alone the final ballot paper. (Sect. 6.2.1)

6.3.5 *Human Rights*

A most necessary element of any governmental structure is therefore not only a written constitution and a bill of rights but the inclusion within these documents of certain democratic rights. Such charters should then be adopted by the people in a multi-option poll, for doubtless there will be certain clauses which could involve a choice between a number of alternatives. If everything were done in this way, then with confidence might the demos start their written constitutions by boldly declaring, 'We the people...'

Such a constitution or bill of rights should contain at least one clause on decision-making and another on the electoral system. Now the people who first decided to abandon fighting and to resolve any disputes by majority vote, (chronology, 600s BC), did not have a fight about it, nor did they take a majority vote on

---

[2] There are 29 States in the USA which allow for referendums.

[3] This Californian referendum was held on 2.6.1998 and 61% voted in favour.

whether or not to adopt the majority vote – as far as I know.[4] Given that the most important decision any democrats have to make concerns the methodology to be used when making decisions, it would seem that the only proper way to do this would be to hold a multi-option vote on the various procedures that are available. At least, by having such a vote, the electorate would come to realize that there are indeed more than two ways of doing things.

6.4 A Comparison of Some Democracies

Previous pages have shown that (a) the choice of electoral system has a direct effect on the subsequent government, (b) the inclusiveness of a parliament will be greater if the threshold of the electoral system is lower, and (c) the government will probably be less or more democratic depending on whether it is either (i) a single-party minority/majority administration in a two-party state or (ii) a majority-, grand-, or all-party coalition in a multi-party state.

Taking these factors into account, a diagrammatic comparison of various democracies during the course of the last 20 years is shown in Fig. 6.1. The vertical axis depicts the effective number of political parties, which is based on the type and threshold of the country's electoral system. The horizontal axis, which is divided (but not in a mathematical way) into different types of government, portrays the extent to which the country concerned exercises single-party or coalition governments. It varies:

- from Canada which always has either single-party majority rule or a single-party minority administration of one party or another;
- via Norway, which changes from single-party rule to majority coalition, depending on the election results;
- to Finland where there is invariably a majority coalition;
- to Germany, which has either a majority or a grand coalition, depending on the mathematics of the election results; (Sect. 5.1.4.1)
- to what this book considers to be the best form of governance to date: the all-party coalitions of Switzerland.

In some countries, a coalition can be very fickle; in others, it may become semi-permanent and act as if it were just the one, single party. In Serbia, for example, the Democratic Opposition of Serbia, a coalition of 15 parties, came together to get rid of Milošević, and once the job was done in 2000, the coalition then fell apart;

---

[4] To the best of my knowledge, there has been only one instance where people have had a referendum on whether or not they should have a referendum. It happened in 1991 in Vlaardingen in the Netherlands, and 67% voted to vote. (Holsteyn 1996: 130)

There was also one referendum on whether to abolish referendums in regard to constitutional change. This took place in Guyana in 1978, when the proposal was approved by 97%. (Butler and Ranney 1994: 281)

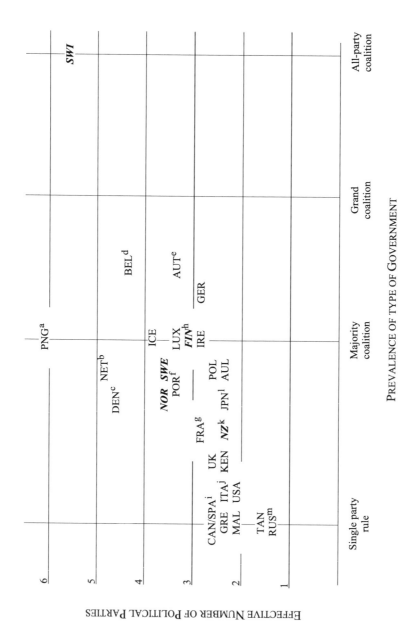

Fig. 6.1 Democratization (continued) (The key to Fig. 6.1 is on page 132.)

Fig. 6.1 Democratization.

(**a**) On gaining independence in 1975, PNG changed from AV to FPP, but back again in 2002, with the added stipulation that voters must cast three preferences. Its multi-ethnic nature of society means that there is an unusually high number of political parties. Furthermore, just as in some countries the distinction between "coalition" and "party" is vague, so here the difference between "partisan" or "independent" candidates can be rather opaque.

(**b**) The Netherlands usually has a majority coalition government of two or three parties, which sometimes are "adjacent" but not always. There is currently (2011) a minority administration: a coalition of two parties with the support of, but without any ministers from, the right-wing Freedom Party.

(**c**) Denmark often has a minority administration in which the largest party is supported by other smaller ones, and it was ever thus: 'Denmark is known for its long periods of government by minority cabinets.' (Lijphart 1977: 111)

(**d**) Belgium's high number of effective political parties reflects the plural nature of that society. Governments are formed on the basis of popular support from both the Fleming and Walloon parties, and thus practice a form of power-sharing. (See also chronology 2010.) The post-election caretaker government consists of three Francophone and two Flemish parties representing a majority and minority of their respective electorates.

(**e**) Post election negotiations on forming a government in Austria have often been problematic and protracted. Particularly controversial was the majority coalition of 2000 when the People's Party joined up with the Freedom Party. After the 2006 election, the former rejoined the Socialists in a grand coalition.

(**f**) The Socialist Party which won an absolute majority in Portugal's 2005 elections formed a cabinet with a number of independent members.

(**g**) Since 1986, France has often enjoyed *cohabitation*, but politics is still a left-versus-right contest between one coalition led by the socialists against another coalition under the UMP.

(**h**) Finland's last minority administration was in the 1970s. For the last 20 years, it has always enjoyed a majority coalition of between three and five parties.

(**i**) Despite having a PR-list electoral system, albeit one in which seats are allocated by the d'Hondt formula which tends to favour larger parties, Spain now has a two-party system – two large parties and a number of very small parties – and either single party majority rule or single party minority administration.

(**j**) Post-war Italy has had 51 different governments in 45 years, most of them weak coalitions. The instability was blamed on the electoral system, PR-list, (and not on the practice of majority voting). So in 1993, they had a referendum for a more majoritarian electoral system, MMP. The problem was still there, so in 2005, Italy reverted to PR-list, with the added proviso of bonus seats (though not quite as many as under Mussolini, App. A, A.1.2) to ensure that the party with the largest minority then gets 55% of the seats in parliament.

(**k**) New Zealand replaced its FPP by an MMP electoral system in 1993. (Sect. 2.6) Since then, the government has been either a majority coalition or, in 2008, a minority administration.

(**l**) Japan changed its electoral system for the Diet from SNTV to a two-tier system of MMP in 1993, with 300 MPs elected in single-seat FPP constituencies and 180 under PR. The Liberal Democratic Party ruled almost continually from 1955 – with just the one break in 1993 – until their three-party coalition was trounced by a five-party coalition led by the Democratic Party in 2009.

(**m**) Initially in 1989, the USSR adopted TRS. (Sects. 3.1.4 and 3.3.2.3) Today, however, Russia is a one-dominant party state (Sect. 5.1.2.1) with a PR-list electoral system under a 7% threshold, designed to perpetuate the prominence of Putin's EP. Just in case he might be too successful, the electoral law has a proviso to give a small proportion of seats to the party which comes second, even if this runner-up fails to clear that threshold.

Key to Figure 6.1

Country	Code	Electoral system	Tier	Referendums Mandatory	Citizens' initiatives
Australia	AUL	AV	1	yes	no
Austria	AUT	PR-list	2	yes	no
Belgium	BEL	PR-list	1	no	no
Canada	CAN	FPP	1	no	no
Denmark	DEN	PR-list	2	yes	no
Finland	FIN	PR-list	1	no	no
France	FRA	TRS	1	no	no
Germany	GER	MMP	2	no	no
Greece	GRE	PR-list*	2	no	no
Iceland	ICE	PR-list	2	yes	no
Ireland	IRE	PR-STV	1	yes	no
Italy	ITA	PR-list*	2	no	yes
Japan	JPN	MMP	2	yes	no
Kenya	KEN	FPP	1	no	no
Luxembourg	LUX	PR-list	1	no	no
Malta	MAL	PR-STV*	1	yes	yes
Netherlands	NET	PR-list	1	no	no
New Zealand	NZ	MMP	2	yes	yes
Norway	NOR	PR-list	2	no	no
PNG		AV	2	no	no
Poland	POL	PR-list	1	yes	no
Portugal	POR	PR-list	1	no	no
Russia	RUS	PR-list	1	yes	yes
Spain	SPA	PR-list	1	yes	no
Sweden	SWE	PR-list	2	no	no
Switzerland	SWI	PR-list	1	yes	yes
Tanzania	TAN	FPP	1	no	no
UK		FPP	1	no	no
USA		FPP	1	no	no

*If no party wins a majority in parliament, the party with the biggest minority gains a number of bonus seats, so that it can then form a single-party majority government

Serbia, however, is still in transition and is not shown in Fig. 6.1. In Germany, on the other hand, the CDU has long been in almost permanent coalition with the Christian Social Union, CSU. Ireland falls somewhere between the two, for while FG and Labour have distinctive policies, they often campaign in the hope of forming a majority coalition government. Italy is another exception, where a form of multi-party politics has descended into a contest of two opposing coalitions. Furthermore, some countries are rather difficult to place: Kenya, for example, changed from single party majority rule to a form of all-party power-sharing in the wake of the 2008 violence (Sect. 3.3.1.2) without any experience of coalition government. Not too much, therefore, can be taken from Fig. 6.1, but it does show a distinct trend.

It would be useful to add a third dimension, to indicate the level of decentralization, but apart from the data which is in the key to Fig. 6.1, the only additional information indicates which states use multi-option voting in either their parliaments and/or national referendums, if but occasionally; these countries are shown in bold italics.

Part of the information represented in Fig. 6.1 is taken from Lijphart (1999: 76–7); some material is obtained from IDEA and the ACE electoral knowledge network;[5] the rest is from the author's own research.

No one government structure is perfect, of course, but some are definitely less adversarial than others, and most of the countries which tend to work in a more consensual manner are amongst the coalitions to the right of the graph.

6.5 Conclusions

'*Democracy* is a concept which virtually defies definition.' (Lijphart 1977: 4) Others have tried: 'its primary meaning is that all who are affected by a decision should have the chance to participate in making that decision.' (Lewis 1965: 64)[6] To this can now be added the phrase from Sect. 2.7: democratic decision-making is a process which identifies either the unanimous viewpoint (where such exists); or, on more controversial issues, the average opinion or consensus; or on really contentious matters and/or especially in any plural society, the most acceptable compromise.

It is certainly worth trying to define the term, if only because until this is done, the world will continue to be plagued by a host of *exclusive* political parties – democratic unionists, democratic Serbs, democratic Croats and so forth – which often use the *inclusive* adjective with little justification. Indeed, 'even the most undemocratic parties [have] the adjective "democratic" in their names.' (Kapuściński 2008: 41)

Accordingly, the first priority (like the first task of this book) is to establish that the simple majority vote is not very democratic unless everyone and every minority agrees both to accept its use and to abide by the outcome. Instead of the right of the majority to rule, there should be the right (and therefore the responsibility as well) of all to come to an accommodation. No majority has the right to dominate and by the same token no minority has the right to veto. Within a culture of human rights, all must come to a compromise.

The same principle should apply at the national level, especially whenever there is to be a regional or national plebiscite. Every voter should be enabled to cast their preferences on a range of options, especially if the issue itself is controversial.

---

[5] Data taken by kind permission of International IDEA from <http://www.idea.int/esd/world.cfm> and <http://aceproject.org/epic-en/CDTable?question=ES001&view=country&set_language=en> International Institute for Democracy and Electoral Assistance, 2011. (Accessed 14 Jan. 2011)

[6] He went on to say, 'Its secondary meaning is that the will of the majority shall prevail,' and then admitted that this somewhat contradicted the primary interpretation.

At the very least there should be at least one compromise option on the ballot paper, and a minimum therefore of three options altogether.

The second priority is to use a non-adversarial electoral system. There will always be some who get elected and others who do not, but that does not mean the system itself has to be so obviously of the win-or-lose variety. Instead, the chosen system should allow the voters to act as the sophisticated creatures they really are and to vote by preference on a range of candidates.

Finally, as far as governmental structures are concerned, not only must parliament represent the people but the government must represent the parliament. All-party, power-sharing coalitions are both right and a right. Accordingly, *inter alia*, the right to an all-inclusive government should also be enshrined in international Human Rights law.

Asking our present political leaders to adopt consensual voting procedures might be rather like asking the monarchs to introduce democracy. Sadly, many of the latter only changed their minds after losing their royal heads, so hopefully the next changes will take place a little more peacefully.

6.6 Democracy Defined

It is now possible to define what we mean by the term "democracy" in regard to voting procedures. The word is associated with a free press, jury trials, a legal system of *habeas corpus*, the right of free association, and so on. The compass of the present volume is restricted to collective decision-making under a fair system of representative government. In Chaps. 2 and 4, democratic decision-making and democratic elections were defined; it is now time to lay down the basis of decision-making in a consensual, representative democracy.

1. The legislature shall be directly elected under a free and fair, proportional and preferential electoral system. This legislature shall be separate from the executive which shall also be elected under an equally free and fair system, either directly by the people or indirectly by parliament. The executive shall be accountable to the legislature, and both shall be subject to fixed terms.
2. Just as a presidency and a parliament should represent the entire country, so too should the government. Accordingly, in any parliamentary democracy, government shall be a (non-party or all-party) power-sharing coalition of national unity; this can best be formed by using a PR matrix vote election in which every MP has a free vote.
3. In so far as is possible, decisions taken in parliament shall reflect the unanimous will, the consensus, or the collective best compromise of that parliament; and these decisions should also reflect the will of the people, their consensus, or their best compromise. Accordingly, all legislation shall be enacted on the basis of the collective will of parliament as identified either in a verbal consensus and/or by

a consensus vote; all such votes shall be free and, where appropriate, i.e. in most instances, multi-optional.
4. The people shall remain sovereign. Within certain parameters, not least those of human rights, the electorate shall have the right to a citizens' initiative to propose a new law and/or abrogate an existing one and/or change the constitution. Parliament may also propose national polls. All such citizens' or parliamentary initiatives shall be subject to independent review and, if appropriate, the relevant voting papers to be presented to the electorate shall be multi-optional, the vote being conducted under the rules laid down for an MBC.
5. All executive and legislative positions shall be subject to job rotations and limited tenures of office.
6. All judicial appointments shall be subject to consensus decisions. In addition, parliament shall elect by an MBC or a QBS a team of at least three persons from this judiciary to act as its consensors.
7. Every jurisdiction shall have a written constitution, and this shall include certain democratic rights in relation to decision-making, electoral systems and inclusive government; such a constitution shall be subject to change only if approved in a national poll.

References

Aristotle (1992) The politics. Penguin Classics, London
Butler D, Ranney A (eds) (1994) Referendums around the world. The AEI Press, Washington
Kapuściński R (2008) The other. Verso, London
Latov V (1974) The Soviet electoral system. Novosti Press, Moscow
Lewis Sir A (1965) Politics in West Africa. George Allen and Unwin, London
Lijphart A (1977) Democracy in plural societies. Yale University Press, New Haven
Lijphart A (1999) Patterns of democracy. Yale University Press, New Haven and London
Ministerie van Buitenlandse Zaken, Ministry of Foreign Affairs, (2000), The Netherlands in brief. Den Haag.
Sheeran MJ (1983) Beyond majority rule. Regis College, Philadelphia
van Holsteyn J (1996) The Netherlands. In: Gallagher M, Uleri PV (eds) The referendum experience in Europe. Macmillan Press, London
West R (1967) Black lamb and grey falcon. MacMillan, London

Epilogue: Majoritarianism in Focus

The pure idea of democracy, according to its definition, is the government of the whole people by the whole people, equally represented.
Democracy, as commonly conceived and hitherto practiced, is the government of the whole people by a mere majority of the people exclusively represented.

(Mill 1861: 92.)

Abstract Given the weight of scientific and historical evidence which confirms that majority voting is a primitive instrument, it is at least odd that the methodology is seldom if ever criticized. This oddity is here examined.

E.1 A Bizarre Absence of Dissent

Just after the UK's 2010 general election in which no single party won a majority, the BBC interviewed Lord (Paddy) Ashdown. Despite his intimate knowledge of NI and his much admired work as UN High Representative in post-war Bosnia, he said, 'In order to be able to run the country, you need to have a majority.' His interviewer John Humphrys, who normally questions only everything, replied meekly, 'Indeed, indeed.'[1] Majoritarianism, for some, is like a tablet of stone.

Why is it that so many people – politicians, the press, professors of political science, as well as the general public – still believe (a) that democracy is majority rule and (b) that the majority vote is the means by which such rule can function. 'Democracy works on the basis of a decision by the majority.' (Government of Ireland 1996: 398) This was how the Irish Constitution Review Group defined it, a group of two professors, six doctors, four bachelors of law and an attorney.

---

[1] BBC Radio 4 *Today* program, 7.5.2010.

Lest there be any doubt, they went on to say, 'the referendum system has worked well in practice...' (*Ibid*: 469)[2]

Part of the trouble lies in the fact that 'the theory of voting... appears to be wholly unknown... to the politicians... and to others actually involved in decision-making...' (Dummett 1984: 5) and all too few realize that there might be something wrong with the theory and/or practice of majoritarianism. In fact, not only do many think there is nothing wrong with the simple two-option majority vote, some actually think there is something wrong with any sort of vote which is *not* a two-option poll. 'An obvious problem in multiple-option referendums is what to do if none of the options receives a majority...' (Gallagher 1996: 245 note 12) Furthermore, some think that multi-option voting is 'impossible' (Government of Ireland 2001: 7) and that politics has to be adversarial. In practice, as has been shown, there are relatively few problems with multi-option referendums and huge complications in two-option voting, even when one of the options gets a "respectable" majority, i.e. neither too small nor too large.

Some observers look at Northern Ireland and conclude that majority rule was a cause of "the troubles". By this they imply that the unionists abused their majority (which of course they did) as if they also abused the majority vote (which they did not, they just used it). Majorities may do what they like, apparently, as long as minorities are protected by bills of human rights and so forth. Alas, existing charters seldom question the majoritarian interpretation of the one particular right which to many is one of the most important: the right of self-determination. In this instance, it is a straight majority vote, and that is that. It is laid down in the Belfast Agreement, just as it was laid down by the Badinter Commission for Yugoslavia.[3]

For several years now, the NIG has been trying to question both the belief in majority rule and the practice of majority voting; there are others, not least those in the SCW, who are doing similar work in France, Britain, the US and elsewhere.

In 1986 in Belfast, the NIG held a public meeting as an experiment in consensus and multi-option decision-making: it worked. Senior members of parties from across the political spectrum, from SF to UUP, were invited to attend and, with the exception of the DUP, they all came. Over 200 participants debated the constitutional position of NI and then, in a ten-option ballot, they cast their preferences. Thus a consensus was found: 'NI to have devolution and power-sharing with a Belfast-Dublin-London tripartite agreement'. It was a foretaste of the Belfast Agreement, 12 years ahead of its time.

For the next NIG public meeting in 1991, a computer program of the MBC was deployed together with technical aids like a data projector to facilitate electronic

---

[2] Other Irish officials think the very opposite. 'The Government is conscious that... prior to the 1983 and 1992 [abortion] referenda, the debate became bitter and polarized...' (Government of Ireland undated: Art. 7.93)

[3] In the early 1990s, a commission under the French constitutional lawyer, Robert Badinter, suggested the (two-option) referendum should be the means by which Yugoslavia could settle its internal differences. As a result, there were well over a dozen such referendums... and four wars. (Emerson P 1999: 60–3)

preference voting. Several MBC, QBS and matrix votes have been conducted since then, in demonstrations or in actual meetings. Every one of these occasions has shown that these Borda methodologies can and do work.

It must be said that very few organizations were able to bring SF and the UUP together in those dark days, let alone facilitate an agreement between them. Despite this proof of the pudding, many NI politicians and academics still eat the stale old bread of majoritarianism.

Political scientists seldom do experiments, and while some professors in this field have supported the NIG, most decline to consider the subject. The Opsahl Commission,[4] for example, though broadly conceived and well respected for its achievements, failed to consider the full potential of the MBC as a decision-making process, (Pollak 1993: 240), and this despite receiving a number of submissions in its favour.

Many journalists, too, are loathe to comment on the nakedness of our democratic structures. They sometimes come to the public meetings, either to interview any big fish who might be there and/or to hear what the SF persons have to say. Alas, as often as not, they fail to comment on the actual methodology of decision-making, referring neither to the inclusive debate nor to the consensus voting procedure; it is as if the methodology has no bearing on the matter.

At other times, the author has tried to promote consensus voting by the quieter approach. On one occasion, for example, a colleague and I sat in a Dublin pub to share a drink and discuss inclusive democratic structures with a senior journalist in *Radio Telefís Éireann,* RTÉ (the Irish broadcasting company). The pint was well drawn, the arguments well laid, and he listened carefully. There then came a small pause before he suggested that this would mean the end of the fixed party structure of politics. The penny had dropped. The two of us smiled and responded positively. At which point he got up and walked out. The subject, apparently, was off-limits.

In like manner, BBC Radio 4's *Today* programme has consistently refused to discuss those decision-making voting procedures which could lead to a less adversarial democratic structure than the one which currently exists in Britain.[5] Many UK academics and activists also appear to be uninterested. There was a chance in 1997 when the British government set up an "independent" review to look into the possibility of a new electoral system for Westminster elections. It asked Lord (Roy) Jenkins (Chap. 2 note 1) to be the chair and, as part of the commission's work, he chose to receive written submissions and hold public hearings in a number

---

[4] Named after its chair, the late Professor Torkel Opsahl, this Commission ran a "citizens' enquiry" into the future of Northern Ireland, before then publishing a lengthy report in 1993. The group consisted of three professors, two journalists, one senior fellow, one senior civil servant and a clergyman.

[5] They *nearly* debated the topic, once. In June 2001, the BBC invited the author to appear live on the *Today* programme on Thursday 7th. At the last minute, they postponed; they re-scheduled for the 9th, and then for 11th, but these too they "postponed". It must now be assumed that they cancelled. On 21.5.2010, Radio 4's *More or Less* programme did debate the BC in an interview with Professor Donald Saari.

of UK cities, including Belfast. The author suggested that a stark *A* versus *B* referendum would be inadequate in what was obviously a multi-option debate and proposed a multi-option vote by quoting the New Zealand model (Sect. 2.6). The said Lord disagreed, and while some of his own commissioners actually visited New Zealand, his final report failed to even mention the fact that their referendum had been a multi-option ballot (Jenkins R 1998).

Part of the trouble lies in the fact that some politicians actually believe the idea of multi-option voting to be too dangerous. Lord Jenkins for one perhaps; Dr Garret FitzGerald, a former *Taoiseach,* is another. At a seminar on decision-making which Professor John Baker organized in University College Dublin, UCD, in Dec. 1999, the author gave a presentation on multi-option decision-making. In response, the now retired premier warned that if the people had what they wanted, they would do all sorts of terrible things: ban income tax, ban immigrants, ban everything. To prevent such an anarchic situation, he continued, the politicians themselves should decide what is good for the people, and as long the latter's elected representatives were benevolent and kind, all would be well.[6]

> [President Theodore] Roosevelt said, "I simply made up my mind what they [the people] ought to think, and then did my best to get them to think it." So did Jefferson.
> (Ketcham 1984: 176).

It would appear, therefore, that Rousseau was right when he warned that the professional politicians would, in time, become as it were a class apart. 'Sovereignty... [lies] in the general will, and will does not admit of representation... the moment a people allows itself to be represented, it is no longer free.' (Rousseau 1975: 240–2.) As it is, many elected representatives often restrict any discussion on political development and fail even to *mention* non-majoritarian decision-making. Furthermore, they see no need, because both the public and the professions think democracy *is* majoritarianism. '[T]here is a surprisingly strong and persistent tendency in political science to equate democracy solely with majoritarian democracy and to fail to recognize consensus democracy as an alternative and equally legitimate type.' (Lijphart 1999: 6)[7]

Admittedly, Lijphart regards a consensus democracy as a consociational coalition, and even he does not consider what could happen if multi-option decision-making procedures were introduced as well. He argues for power-sharing in the allocation of ministerial posts; he suggests governments and parliaments should try to come to a consensus if they can; but he admits that, 'The proportional composition of cabinets and other decision-making bodies does not solve the problem of how to

---

[6] Dr FitzGerald, often referred to as 'Garret the Good' in the Irish media, was *Taoiseach* from June 1981 to Feb. 1982 and again from Dec. 1982 to Jan. 1987.

[7] Larry Diamond is one such example. With 'complexifying' words like 'democraticness', he writes, 'a two-party-dominant system appears to foster policy effectiveness' and 'power-sharing... could prove counter-productive to democracy...' (Diamond 1999: 98–104)

achieve proportional influence when the nature of the decision is basically dichotomous: for instance, should a certain action be taken, yes or no?' (Lijphart 1977: 39)

If problems are to be regarded as dichotomous, people will not 'recognize consensus democracy as... equally legitimate.' Instead, as Lijphart acknowledged, many political scientists argue that 'a strong political opposition is the *sine qua non* of contemporary democracy...' (Quoted in Lijphart 1999: 6) Sadly, he does not ask why so many disputes *should* be regarded as 'basically dichotomous'.

That, I think, is the cause of the problem. We return to the right-or-wrong, true-or-false syndrome, which all too easily slides down a slope and puts everything into pairs: left-and-right, day-and-night, male-and-female. These however are not all opposites of the strictly either/or variety; indeed, in many instances, they compliment each other. The obvious example is the male-and-female pair, for without a coming together of the two, nothing can be (pro)created. So too, in politics: without each other, we cannot be democratic.

Democracy should be pluralist, and a pluralist democracy should enable everyone to influence that which then becomes the confluence, the consensus, the general will, the collective "wisdom of crowds". What's more, the need for democracy to be pluralist should be a truism because the very survival of our species depends, *inter alia*, upon its diversity. Such political diversity, such subtlety, such richness and sophistication cannot exist if politics simplifies everything into two supposedly "basically dichotomous" opposites.

Political diversity did not survive in the Soviet one-party state, where individuals who did not conform were declared to be 'an enemy of the people', *vrag naroda*. Thus was a minority (sic) of at least 24 million people murdered in the labour camps of Siberia. Stalin also "justified" his actions by promoting the idea of an external enemy. First it was Western imperialism, next came fascism and then, after the war, Western capitalism again. Like the kings of old, he achieved internal hegemony by virtue of an external enemy. Political diversity cannot flourish in a two-party state either, for the latter promotes not pluralism but dualism; furthermore, in so doing, it often provokes division if not indeed violence, and both "major" parties in a two-party state frequently deploy the notion of the internal adversary.

Admittedly, the "enemy" is not to be killed or sent to the snows of Siberia; rather, they should be regarded as opponents to be outvoted and put into only the political cold. From there, this opposition joins their political opponents to regard all those who do not follow the party line of either party X or of party Y as being quite beyond the Pale. Everything, it seems, is dichotomous. 'Those who are not with me are against me,' to quote both the bible and Stalin;[8] it is a sentiment often used by both X and Y in an attempt to "force" everyone to take sides.

---

[8] St. Luke Ch. 9 v. 50, Ch. 11 v. 23 and St. Matthew Ch. 12 v. 30. This expression was also used by János Kádár, the Hungarian Communist Party leader; see *Time* Magazine, 11.8.1986, p. 8, and something similar has 'often been quoted at Communist Congresses.' (Duverger 1955: 348) Likewise, in his autumn 2001 'war against terrorism', President Bush also declared that 'those who are not with us are against us'.

How is it, then, that while arguing for tolerance and compassion, while promoting inter-communal harmony and a "multi-multi" society, many people simply do not realize that political diversity is as important to our species as bio-diversity is to the ecosystem; and that, as a democratic structure, the two-party state is both artificial and dangerous. Is it because they do not understand that by adding up totals for-or-against, they are exacerbating a divide, whereas by adding up points they might be helping to heal it? Is it because the very idea of consensus suggests they might have to compromise their beliefs? Do some politicians find it impossible to live without internal division, just as others cannot contemplate life without an external enemy? Do the professors and politicians really not understand that majority voting is exclusive, hopelessly inaccurate, and even, in many instances, a cause of war?

References

Diamond L (1999) Developing democracy. John Hopkins University, Baltimore
Dummett M (1984) Voting procedures. Oxford University Press, Oxford
Duverger M (1955) Political parties. Methuen & Co., London
Emerson P (1999) From Belfast to the Balkans. The de Borda Institute, Belfast
Gallagher M (1996) Conclusion. In: Gallagher M, Uleri PV (eds) The referendum experience in Europe. Macmillan Press, London
Government of Ireland (1996) Report of the constitution review group. Government of Ireland, Dublin
Government of Ireland (2001) Sixth progress report. The Referendum, Constitution Review Group, Government of Ireland, Dublin
Government of Ireland (undated) Green paper on abortion. Government of Ireland, Dublin
Jenkins L (1998) The report of the independent commission on the [UK] voting system. The Stationery Office, London
Ketcham R (1984) Presidents above party. University of North Carolina, Chapel Hill
Lijphart A (1977) Democracy in plural societies. Yale University Press, New Haven and London
Lijphart A (1999) Patterns of democracy. Yale University Press, New Haven and London
Mill JS (1861) Considerations on representative government. (2004) Pennsylvania State University
Pollak A (ed) (1993) A citizens' enquiry, the Opsahl report on Northern Ireland. Lilliput Press, Dublin
Rousseau J-J (1975) The social contract and discourses. JM Dent and Sons, London

Appendix A: The Dictators' Referendums

Abstract The two-option majority vote has often been used by those whom history would judge to have been bloody dictators. The following short stories summarize the worst of these ballots.

A.1 Introduction

Most dictators like to "justify" their own actions. Hitler, for example, wrote *Mein Kampf*; Máo produced his little red book; and Gaddafi tried a small green one. Others have been rather more prolific: Lenin wrote 24 volumes of political tracts; Stalin, who knew he was better, wrote 54; and the world record surely goes to Enver Hoxha, who clocked up 84 publications.

Of these six rulers, only Hitler (Sect. A.1.3) and Gaddafi[1] used a referendum. As leaders of the bolsheviks – the members of the *bolshinstvo*, the majority – maybe both Lenin and Stalin thought their policies did not need any formal approval; or maybe the main reason was because, on the one occasion when they tried to be democratic, just after the so-called revolution of 1917, they lost. The bolsheviks, the supposed majority, (App. C, C.1.2) held an election; but the actual majority was won quite convincingly by the Social Revolutionaries, SRS.[2] Lenin therefore sent in the troops and took control by military force. By any definition, it was a *coup d'état*. And thus, as an effective instrument of change, the USSR ballot box became redundant.

No soviet leader held a referendum until, right at the end, Gorbachev used one, more in desperation than from democratic conviction (Sect. 1.1.2.7). The USSR did

---

[1] In 1971, 99% approved the founding of the new state of Libyan Arab Jamahiriya.

[2] The Bolsheviks won just 175 seats of the 707-seat Assembly. Admittedly, this was more than the Mensheviks, who gained only 16. In contrast, the SRS won 370 seats and thus a 52% absolute majority.

have some elections, when comrades could vote yes-or-no on the party nominee.[3] As far as the leaders of the CPSU were concerned, however, they the party represented the majority, they *were* the majority. Furthermore, being "the majority" was a "justification" for their actions, just as it so often is in many a western "democracy".

Other dictators have chosen to vindicate their actions in non-literary ways, and what better than the democratic process itself? It should be noted that some of them changed their electoral system by scrapping PR for example; some changed their party structure by banning other political parties; but no dictator has ever seen the need to change the two-option majority vote. It is, as was shown in Chap. 1, a brilliant means by which to manipulate people, not least because most people think that it is actually democratic and *not* a tool of misrule. Perfect! So all the dictator has to do is to persuade the people that they want what he wants, in the manner of Messrs. Blair and de Gaulle. (Sect. 1.1.2.8) Then, if the people do not want democracy and vote in his favour, what else can the poor dictator do but dictate?

A.1.1 France

Napoleon organized a *coup d'état* in November 1799. Ten years earlier, *les citoyens* had been storming *La Bastille* and singing *La Marseillaise*, with cries of *liberté, égalité et fraternité*. Now that all sounded pretty democratic and, during the course of this decade, France had already enjoyed – if that's the right word – three referendums.

While the 30-year old emperor-to-be nevertheless wanted to do things *comme ci*, there were others who wanted to dictate *comme ça*, not least the Royalists who had tried to blow him up with a *'machine infernale'*; they missed, by just a few seconds. So a new constitution, which just happened to give a lot of power to Napoleon the Consul was introduced on Christmas Day, 1799. Then, just to make it all democratic, there were the three referendums shown in Table A.1, 'exercises in official manipulation.' (Ellis 1991: 22)

Table A.1 Napoleon's referendums

Date	Purpose	% in favour	Turnout (%)
07.02.1800	Approve Napoleon as consul	99.9	43.1
02.08.1802	Approve Napoleon as consul for life	99.8	51.2
18.05.1804	Approve Napoleon as Emperor	99.7	43.3

---

[3] In one Soviet polling station in Brezhnev's time, there were 12 booths; 11 of them were marked "*Da*" and one "*Nyet*". On getting a ballot paper for the one and only candidate, the voter could proceed to any of the "*Da*" booths, vote "*Da*", and go home. Alternatively she could go to the one "*Nyet*" booth and vote there… but if she did, she would immediately be surrounded by a host of apparatchiks asking, "Oh what's wrong comrade, are you not feeling well today?" The author heard this story when he was living in Kiev in 1987.

A.1 Introduction

Table A.2 Mussolini's referendums

Date	Purpose	% in favour	Turnout (%)
24.05.1929	Approve fascist regime	98.3	89.9
26.03.1934	Approve fascist regime	99.9	96.6

A.1.2 Italy

In 1922, King Victor Emmanuel II asked Mussolini if he would like to be the PM. The latter said yes and then marched on Rome with his fascist supporters, where he chaired a cabinet of four fascists and 10 others.

It all started in 1919, just after WWI, when the future dictator founded the Fascist Party, a term based on the word "fasci" meaning groups. In the first post-war elections in November that year, no fascists were elected at all. In May 1921, however, the left split, and 35 of Mussolini's candidates were successful. Then, with a little more chaos in the country, not least from his own fascist thugs, he received the above royal invitation.

Once in power, he changed the electoral law so that the party with 25% in the polls won 67% of the seats – a grand rule if only one party gets over 25%. In the next election, it all went his way and he actually got 64% of the vote. (See also Fig. 6.1 note *j*.) Only a few loose ends remained: he suppressed all the opposition parties, formalized the one-party state, and then held a referendum, just to make it all democratic.

A.1.3 Germany and Austria

When the Chancellor, Franz von Papen, asked Hitler if he would like to join the cabinet, the latter actually wanted to be the chancellor. As in Italy, the story starts in 1919 when a relatively unknown Austrian joined a new party, the German Workers' Party, DAP. Hitler then changed the name to National Socialist DAP, from which came the word "nazi". Initially, they did not do very well. In the 1924 elections they gained just 14 seats, and 4 years later it went down to 12. In the economic gloom of the Great Depression, however, with everything made that much worse by the reparations clause of the Treaty of Versailles, the NSDAP increased its vote enormously: in 1930, it won 6.5 million votes, 18% of the total, to thus gain 107 of the 608 seats.

On the strength of this, Hitler stood for the presidency and, in the second round, won 27% to Paul von Hindenburg's 53%. So, unable to be president, Hitler focused on the chancellorship. At the general election, he gained 37% of the vote and 230 seats. When Hitler declined to join the cabinet, von Papen tried to weaken the NSDAP by calling another election, but the Nazis fell back only slightly to 196 seats. As a result, von Papen, no longer the chancellor, vacillated and persuaded Hindenburg

Table A.3 Hitler's referendums

Date	Purpose	% in favour	Turnout (%)
12.11.1933	Approve Nazi government	93.4	92.2
19.08.1934	Approve Hitler as leader + chancellor	88.2	94.7
29.03.1936	Approve Reichstag list and Führer	98.1	98.9
10.04.1938	Approve Anschluss	99.7	99.7

to appoint Hitler to the post on 30.1.1933. Two days later, Hitler called yet another election and now gained 44%. He was almost there.

What followed was a nasty piece of logrolling by which the Centre Party voted for Hitler's Enabling Act on the basis that, in return, Hitler would give them segregated education. 'The Catholics in particular were rather reassured by Hitler's insistence that the position of Christianity would be untouched in the future...' (Fulbrook 1991: 68) The only ones to vote against were the SPD – the communists had already been banned – and thus Hitler got the necessary 2/3rds majority to reduce the Reichstag's powers.

He was nearly home and dry. One or two small formalities were still required: all political parties apart from the NSDAP were banned; another election was held under a single party list, in which the NSDAP took all of the seats; and the November 1933 referendum was held, just to make it all democratic.

A.1.4 *Romania*

Amidst the machinations of the super-powers, the Romanians, like those of most other Balkan countries, did not have much chance really. They tried democracy after WWI and, for a time, it worked. First were the Liberals who, like many another party, adjusted the electoral law to suit what they thought were their own interests: the party with 40% of the vote would get 50% of the seats. At the next election, however, they failed to jump their own hurdle and power went to the National Peasant Party instead. This administration also worked fairly well until King Carol II returned to take more and more power away from parliament before eventually becoming a dictator-monarch. At the same time, a further force was at large, the fascist Iron Guard. Initially, the King worked with these paramilitary groups, but then decided he would dictate without them.

Meanwhile, Germany wanted Romanian oil; the USSR wanted some Romanian territory, Bessarabia and Bukovina; and Hungary wanted some land as well, Transylvania. Yet by 1939, all four countries were allies. King Carol asked Hitler to tell Stalin not to be so greedy, but in vain. As a result, he (the king) had to go, so off he went with his mistress, and in came King Michael with the new dictator, General Ion Antonescu, along with a referendum, just to make it all democratic.

A.1 Introduction

Table A.4 Antonescu's referendums

Date	Purpose	% in favour	Turnout (%)
24.02.1938	Approve constitution	99.9	92.0
05.03.1941	Approve Antonescu government	99.9	–
09.11.1941	Approve Antonescu government	99.9	–

Table A.5 Duvalier's referendums

Date	Purpose	% in favour	Turnout (%)
14.06.1964	Life presidency for Duvalier	99.9	–
31.01.1971	Confirm Duvalier's power to choose successor	100	–

A.1.5 Haiti

The US decided that Haiti was both politically and economically unstable, so from 1915 to 1934, they chose to run it themselves. Accordingly, in 1918 a 'US designed constitution... that gave US corporations the right to buy up Haiti's lands... was ratified by a 99.9% majority, with 5% [turnout].' (Chomsky 1994: 36) This level of support may have been a little inflated, however, because 'none of the "no" votes were counted in 96 of the 97 polling stations'[4].

Then came a *coup* or two, before Dr Frances Duvalier was elected to the presidency in 1957. In keeping with tradition, he also became a dictator, Papa Doc, and with the help of the two referendums shown, he reigned until his death in 1971. His son, Jean-Claude or Baby Doc, took over, and announced some constitutional reforms in 1985. The people, however, considered them to be inadequate and protested. So he took his family off to live in exile in France.

What could have been a democratic future did not immediately materialize. The new leader, the left-wing President Jean-Bertrande Aristide, was deposed in yet another *coup*, so the US returned in 1994, albeit under a UN mandate, and only then was Aristide reinstated. All was well, seemingly, and in 1996, his colleague René Préval was elected. Alas, they then fell out, so Aristide formed a new party and was re-elected president in 2000, but again, not for long. Disturbances in 2004 led to his exile; in came the UN; and Préval was re-elected in 2006. After the massive earthquake in 2010, Baby Doc came back in Jan. 2011, only to be arrested, and Aristide also prepared to return.

---

[4] From the Centre for Research on Direct Democracy website. http://www.c2d.ch/detailed_display.php?lname=votes&table=votes&page=1&parent_id=&sublinkname=results&id=38594 (Accessed 23 May 2010).

Table A.6 Pinochet's referendums

Date	Purpose	% in favour	Turnout (%)
04.01.1978	Approve Pinochet's Defence of Chile	78.7	91.4
11.09.1980	Approve regime	68.5	92.9
05.10.1988	Extend president's term	43.0	97.5

Table A.7 Some Iranian referendums

Date	Purpose	% in favour	Turnout (%)
10.08.1953	Mossadegh's policies	99.8	–
21.01.1963	The "white revolution"	99.9	91.8
30.03.1979	Approve Islamic Republic	99.3	84
02.12.1979	New Islamic Constitution	99.5	65
28.07.1989	New Islamic Presidency	97.6	99.8

A.1.6 Chile

In 1973, Pinochet organized a military *coup* and seized power; then he asked the people, just to make it all democratic.[5] He asked them to give him their approval in a second referendum in 1980 and, in so doing, he promised he would ask them again in 8 years' time.

When that time came, he thought he would win again; but he lost. He nevertheless accepted the verdict, fresh elections were held and although he retained control of the army, a new centre-left administration took over the government.

A.1.7 Iran

In 1951, parliament nationalized the oil industry, much to the annoyance of its British owners. Just in case anyone thought this policy was not democratic, the PM, Mohammed Mossadegh, held a referendum which gained 99.8% support. The US and UK then organized a *coup d'état* to depose him and install in his place Mohammed Reza Pahlavi, the Shah.

To show how popular were his own policies, the Shah also ordered a referendum, the 1963 poll; it was another landslide. In 1979, however, after much political unrest, he was forced to go into exile. In came the Ayatollah, Ruhollah Khomeini, a Shi'a, and he organized yet another referendum to establish the Islamic state. Some Sunni Turkoman rebels did not like it very much and called for a boycott.

---

[5] Chile has had other dictatorial referendums (see chronology, 1818); we confine ourselves here to the most recent story.

Table A.8 Some Yugoslav referendums

Date	Purpose	% in favour	Turnout (%)
01.07.1990	Constitutional amendments in Serbia	97	–
19.05.1991	Croatian independence	93	84
11.10.1992	Early vote for Yugoslav presidency	95	46

Table A.9 Saddam Hussein's referendum

Date	Purpose	% in favour	Turnout (%)
15.10.2002	Re-election of president	100.0	100.0

On 3.8.1979, elections were held for a constituent assembly, to draw up a new constitution. Some 80% of the 417 candidates were clerics and of the 73 seats, they won 60. (Orlovsky 1980: 614) There then followed the 1989 referendum to proclaim Shi'ite Islam as the official state religion and, in an equally democratic way, to declare Khomeini as the political and religious leader for life.

A.1.8 *Croatia and Serbia*

Two more democratic dictators, Franjo Tudjman and Milošević, also deserve a mention, not least because, while other dictators have been first allies and then enemies – Hitler and Stalin, the prime example – the two Slavs managed to be both friend and foe simultaneously! In 1991 they planned a secret carve-up of Bosnia and in the same year they went to war in Croatia. (Emerson 1999: 26; Glenny 1996: 149; Silber and Little 1995: 143–4).

A.1.9 *Iraq*

Just in case anyone in the twenty-first century was still unaware that a majority vote could be manipulated, Saddam Hussein achieved that which Chile had managed in 1818 and Syria in 1999, namely, 100% support.

A.2 Conclusions

In the 1920s and '30s, with the very severe conditions created by WWI and the Great Depression, many democracies both fledgling and mature were confronted by seemingly intractable problems. Under these conditions, many crumbled and by 1938, Europe was under the jackboot of 16 dictatorships.

Of those which did not crumble, 'The Scandinavian countries... made effective use of consensus politics. Britain... [used] a National Government [and] France managed... through the expedient of broad-based coalitions.' (Lee 1987: 22) The others were Belgium, Ireland, the Netherlands and Switzerland. On balance, therefore, a form of coalition government may be not only the more desirable, but also the more durable.

References

Chomsky N (1994) World orders, old and new. Pluto, London
Ellis G (1991) The Napoleonic empire. Macmillan, London
Emerson P (1999) From Belfast to the Balkans. The de Borda Institute, Belfast
Fulbrook M (1991) Germany 1918–1990 the divided nation. Fontana Press, London
Glenny M (1996) The fall of Yugoslavia. Penguin, London
Lee SJ (1987) The European dictatorships. Routledge, Abingdon
Orlovsky S (ed) (1980) Facts on file yearbook 1979. Facts on File Inc., New York
Silber L, Little A (1995) The death of Yugoslavia. BBC Penguin, London

Appendix B: The People Have Spoken*

Abstract The following is a list of all those national or "would be national" referendums in which the winning option gained 51% or less.

B.1 By a Whisker

			Yes (%)	No (%)
14.01.1866	Switzerland	Weights and measures	50.4	49.6
14.01.1866	Switzerland	Religious liberty	49.1	50.9
12.05.1866	Switzerland	Revision of constitution	49.5	50.5
13.04.1910	Australia	Finance	49.0	51.0
31.05.1913	Australia	Six separate polls	49.1–8	50.9–2
10.12.1914	New Zealand	Prohibition	49.0	51.0
19.12.1919	Australia	Legislative powers	49.7	50.3
21.03.1920	Switzerland	Labour conditions	49.8	50.2
21.03.1920	Switzerland	Gambling houses	51.0	49.0
06.10.1922	Sweden	Prohibition	49.0	51.0
26.10.1930	Liechtenstein	Press	49.9	50.1
06.12.1931	Switzerland	Taxation of tobacco	49.9	50.1
15.08.1932	Estonia	Constitutional reform	49.2	50.8
21.06.1937	Luxembourg	Restrictions on extremist parties	49.3	50.7
14.09.1946	Faroes	Separation from Denmark	50.1	49.9

(continued)

---

*This phrase was used by the then *Taoiseach*, (PM) Bertie Ahern, after the 2002 poll on abortion. The obvious response was to ask, "So, what did they say?" (the author's letter, *Irish Times*, 8.3.2002). It was also spoken by his predecessor, John Bruton, after the 1995 Irish divorce referendum. Most of the information used in this Appendix has been sourced either from *Referendums around the World* (Butler and Ranney 1994) and/or from a superb website run by the *Université de Génève*. <http://www.c2d.ch/index.php> (Accessed 8 Nov. 2010).

P. Emerson, *Defining Democracy*,
DOI 10.1007/978-3-642-20904-8_9, © Springer-Verlag Berlin Heidelberg 2012

			Yes (%)	No (%)
28.09.1946	Australia	Two polls on marketing and industrial relations	50.6/3	49.4/7
11.11.1949	Switzerland	Direct democracy	50.7	49.3
22.09.1951	Australia	Communism	49.4	50.6
13.03.1955	Switzerland	Consumers' protection	50.2	49.8
24.09.1972	Switzerland	Export of arms	49.6	50.4
30.11.1975	Liechtenstein	Majorities	49.7	50.3
05.11.1978	Austria	Nuclear power	49.5	50.5
18.02.1979	Switzerland	Vote at 18	49.2	50.8
07.09.1980	Liechtenstein	Art museum	50.3	49.6
02.06.1982	Switzerland	Law about foreigners	49.6	50.4
27.02.1983	Switzerland	Federal energy policy	50.9	49.1
01.12.1984	Australia	Senators' terms	50.6	49.4
06.09.1987	Turkey	Amnesty for politicians	50.2	49.8
26.11.1989	Hungary	Delay presidential election	50.1	49.9
02.06.1992	Denmark	Approve Maastricht treaty	49.0	51.0
20.09.1992	France	Approve Maastricht treaty	51.0	49.0
06.12.1992	Switzerland	European Economic Area membership	49.7	50.3
25.04.1993	Russia	Early elections for president	49.5	50.5
11.06.1995	Italy	Administrative assemblies	49.97	50.03
11.06.1995	Italy	Change mayoral election rules in larger communes	49.3	50.7
24.11.1995	Ireland	Allow legislation on divorce	50.3	49.7
01.11.1995	Quebec	Independence	49.4	50.6
08.12.1996	Uruguay	Constitutional reforms	50.5	46.2
21.05.1997	Ecuador	Parliamentary leadership	50.7	49.3
18.09.1997	Wales	Devolution	50.3	49.7
15.03.1998	Madagascar	Constitutional reforms	50.9	49.0
28.06.1998	Portugal	Legalizing abortion	49.1	50.9
18.06.2000	Liechtenstein	Citizenship	50.1	49.9
10.06.2001	Switzerland	Deployment of Swiss troops in UN peacekeeping	50.9	49.1
07.03.2002	Ireland	Abortion	49.6	50.4
27.08.2002	Micronesia	Simple/weighted majority votes in parliament	49.9	50.2
27.08.2002	Micronesia	New VAT rules	50.5	49.5
24.11.2002	Switzerland	Against abuses of asylum	49.9	50.1
25.05.2003	Armenia	Constitutional reform	50.3	49.7
07.12.2003	Martinique	Create a territorial collectivity	49.5	50.5
29.09.2004	Switzerland	Postal services for all	49.8	50.2
25.09.2005	Slovenia	Regulate state broadcasting	50.7	49.3
27.11.2005	Switzerland	Labour law	50.6	49.4
05.11.2006	Guam	Raise the drinking age	49.2	50.8
02.12.2007	Venezuela	36 changes from President Hugo Chávez on the constitution	49.4	50.7
		33 more changes	49.0	51.0
24.02.2008	Switzerland	Taxes on private enterprise	50.5	49.5
04.11.2008	American Samoa	Parliament to override governor	49.6	50.4

B.2 Conclusions

As shown in Chap. 1, a referendum result might not mean very much if it is won by only 51–49%; if, however, it is more than 99–1%... well, even then, it sometimes does not mean very much. The Norwegian poll in 1905, when 99.9% of an 84.8% turnout voted to separate from Sweden was probably fair enough, even if it were an unfortunate precedent for so many other communities who then used this "Russian dolls" approach to self-determination. (Sect. 1.2.5) Whether the Egyptians, who from 1956 to 1980 voted with a 99.9% majority on 11 separate occasions, really wanted union with Syria, is perhaps debatable; but 99.9% of the Syrians wanted it too.

In like manner, Iran has had five referendums (App. A, A.1.7) and all of the first four were approved by a 99% majority. Democratization, however, is afoot: the fifth and latest in 1989 was won by a mere 97.6%. Syria, meanwhile, has held 15 referendums, the latest of which was in 2007: the smallest turnout was 86.8% in 1953, and their lowest winning score was in 1971: 96.6%.

Reference

Butler D, Ranney A (eds) (1994) Referendums around the world. The AEI Press, Washington

Appendix C: Won By One

Abstract History, it seems, is often subject to the personal whim and caprice of just a few individuals. Indeed, in several countries, and sometimes on several occasions, crucial majority-vote decisions have been resolved on the basis of only one person's vacillation. In some instances, the individual concerned was logrolling; occasionally, by means fair or foul, he – it was usually a he – was cajoled. Either way, the effect was that decisions were sometimes swung this way or that by the one who knew or cared least about the outcome. A few brief stories are worth re-telling, if only to show how frail is the polity of majoritarianism.

C.1 Introduction

The following information – five short case studies plus two lists, one of decisions (C.2) and one of elections (C.3) – is by no means a comprehensive compilation of those votes which have been won or lost either by just one vote or by less than 1%.

C.1.1 Ireland

In the wake of the 1798 rebellion, the British decide to get rid of the Irish parliament and thus get rid of the Irish problem. Accordingly, Grattan's parliament holds a debate on the union of Ireland with Britain, whereupon 'the most palpable, undisguised act of public tergiversation' takes place. (Barrington 1843: 491) On 22.1.1799, a certain Mr Trench changes sides and Lord Castlereagh wins the vote by a majority of one. The said Trench is made a lord. (*Ibid*: 506)

All is not lost, however, and a proposal to make Ireland independent for ever gains a majority of six. Not to be outdone, Lord Castlereagh approaches the art of persuasion with a little more vigour and 'no member who [can] be seduced, intimidated or deceived, [can] possibly escape the nets that [are] extended to secure him.' (*Ibid*: 497) 19 are 'rewarded by offices for their votes' and one member is 'openly seduced in the body of the House'. (*Ibid*: 508). In all, by making a few more lords, dishing out some regiments, consecrating a couple of bishops, and making one – the same Trench – the 'Ambassador to Holland', Castlereagh 'purchase[s]' 25. (*Ibid*: 581) Thus, on 5.2.1800, he is able to 'seduce 43 [to]... out vote the Anti-Unionists'[1] (*ibid*: 509) and that, apparently, is the end of the Irish problem.

C.1.2   Russia

In 1903, 43 comrades of the Russian Social Democratic Workers' Party meet in Brussels, but the close surveillance of the police prompts them all to move to London. While the main topic on the agenda is the revolution, they start by arguing about a clause on party membership; in the subsequent vote, the 'hard' Lenin loses by 23–28 to the 'soft' Jules Martov. Never mind comrades, says Lenin, 'I do not think that our differences are so important...' (Deutscher 1982: 71)

Then, however, four of Martov's comrades walk out. Another vote is taken, this time on who is to control the party newspaper, and Lenin wins by 'the accidental arithmetic of a single ballot', 19 votes to 17 with three abstentions. (*Ibid*.) Now this vote, he tells the comrades, *is* important. So they split and the bolsheviks or *bolsheviki,* (members of the majority, *bolshinstvo, большинство*), part company from the mensheviks, (the minority or *menshinstvo*), who are comrades no longer. (Chap. 3 note 5.)

C.1.3   Britain

In May 1978, Jim Callaghan, the British PM, is in trouble because he does not have a majority in parliament but only the largest minority. The Tories smell blood. A vote of confidence, they cry, but they lose by 282 votes to 287. Callaghan survives by chatting up the Liberals and then the Unionists, but still the Tories bark at his heels. Indeed, in December, he survives two more votes by 312–300 and 300–290.

The New Year brings nothing new, and in March the opposition tries again; this time, it is going to be close. Nearly everyone knows which way nearly every MP will vote, and virtually the only uncertainty lies in whether or not any might not turn up on the night. There is just one other doubtful quantity, a certain Frank Maguire MP, a republican by trait and a publican by trade, who realizes that the entire future course of British history depends upon his good self, an Irishman.

The debate is called and all eyes are on Frank. Speakers say what everyone knew they were going to say, while Frank says nothing. Eventually, the division bell

---

[1] Governments very rarely perpetrate 'the most extraordinary act of legislative suicide' (Barrington 1843: 515) and vote for dependence. Apart from this Irish saga, one other incident comes to mind when, in 1940, the three Baltic States – Estonia, Latvia and Lithuania – voted to be absorbed into the Soviet Union. Stalin's tanks were already on the streets.

rings, 621 MPs rise to vote, and all eyes are still on Frank... who abstains. Callaghan loses by one vote, 311–310. Frank, they ask, why? "I wanted to abstain in person," says he.

As a result, an election is called and, on the basis of 44% of the vote – the same percentage as was achieved by Hitler 45 years earlier – Thatcher gains an overall majority of 52% of the seats in parliament and stays in power for the next 11 years. (Gee thanks Frank.)

C.1.4 India

In the 1996 election the BJP fails to get a majority but so too does every other party. Two years later, the BJP comes to power as head of a rather shaky 14-member coalition but, on 17.4.1999, the inevitable vote of confidence is called: the government loses by 270 votes to 269. In the subsequent election, the BJP under Atal Behari Vajpayee returns to power with a comfortable majority of 299 of the 545 seats, this time at the head of a 24-party coalition. To what extent its success can be explained, either by the atomic bomb referred to in Sect. 3.2.1.9 or by the threat of yet further conflict with Pakistan over Kashmir, is a matter of speculation.

C.1.5 USA

On 12.12.2000, the US Supreme Court decides by five votes to four that Bush is to be the next US President. He gains 50,456,167 votes or 47.88% whereas Al Gore polls 50,996,064 votes or 48.39%. That, it seems, is beside the point. The issue is Florida, where Bush wins 2,912,790 votes to Gore's 2,912,253, give-or-take a few pregnant chads. This means Bush wins all 25 Florida seats and hence a majority of 271–266 in the electoral college.

Congress is evenly balanced, 50:50, Democrats and Republicans. So whenever the members vote on party lines, the outcome depends on the casting vote of the Vice-President, Dick Cheney. Therefore, the Republicans could win everything, by one. Unless a Republican retires or resigns, as when Senator James Jeffords becomes an Independent on 24.5.2001. After this, they could *lose* everything by one, and the Democrat majority leader can rule the roost instead.

* * * * *

Lots of other countries have sometimes had some tight majority votes as well. In a few cases, the outcome depended upon the one individual who was persuaded, threatened or bribed. Here are a few of these stories.

C.2 Decisions

23.2.1782	Britain	'At two in the morning,' (Hansard) a motion to end Britain's participation in the US war of independence, (in which Jean-Charles de Borda captains a French frigate), is lost by one vote: 194 to 193.
9.1.1794	USA	A petition is submitted to the House of Representatives to recognize German as an official language; it is rejected by 42–41. Hence the Muhlenberg legend, named after Frederick, the first speaker, although he himself abstains.
23.3.1831	Britain	The second reading of the First Reform Bill, extending the male franchise, reducing the number of "rotten boroughs", but not yet introducing the secret ballot, is passed by just one vote.
27.3.1866	USA	President Johnson vetoes the Radicals' Civil Rights Bill, so the Radicals try to impeach him. By a single vote, however, they fail to gain the necessary two-thirds majority in the Senate.
30.1.1875	France	Much to the surprise of the monarchists, the National Assembly passes a rather innocuous law which, as it were by default, recognizes the Third Republic; the vote is 353–352. Maréchal Patrice de Mac-Mahon, a monarchist (of Irish descent) becomes the president, but he is perhaps best remembered for another mistake: "Typhoid fever is a terrible sickness," he says, "Either you die from it or you become an idiot. And I know what I'm talking about, I had it".
30.3.1900	Netherlands	The conservative minister F.D. graaf Schimmelpenninck achieves notoriety by falling off his horse. He thus fails to vote against a bill for compulsory education which is passed by one vote, 50 to 49.
16.8.1927	Ireland	On paper, the FF opposition has a majority of one; a vote of no confidence is called. Alas, come the vote, one of its members, a Mr Jinks, the member for Sligo, is missing. The result is a tie. The speaker then uses his casting vote and the *Taoiseach*, WT Cosgrave, survives, just. The opposition shouts, 'One vote! Resign, resign!' but he replies, 'One vote! That is democracy.' (Letters, *Irish Times*, 7.3.1996). The 'accepted version [of history, however,] is that Mr Jinks [is] plied with drink and put on the train to Sligo by [one] Mr Smylie of the *Irish Times*'. (Jordan 2006: 154) Mindful of his good fortune, Mr Cosgrave gives a race horse the name Jinks and it wins the 1929 Two Thousand Guineas.
14.5.1959	Sweden	In a 1957 three-option referendum on pensions, 46% say "this", 15% "that", 35% "the other" and 4% nothing. So "this" wins, say "these". But "those" and the "others" say they have an "anti-this" majority. So parliament votes, "these" against "those", 115–114, with one abstention.
24.8.1963	Norway	In 1961, parliament consists of 74 Conservative, 74 Labour and 2 Socialist, so the two left-wing parties form the government. A report into coal mine accidents leads to a vote of confidence, the two Socialists switch, and the Conservatives take over. However, when the latter present their programme for government, the Socialists switch back again.
14.12.1964	Sri Lanka	In June 1964, two parties form the government. The junior partner then splits into two, but there is also dissension in the senior partner, and the Leader of the House crosses the floor to defeat the government on its "throne speech" by just one vote.

(continued)

C.2 Decisions

27.4.1972	Germany	The CDU opposition puts Chancellor Willy Brandt's policy of *détente* to a constructive vote of no-confidence (Sect. 1.1.2.3) but they fail to get an absolute majority by two votes because, it is said, one Karl Wienand has offered a 50,000 DM (c. £15,000) bribe to at least one CDU member to change sides. On the morrow, the budget vote is tied, 247 to 247.
17.1.1982	Ireland	Mr Jim Kemmy, a former member of the Labour Party, votes against the FG/Labour Party coalition budget, which is thus defeated by 82 votes to 81. In the subsequent election FF is returned to power and Haughey to the post of *Taoiseach*.
1994	Finland	'Most decisions in the Finnish Parliament [c. 85%] are made without voting,' but even on this limited agenda, there were '8 such [won or lost by one] votes' in 1994 'plus 3 ties'. (Correspondence from the Finnish embassy.)
27.11.1997	Austria	In the National Council, one law on homosexuality is "defeated" by 91:91, but another is passed by 90:89.
9.10.1998	Italy	The government of President Romano Prodi collapses by 313–312 votes because one member of Prodi's coalition changes sides.
9.11.1999	Moldova	While Estonia thinks an absolute majority in a 101-member chamber is 51, the Moldovan constitutional Court says it is 52. The latter government with this minimal level of support collapses after only 8 months in power.
18.5.1999	Netherlands	*De nacht van Wiegel,* the Wiegel-night. A law to introduce referendums into the Dutch constitution fails by one vote. On the next day, the government collapses as a result of the Dutch liberal, Mr Wiegel, who votes against.
1999–2000	Denmark	'In the parliamentary year 1999–2000, five votes are decided with a margin of only one vote,' says a letter from the Danish Embassy; 'this happens quite often.'
4.8.2000	EU	273 votes are in favour while 273 are against the European proposal to ease cross-border take-overs for the multi-nationals.
19.5.2005	Canada	On its first reading, much to everyone's surprise, the minority government's budget is supported by the opposition. Come the second reading, however, amidst allegations of government corruption, the vote is 152:152. The speaker now uses his casting vote to maintain the debate, which then centres on accusations of the opposition cajoling one of the independent MPs by bribery.
24.7.2005	Bulgaria	By a margin of one vote, Sergei Dmitriev Stanishev is approved as PM. The cabinet he then proposes, however, is disallowed by the same margin.
11.3.2010	Sweden	The government recognizes the 1915 Ottoman genocide in Armenia by 131–130.
14.12.2010	Italy	In 2008, Silvio Burlusconi's coalition gains only 47% of the vote but 55% of the seats. (Fig. 6.1, note *j*) So when one of his coalition partners withdraws, the vote of no confidence becomes inevitable. He should have lost by one but he survives by 314 votes to 311, because two members of the Values Party change sides. There are many allegations of vote buying.

C.3 Elections

17.2.1801	USA	In the electoral college vote for the presidency, Thomas Jefferson wins 73 votes but so does another member of the same party, Aaron Burr. After 35 ballots spread over 6 days, the House of Representatives chooses the former.
4.3.1877	USA	Samuel Tilden (Democrat) wins 4.3 million votes, while Rutherford Hayes (Republican) gains only four million. This gives Tilden 184 votes in the electoral college to Hayes' 166, with 19 votes in three states in dispute. A bipartisan commission is asked to settle the issue and Hayes, the loser, wins, 185–184.
19.9.1949	Germany	To become West Germany's first post-war Chancellor, Konrad Adenaur needs a majority of the 402 MPs and he gets just 202.
17.1.1956	Finland	Beating his rival for the presidency by 151–149, Urho Kekkonen goes on to become the country's longest serving president, surviving in office until 1982. (The rules have now been changed to limit the office holder to just two terms.)
1.6.1961	Zanzibar	A coalition of two parties wins 49.4% of the FPP vote, thus to win 13 seats; while their opponents with 50.6% get 10.
17.8.1970	Lebanon	Suleiman Frenjieh fails to get a two-thirds majority in the first round; the second round is declared invalid when the total number of votes in the 99-person chamber tops 100; but 'Franjieh's gunmen [bring] their firearms into the chamber.' (Fisk 2001: 76) He now wins by 50 votes to 49.
31.12.1989	Poland	In a joint meeting of both houses of parliament, Wojciech Jaruzelski is elected president by one vote.
10.10.1999	Portugal	In the general election, the socialists win exactly half of the seats in parliament, 115 out of 230.
2.11.2001	NI	The First Minister David Trimble loses the unionist majority by 30 to 29. So some of the MLAs designated as "others" (Sect. 2.2.1.5) become "unionist", just for the day, and he now gains the necessary 31 out of 60 majority.
10.12.2001	Trinidad and Tobago	United National Congress gets 18 seats from 49.9% of the vote, while the People's National Movement also gets 18 seats, from the slightly smaller total of 46.5%.
5.4.2006	Iraq	Mr Ibrahim Jaafari wins the nomination to head the next government by a single vote but his Shia bloc, with the biggest minority from the December 2005 elections, is still short of an overall majority.
3.2.2008	Serbia	In the second round of the presidential election, Boris Tadić of the Democratic Party is re-elected with 50% of the vote. His rival, Tomislav Nikolić of the Serb Radical Party, whose leader Vojislav Šešelj has been indicted for war crimes and is in The Hague, gains 48%.
7.12.2008	Ghana	In the parliamentary elections, the National Democratic Congress wins 114 seats, which is exactly half of the parliament, and in the second round of the presidential elections held on 28th, John Atta Mills wins 50.2% of the vote while his rival Nana Akufo-Addo gains 49.8%. Unlike the events which followed the election in Kenya (Sect. 3.3.1.2), the changeover in Ghana is peaceful.

(continued)

7.3.2010	Iraq	With 24.7% of the vote, the party of the former PM, Iyad Allawi, gains 91 seats out of 325, while the PM, Nouri al-Maliki, with 24.2%, wins 89. (See also Sect. 3.3.5.2 and chronology 2010.)
6.5.2010	UK	The UK general election is won by none. The Tories get 306, Labour 258, Lib-Dem 57, DUP 8, the Scottish Nationalist Party, SNP, 6, SF 5, *Plaid Cymru* 3, SDLP 3, Alliance 1, GP 1, Ind. 1. A majority equals 326, or 323 if SF stays away.
		So there could be a minority administration:
		(a) 306 or (b) 306 + 8 or (c) 258 + 57,
		or a majority one:
		(d) 306 + 57 or (e) 258 + 57+ 6 + 3 + 1 + 1 + 1 or (f) 258 + 57+ 8 + 6, or (g) some other combination, or there could be (h) a GNU.
		After just 5 days of negotiations, a coalition government is formed, (d) 306 + 57, heralding, they say, a new era of consensual politics.
21.8.2010	Australia	In Dec. 2009, Tony Abbott is elected leader of the Liberal Party by one vote, 42–41 with one abstention. In the 2010 general election, he ties with Jackie Gillard of the Labour Party at 72 seats each, but the latter forms an administration with the help of one GP MP and some independents.

References

Barrington Sir J (1843) The rise and fall of the Irish nation. James Duffy, Dublin
Deutscher I (1982) Stalin. Pelican, Harmondsworth
Fisk R (2001) Pity the nation. Oxford University Press, Oxford
Jordan AJ (2006) WT Cosgrave, founder of modern Ireland. Westport Books, Dublin

Appendix D: Some Multi-Option Referendums

Abstract Most multi-option referendums have been both peaceful and successful. Here are some of them.

D.1 Introduction

The world's first multi-option vote was held in New Zealand in 1894 on the question of prohibition, a topic to which they have often returned. Their only other multi-option ballot was held on electoral reform (Sect. 2.6).

Another interesting case history concerns the multi-option poll held in Newfoundland. The politicians had decided the voters should be given a simple choice of *A* versus *B*. The people, however, thought otherwise, and many went out onto the streets to ask for a third option *C*. So the latter was added to the ballot and it won, although it did take two rounds (Table D.1).

One of the nicest examples of pluralism is the poll which took place in Guam. There were six options on the ballot paper but there was also a blank option, just in case the voter, or a group of voters, wanted something else. A blank option was also a feature of polls in Finland, Sweden (Sect. 1.1.2.15), Switzerland, and Bolivia, where in 1931 any blanks were counted as "yes" votes.

Multi-option voting has also been used (a) in Chile (1925), where they held a three-option poll on the constitution; (b) a number of times in Liechtenstein (e.g., 1951); (c) in Uruguay where the first one was a three-option ballot on the constitution (1958), while another on the same theme was a five-option poll (1966); (d) once in Cambodia (1960) with four-options, although the methodology was rather loaded; (e) in Singapore (1962) there were three options; (f) in Puerto Rico (1967) as in Table D.1; (g) in the Northern Mariana Islands, which had a nine-option ballot, (chronology, 1969); (h) in Australia (1977) when one of four tunes was

Table D.1 Some multi-option referendums

FINLAND	Prohibition: 3-option 44% turnout		
1931	Abolition 71%	Some relaxation 1%	Continuation 28%

NEWFOUND- LAND	Constitutional status: 3-option, 2 rounds 88% turnout		
1948	Commission Government	'Responsible Government'	Confederation with Canada
	14% 88% turnout	41%	45%
	-	48%	52%

PUERTO RICO	Constitutional status: 3-option 66% turnout		
1967	Commonwealth 60%	Statehood 39%	Independence 1%

GUAM	Constitutional status: 6-/7-option, 2 rounds 38% turnout						
1982	Statehood	Independence	Free Assoc.	Territorial with US	C'wealth with US	Status Quo	Other (specify)
	26% 91% turnout	4%	4%	5%	49%	10%	1%
	27%	-	-	-	73%	-	-

SWEDEN	Nuclear power: 2-/3-option, 1 round 74% turnout		
1980		FOR	AGAINST
	Go from 6 to 12 reactors	Go from 6 to 12, state ownership	Go from 6 to 0 in 10 years
	19%	39% 58%	39% 39%

NEW ZEALAND	Electoral Reform: 5-option, 2 rounds non-binding – 55% turnout				
1992			FOR		AGAINST
	MMP	PR-STV	AV	AMS	FPP
	58%	16%	6%	5%	15%
1993	binding–83% turnout				
	54%	-	-	-	46%

D.1 Introduction   165

chosen to be the national anthem; (i) in Andorra (1982) where the vote was on three forms of electoral reform; (j) in Benin (1990) there were three constitutional options; (k) so too in the Cook Islands (1994); and (l) in Slovenia (1996) where there were three options on electoral reform, but this poll was somewhat unsuccessful because they held three majority votes and lost all of them.

A Chronology of (Western) Democracy

Abstract Democracy has been developed in many societies, albeit initially, in many instances, only for the (old) males. This chronology of mainly Western democracy lists some of its setbacks and bizarre consequences, as well as a few other happenings. Most of the information comes from sources mentioned in the bibliographies and/or correspondence with the relevant embassies. Dates in curly brackets, { }, are cross references to the previous and/or subsequent years relevant to the invention and/or promotion of the voting procedure concerned.

c. 2500 BC	Sumer	'Gilgamesh... scrupulously [refrains] from action in the matter of peace and war until he obtains the consent of the assembly...' (Jacobsen 1943: 165) It seems 'the ruler must lay his proposals before the people, first the elders, then the assembly of the townsmen, and obtain their consent, before he can act' (*Ibid*: 166).
c. 700 BC	Greece	Monarchy is replaced by the Council of the *Aeropagus*, a forum restricted to the rich.
600s BC	Greece	While Sparta enjoys a sort of majority decision-making by shouting, 'It is likely that the vote was used in... the Areopagus both for elections and judicial decisions.' (Larsen 1943: 172) In the Homeric assemblies, it is fair to speculate that 'the counting of votes came in as an alternative to civil war.' (*Ibid*.)
593 BC	Greece	Solon becomes an *archon* in the *Aeropagus* and initiates reforms, one of which extends the right of participation to the poor. Perhaps, too, he gives 'formal recognition of the taking of political decisions by majority vote.' (Ste Croix 2005: 75)
507 BC	Greece	Democracy is first recorded in Athens in the Constitution of Cleisthenes. Decisions are taken by majority vote by a show of hands. Some officials are chosen by lot and 'in this way their election [is] committed to God,' (*ibid*: 95). Others are elected in special constituencies designed in such as way as to effect 'what seems to be the earliest system of proportional representation,' (*ibid*: 165), but there are 'Restrictions on re-election... no Athenian [can] be a councillor more than twice,' (*ibid*: 165–6).

(continued)

487 BC	Greece	Hipparchus is the first person to be ostracized, the people voting with bits of pottery called *ostraka*.
487 BC	Greece	Selecting officials by lot or sortition is first adopted in Athens for the appointment of magistrates.
460s BC	Greece	The word *demokratia* is coined. (Rhodes 2003: 19) For the first time, elected councillors are paid.
403 BC	Greece	At the trial of King Pausanias, charged after intervening in Athens and helping to restore democracy, 15 vote for his condemnation, but 19 vote for his acquittal. It is 'in the law courts that the use of the secret vote [is] most highly developed.' (Larsen 1943: 169–70) {1856, Australia}
400s BC	Greece	The professional speech writer appears.
c.380 BC	Greece	Plato writes *The Republic* and suggests, *inter alia*, that, 'in his ideal state women will be equal status to men...' (Thorley 2004: 80)
335–2 BC	Greece	Aristotle writes *Politics*.
223 BC	Greece	A constitutional convention is held in which the Achaens ratify the constitution of the Hellenic League.
197 BC	Greece	In the Achaean Confederacy, cities have one, two or three votes, according to size. (Larsen 1955: 101)
194 BC	Greece/Rome	Greece is now under Roman supervision, and representative democracy is adopted in Thessaly.
189 BC	Greece	The Achaens vote unanimously for war against Sparta.
154 BC	Greece	Perhaps the world's first openly multi-option debate takes place when both Crete and Rhodes, currently at war with each other, ask the Archaeans to be an ally. Without instructions from Rome, the latter choose a third option and support neither.
146 BC	Greece/Rome	Corinth is destroyed, but many Greek democratic institutions survive.
64 BC	Rome	Marcus Tullius Cicero is elected consul when he wins 'a vote from every century, either as their first or second preference,' perhaps the first recorded instance of preference voting. (Harris 2007: 473)
50 BC	France	Druids hold annual meetings. (Larsen 1955: 143)
105 AD	Rome	In a court of law, Pliny the Younger proposes plurality voting.
304	Rome	Flavius is the first son of a slave to be elected to public office.
400s	Rome	Assembly of plebians. 'In all Roman assemblies,' however, 'it [is] impossible to amend a proposal, [and] the presiding magistrate [asks] the assembly to vote yes or no...' (Crawford 1992: 195)
c. 500	England	King Arthur sits at his round table, or so legend has it.
560	Ireland	The last "*Feis* of Tara", a triennial assembly of all the leading men of Ireland is held under King Dermot, in accordance with the Brehon Laws.
c. 600	Scandinavia	Assemblies of free Vikings known as the *Ting* settle disputes, pass laws and elect their kings, and the latter then swear their allegiance to the *Ting*.
930	Iceland	'The first ever democratic national assembly,' which was also a 'marriage mart,' (Turner 2010: 592)...
1000	Iceland	... adopts Christianity as the state religion by majority vote.
1073	Rome	For the first time, the college of cardinals chooses a new pope by means of an election; the methodology is a simple majority vote.
1085	Italy	Pisa is the first city-state in Italy to defy both papal and imperial suzerainty and appoint its own consul.

(continued)

A Chronology of (Western) Democracy

1179	Rome	Weighted majority voting is introduced for electing the pope. (1073 and Sect. 3.2.1.4)
1215	England	Magna Carta is signed.
1259	England	*Provisions of Westminster* are followed by the first democratic election since the Dark Ages, albeit under a somewhat limited franchise: only four persons vote.
1268	Venice	A form of approval voting {1433} is used to elect the doge; the electors are chosen partly by lot.
1271	Rome	On the pope's death, the cardinals meet to elect a successor. The lay church waits patiently outside. Weeks, months, even years go by without any news from inside, so eventually the faithful conclude that the conclave will be more effectively inspired by the Holy Ghost if they take the roof off. The result then quickly emerges. It has taken 33 months.
1290s	Ireland	A national parliament is set up with no nationals: they are all English
1294	Switzerland	Citizens vote for the first time on a policy issue.
1299	Spain	Ramon Lull invents the pairings (Condorcet) system, {1785} and perhaps also the BC {1433}.
1340s	England	The position of "speaker" is instated.
1378	Rome	The Council of Constance is called to sort out the fact that there are three popes. A system of qualified majority voting is used, if but to ensure the Italians do not rule the roost. All three claimants lose, and a new pope is elected.
1400s	Switzerland	A sort of referendum takes place.
1433	Holy Roman Empire	Nicholas Cusanus re-invents a BC {1299 and 1770} as well as a forerunner of approval voting {1268 and 1987}. (Sigmund 1963: 212)
1532	England	The first parliamentary public division takes place when Henry VIII wants to annul his first marriage. He reckons he is more likely to get a majority in favour if he personally tells those voting to stand in full public view to one side or the other, while nearby in The Tower his henchman whets the executioner's axe.
1549	Russia	Tzar Ivan IV, the Terrible, calls his first *Zemskii Sobor*, a gathering of the representatives of the estates, similar to those in other European countries.
1603	(Germany)	Johannes Althusius lays down the basis of consociationalism.
1636	(USA)	Rhode Island becomes the first secular jurisdiction with complete separation of church and state, (and a thriving economy based on the distillation of alcohol).
1645	England	The Levellers meet but the organization lasts for only 4 years.
1648	(Germany)	The Peace of Westphalia brings the Holy Roman Empire to an end and denotes the ubiquity, at least in Europe, of the sovereign nation state.
1655	France	Louis XIV tells "his" parliament, *'L'état, c'est moi.'*
1670s	England	'The first modern political party [is] forged…' (Wootton 2008: 79)
1682	France	There is the 'first attempt in print to argue that atheists were as likely to be good citizens as other men.' (Wootton 1986: 75)
1714	Britain	George I becomes the world's first truly constitutional monarch; this is partly because he is a Hanoverian who cannot speak English.

(continued)

1729	Britain	Sir Robert Walpole is given the title of Prime Minister, initially as a term of abuse.
1770	France	M de Borda re-re-invents the BC {1433 and 1860}.
1778	USA	Massachusetts becomes the first US state to hold a legislative referendum.
1785	France	Condorcet re-invents the pairings (Condorcet) system, {1299}, but also discovers the paradox of voting.
1787	USA	The Constitutional Convention starts its deliberations in Philadelphia and drafts a new constitution: 'We the people...'
1789	USA	George Washington, a non-party candidate, becomes the first US president.
1789	France	The "Third Estate" proclaims itself to be the National Assembly and then comes the Revolution, followed 2 years later by a constitution which establishes 'an electoral franchise which [is] very close to universal male suffrage.' (Fontana 2008: 119)
1791	USA	Proportionality is considered: Jefferson proposes divisors while Alexander Hamilton opts for quotas.
1791	France	Avignon holds a plebiscite to become part of France.
1793	France	The first national referendum takes place when a new constitution is approved by 99.3% on a 27% turnout.
1800	France	As President of (*l'Académie des Sciences* or) *l'Institut de France*, Napoleon throws out the BC (Sect. 3.1.2) and holds the world's first "dictator's referendum" (App. A, A.1).
1807	Britain	The slave trade is abolished.
1818	Chile	The world's first "totally democratic dictatorship" is formed when 100% of the vote supports the new constitution of Bernardo O'Higgins, the proclaimed "director supremo".
1821	Britain	Thomas Hill suggests a form of PR-STV. {1855}
1826	Britain	The term "His Majesty's Opposition" is first used in the House of Commons by one John Hobhouse, later Lord Broughton.
1830s	Switzerland	The citizens' initiative comes into being.
1831	France	TRS is first used. In the years to come, the French government repeals and re-enacts it four times.
1844	USA	Thomas Gilpin proposes a form of PR-list elections.
1848	Austria	Revolutions threaten the old imperial order, but not only in the Austro-Hungarian Empire.
1855	Denmark	Carl Andrae re-invents PR-STV. {1821 and 1857}
1856	Denmark	The first national elections under PR use a form of STV.
1856	Australia	Victoria and South Australia re-introduce secret voting. {403 BC}
1857	Britain	Mr Hare MP, a Tory who believes in individual choice, re-re-invents PR-STV {1855}. Alas, his fellow Tories take a more 'party-ocratic' approach and rule out his 'hare-brained scheme'.
c. 1860	Denmark	Hother Hage re-re-re-invents the BC. {1770 and 1884}
1869	Belgium	HR Droop proposes his quota.
1884	Britain	Rev. Charles Dodgson (alias Lewis Carroll) re-re-re-re-invents the BC {1860 and 1971} and invents a forerunner of QBS. {1984}
1891	Switzerland	A PR-list electoral system is used for the first time.
1891	Greece	Publication of the Athenian constitution. An original copy, written on papyrus under Aristotle, is the only one of 158 Greek state constitutions to have survived.

(continued)

A Chronology of (Western) Democracy

1893	New Zealand	The world's first democracy, with full male and female multi-ethnic franchise...
1894	New Zealand	... holds the world's first multi-option referendum. (App. D, D.1)
1905	Russia	The 'greatest... and most successful strike in history...' (Riasanovsky 1977: 452) precedes the foundation of the first soviet or council. Shortly afterwards, Tzar Nicholas II sets up the *Duma* or parliament.
1911	Australia	Compulsory enrolment is introduced.
1913	China	First national elections are held. The Guómíndǎng comes top with 269 of the 596 seats, but is disbanded later that year by Yuán Shíkǎi, the president, who wants to be Emperor.
1917	Russia	A revolution in March is followed by Lenin's *coup* in October.
1919	Australia	Preferential voting (AV) is used for the House of Representatives and the Senate.
1919	France	The Treaty of Versailles is signed, the League of Nations is founded, and several democracies emerge in Central Europe.
1920	UK/Ireland	Britain imposes PR-STV on Ireland, North and South.
1922	Italy	Fascism appears in Europe as Mussolini becomes PM.
1933	Germany	The Weimar Republic collapses and Hitler comes to power.
1936	Spain	The civil war starts, and this leads to four decades of rule under the fascists of General Franco.
1941	The World	By this time, there are only 11 democracies in existence.
1942	Britain	Duncan Black coins the term "single-peaked" and later completes his *Theory of Committees and Elections.* (Black 1958: 14 *et seq.*)
1945	Cambodia	The world's smallest minority, one person, votes against independence, while 541,470 vote in favour. (See also Albania 1981.)
1946	UN	The Charter of Human Rights is launched.
1947	India	On gaining independence, India becomes the world's most populous democracy. Other countries in Asia and Africa soon follow the democratic path, and many inherit Britain's FPP and the West's majority vote.
1949	W Germany	A two-tier electoral system, MMP, is introduced.
1950	Costa Rica	Abolishes the military.
1951	USA	Kenneth Arrow publishes his soon to be famous theorem to suggest a perfect voting system is impossible. He later wins a Nobel prize. (Arrow 1963: 46 *et seq.*)
1956	Hungary	Peaceful demonstrations in October are confronted by Soviet troops whose invasion is made easier by the existence of a direct USSR/Hungarian border which Stalin had "acquired" during WWII.
1957	India	In the state of Kerala, Comrade EMS Namboodiripad becomes Chief Minister of the world's first democratically elected communist government.
1957	USA	Senator Strom Thurmond sets a US record with a 24-hour filibuster, (The *Guardian*, 6.12.2000)
1959	Switzerland	An all-party coalition form of governance is established.
1959	Liberia	President Tubman sets a world record for an electoral majority, defeating his opponent by 530,566 votes to 55.
1960	UN	The President of Cuba, Fidel Castro, gives a speech to the General Assembly which lasts for 4 hours and 29 minutes.

(continued)

1960	Sri Lanka	Sirimavo Bandaranaike becomes the world's first female head of state.
1968	Czechoslovakia	The velvet revolution, a pacifist uprising, is brutally squashed by the USSR.
1969	N Mariana	The Commonwealth of the Northern Mariana Islands holds a nine-option ballot on its constitutional future, a world record for pluralism. A majority of 61% vote to join in association with Guam. Guam, however, says no.
1971	Nauru	Desmond Dowdall, re-re-re-re-re-invents the BC {1884 and 1978} and a modified form is adopted as an electoral system, (Chap. 4, note 8).
1974	Yugoslavia	Josip Broz Tito writes the world's longest constitution.
1974	Portugal	The Carnation Revolution overthrows the Salazar dictatorship in a bloodless coup; this also leads to the establishment of democratic regimes in many former colonies.
1978	UK/Ireland	The author re-re-re-re-re-re-invents the BC {1971} and adds the partial vote thereby developing the MBC. He also invents the matrix vote.
1978	China	The "democracy movement" displays posters on the streets of Běijīng.
1981	Albania	In an election held to cover up the mysterious death of the former Premier, Mehmet Shehu, one person votes against; everyone else, 1,627,968 altogether, votes "yes" for Hoxha's officially approved candidates 'in an atmosphere of revolutionary enthusiasm'. (See also Cambodia 1945.)
1984	UK	Sir Michael Dummett re-invents QBS. {1884} (Dummett 1984: 284–93 and 1997: 151–7)
1985	USSR	Gorbachev introduces *perestroika*.
1987	USA	Stephen Brams and Peter Fishburn re-re-invent approval voting. {1433}
1989	USSR	The Soviet Union's first elections since 1918 are held to contest the new Congress. Yeltsin gains a sort of world record majority, winning 5,118,745 votes out of a total of 5,727,937. (See Liberia 1959.)
1989	China	Hundreds of democracy campaigners are killed in Tiananmen Square, Tiān'ānmén Guăngchăng.
1989	Germany	The Berlin wall comes down.
1989	Brazil	Participatory Budgeting starts in Porto Alegre, and some limited use is made of the BC {1978}.
1990	USA	A world record ballot paper, 224 pages long, is used in Arizona.
1991	Yugoslavia	Serjdo Bajramović, a Serb (with a Bosniak name) is elected on what must be a world record minimum turnout of 0.03%; his constituency is in Kosovo.
1991	Bulgaria	In parliamentary elections, the Christian Radical Democratic Party wins what may be the world's lowest ever level of support, 0.00001% of the valid vote, a total of just five votes.
1991	USSR	A world record majority for a referendum is achieved when 105 million people vote to maintain the USSR. (Sect. 1.1.2.7) The Union nevertheless falls apart within the year.

(continued)

A Chronology of (Western) Democracy   173

1991	Armenia	In the above Soviet ballot, the lowest ever referendum turnout is recorded when 0.02% cast their vote; the majority in favour, 72%, is nevertheless deemed to be valid.
1992	Lesotho	All 100% of the parliamentary seats are won on the basis of just 75% of the FPP vote.
1995	Russia	In the *Duma* elections, '44.8% [of the electorate] vote for parties not receiving any seats,' making the result 'among the most disproportional in the history of [PR]...' (Rose and Munro 2003: 274)
2000	The World	In elections worldwide, c. 2,000,000,000 people use FPP, despite its being very old; 250,000,000 use MMP, half of which is equally ancient; nearly 1,000,000,000 use PR-list, which is a little better; and just two small minorities of the 2,000,000 living in Slovenia along with 9,000 in Nauru use a form of BC.

Over 4,000,000,000 persons live in democracies. Decisions therein are nearly always taken by simple majority vote. The parliamentary exceptions are Scandinavian, but even then only rarely; a much larger number of countries, however, occasionally use multi-option referendums. (App. D, D.1) |
2001	Bulgaria	Simeon II, the former king, wins 120 seats in the 240 member *Narodno Sabranie*, and thus becomes the world's first modern "democratic monarch".
2002	PNG	Several candidates win an FPP election with some of the world's smallest "largest minorities" of five per cent of the vote. (Sect. 3.2.2)
2004	Ukraine	The "orange revolution" follows a fraudulent election; (in all three contests, the author is an OSCE observer). Along with the earlier "rose revolution" in Georgia (the election of which he also witnesses), the events in Kiev do not really deserve the same category as Prague's "velvet revolution" of 1968, and neither do the "tulip" and "cedar revolutions" in the Kyrgyz Republic and Lebanon, one year later.
2005	China	'All thinking Chinese... agree that China has to move forward if not to a pluralist democracy then to a greatly modified system in which the "ruling party" seeks its mandate from the public and submits to genuine scrutiny of its behaviour and performance...' (Gittings 2005: 327)
2009	India	The world's largest democracy goes to the polls. Over 700 million registered voters cast their FPP ballots in over 800,000 polling stations – the smallest of which, in the middle of a forest, caters for only one elector.
2010	Iraq	The March election produces a close result. (Sect. 3.3.5.2) Subsequent negotiations on forming a new cabinet are fraught with difficulties. Eventually, taking over from the Dutch, Iraq creates a new record for the time it takes for a parliament to form a government: 249 days... but not for long – a small postscript – Belgium re-claims the accolade on 17.2.2011: 250 days, and still counting.

Glossary

NB Items marked § are described elsewhere in this glossary.

Absolute majority see majority.

AMS The *additional member system* is a partially proportional electoral system based on one ballot and two counts, the first under FPP§ in small constituencies, the second under PR-list§ in larger regional or national constituencies. (See also MMP.)

Approval voting... ...can be used in decision-making or in a (non-PR) election. Voters vote for as many options/candidates as they wish; each "approval" has the same value, and the option/candidate with the most approvals wins.

Arrow's theorem See Impossibility theorem.

Autocracy Rule by a minority of one, an autocrat.

AV The *alternative vote* can be used in decision-making or in a (non-PR) election. It is a form of preference voting in which the electorate votes 1, 2, 3... for their first/second/third... preferences, voting for as many or as few as they wish. If in the count no option/candidate gets 50% + 1 of the first preferences, the least popular option/candidate is eliminated and its votes are transferred according to its second preferences. The process continues until an option/candidate gets or exceeds 50% + 1, or until only one option/candidate remains. (See also PR-STV.)

BC *Borda count*. This points system can be used in decision-making or in a (non-PR) election, although it is more suitable in the former application; for its use in PR§ elections, see QBS.

The BC is a form of preference voting in which the electorate votes 1, 2, 3... as in AV§. Where there is a choice of n-options or candidates, a first preference gets n points, a second preference gets $n\text{-}1$, a third preference gets $n\text{-}2$, and so on; the winner is the option/candidate with the most points. (See also MBC.)

Binary A binary decision-making process is one where every decision is a two-option, for-or-against choice, or a series of such majority votes.

Block vote This is a (non-PR) electoral system of FPP§ in multi-member constituencies where voters may support as many candidates as are to be elected.

The term is also used to describe the vote of, for example, a trade union delegate, whose single vote may supposedly represent many members.

Borda See BC.

Citizens' initiative This is a mechanism whereby a certain number of citizens can demand a referendum§ on a topic of their own choosing.

Clone A clone is an option which is very similar to another one.

Coalition

    Majority A majority coalition is a union of some parliamentary parties in a government which then commands a simple majority§ in that parliament.

    Grand A grand coalition involves the two biggest parties and thus enjoys a large majority.

    All-party An all-party coalition is a power-sharing government involving all the main parliamentary parties.

Composite An amalgam based on two or more compatible options/policies.

Condorcet A Condorcet count or pairings vote can be used in decision-making or in a (non-PR) election. The voters cast their preferences on the options/candidates, voting 1, 2, 3… as in AV§; in the count, pairs of candidates are examined separately and in, say, a three-option contest, if *A* is more popular than *B and* if *A* is more popular than *C,* then *A* is the Condorcet winner. (See also paradox.)

Consensor In consensus§ decision-making, the chair or facilitator is assisted by a team of impartial *consensors* who monitor the debate in order to recommend which voting mechanisms if any are to be used, and which options are to be included on any relevant ballot paper.

Consensus (See also consensus coefficient.)

    Verbal A verbal consensus is an agreement, sometimes taken after lengthy discussions and after all concerned have agreed to a compromise, without resort to a vote.

    "*votal*" An agreement taken (after lengthy discussions and) after all have agreed to identify their best compromise via an MBC§ vote is a consensus decision, sometimes called a *votal* consensus.

Consensus coefficient If S_A is the MBC§ score of option *A*, if V is the valid vote§ and if *n* is the number of options/candidates to be voted on, the consensus coefficient of option *A*, C_A, is defined by the formula: $C_A = S_A/V.n$.

That is, the consensus coefficient is the MBC§ score divided by the maximum possible score; and it varies from bad to good, from zero to one.

Consensus voting The term applies to those inclusive methodologies in which the outcome is the most popular amongst everybody, and not necessarily just the majority. (See also MBC, QBS and matrix vote.)

Consociationalism is a form of government where decisions are taken by simultaneous majorities§ from both or all communities, eg. from both unionist and nationalist (Northern Ireland); from both Czech and Slovak (Czechoslovakia); from all three Bosniak, Bosnian Croat and Bosnian Serb (Bosnia). In effect, every relevant grouping has the power of veto§.

Constituency A constituency is a geographical area represented by one or more elected representative(s). Single-seat constituencies are used in non-PR electoral systems; multi-member constituencies have two or more representatives.

The word 'constituency' may also be used in a non-geographical sense, to describe a particular group of people who, *inter alia,* relate to one or more representatives.

Cycle See paradox of voting.

Democracy Rule by the people, *demos*. It can be direct as it was initially for certain rich males in ancient Greece, or indirect, via a parliament of elected representatives.

Consensual A consensual democracy is rule by representatives of all the main political parties/opinions; decisions are taken in consensus§.

Consociational A consociational democracy is rule by a cross-community all-party coalition§; decisions are taken together, as in consociationalism§.

Majoritarian A majoritarian democracy is rule by a single party or group of parties which has the support of a majority§ of elected representatives; decisions are taken by majority vote.

d'Hondt See divisors.

Dictatorship A voting methodology should not allow the preferences of any one individual to determine the outcome, a condition known as Dictatorship. (See also impossibility theorem.)

Divisor system Both divisors and quotas§ are rules of thumb for allocating seats according to party strengths. With the former, every party's vote total is divided by a prescribed set of divisors to give a series of descending scores. Seats are awarded to the parties with the highest resulting scores.

Different sets of divisors include the following:

d'Hondt 1 2 3 4 ....

St. Laguë 1 3 5 7 ....

Modified St. Laguë 1.4 3 5 7 ....

Each set may give marginally different results.

Droop See quota.

Electorate All those eligible to vote.

Filibuster A long speech, the main purpose of which is to obviate any vote.

FPP *First-past-the-post*. This is a (non-PR) electoral system where the voter casts one 'x' only. If there are only two candidates, it is a majority vote and the candidate with the majority§ of the votes is the winner. With three or more (a plurality§ of) candidates, the candidate with the most votes wins; this may be an absolute majority of the votes, or it may be just the largest minority, a plurality. Thus FPP elections with three or more candidates can be termed plurality votes§.

Franchise The right to vote in public elections, especially in state or parliamentary elections.

Gerrymander The "art" of adjusting constituency boundaries so that your own party benefits.

Grand coalition See coalition.
Guillotine An order to suspend debate and move to a vote.
Hare See quota.
Hung parliament One in which no one party has an absolute majority§.
Impossibility theorem Ideally, a voting methodology should satisfy the conditions of non-dictatorship§, independence§, Pareto§ and universality§; alas, according to *Arrow's theorem*, such a methodology is impossible.
Independence The condition of independence suggests that the popularity of an option, as identified in a vote, should remain unchanged, even if some other option, a clone§ or an irrelevant alternative§, is included on the ballot. (See also impossibility theorem.)
Irrelevant alternative If in a multi-option ballot, with options *A, B, C, D* and *E*, the most popular option is, say, *D*, then *D* should still be the most popular option even when an additional but less popular option, an irrelevant alternative like *F*, or a clone§ like *B'*, is also included on the ballot. (See also impossibility theorem.)
IRV *Instant run-off voting* is the name used in the Americas for AV/STV.
Majoritarianism The belief in and/or practice of majority rule.
Majority See also coalition.
  Absolute An absolute majority is 50% or more.
  Consociational See consociationalism.
  Qualified A qualified majority is used in the EU where different countries have different numbers of votes depending on their size, and where the result depends on a certain weighting,
  Relative/simple A relative/simple majority may be only the biggest minority.
  Weighted A weighted majority involves 2/3rds or some such other ratio greater than 1/2.
Majority rule A form of democracy based on decision-making by majority vote.
Majority vote See FPP.
Matrix vote The matrix vote is a PR§ electoral system by which an electorate can elect a fixed number of persons to be members of a team which may involve very different positions. It is ideally suited (a) for the election of the chairperson, secretary, treasurer, etc. at an association's AGM; and (b) for a power-sharing administration in which the parliament or assembly elects a cabinet or an executive. The matrix vote is based on a QBS§ and an MBC§ count.
MBC A *modified Borda count* can be used in decision-making or in a (non-PR) election. It allows for partial voting as follows: if someone casts preferences for all *n* options/candidates, points are awarded as in a BC§: $n, n-1, \ldots, 1$; if, however, an individual votes only for *m* options/candidates, points awarded are $m, m-1, \ldots 1$.
MMP *Multi-member proportional* is a PR§ electoral system based on two ballots and two counts, the first is under FPP§ in small constituencies, the second under PR-list§ is in larger regional or national constituencies. (See also AMS.)
Modified St. Laguë See divisors.

Glossary

Monotonicity A voting procedure is said to be monotonic if, in all circumstances, an increase in support for an option/candidate leads to that option/candidate having a greater chance of success.

Multi-member See constituency.

Oligarchy Rule by a small clique, faction or class.

Pairings See Condorcet.

Paradox of voting A paradox of voting or cycle can occur in binary§ or Condorcet§ voting when there are three or more persons voting on three or more options. If, for example, in a "society" of three people, Messrs **J**, **K** and **L**, Ms **J** has first-second-third preferences *A-B-C*, Mr **K** has *B-C-A*, and Ms **L** has *C-A-B*, then in any system of majority voting and if all three vote sincerely, *A* will be more popular than *B*, *B* more popular than *C*, and *C* more popular than *A*. This can be written as:
$A > B, B > C$ and $C > A$ or
$A > B > C > A > \ldots$

Pareto condition If everyone prefers option *D*, say, to option *B*, then any voting methodology which complies with the Pareto condition should have an outcome in which *D* is superior to *B*. (See also impossibility theorem.)

Partial vote In a ballot in which the voter is asked to cast (up to) n preferences, a ballot of only m options, where $1 \leq m < n$, is a partial vote. (See MBC.)

Party-ocracy Rule by the party or parties.

Patronage Party political patronage applies to those instances when a party leader appoints certain individuals to positions of power and/or prestige in return for 'loyalty' or other 'favours'.

Plebiscite A referendum§ on the topic of national sovereignty.

Plural society A society which includes two or more different ethnic or religious groups.

Plurality The largest minority. (See FPP.)

Plurality voting allows the voter to cast only one 'x'. It can be used in decision-making or in a (non-PR) election. In the latter instance, it is like FPP§ whenever there are three or more candidates.

Points system See BC/MBC.

PR *Proportional representation* refers to an electoral system which is designed to ensure that the number of party candidates (and sometimes independents) elected are in proportion to the number of votes gained. PR systems are used in multi-member constituencies§.

Preferendum A Borda preferendum is an MBC§.

PR-list In PR-list elections, each party "lists" its candidates in its own order of priority. Seats are awarded to parties on the basis of a divisor or quota system and, if party *X* wins n seats, then in a closed list system, the first n names from the top of the list, or in an open system, the n most popular candidates, are deemed elected.

PR-list closed An electoral system in which the voters vote for one party only.

PR-list open In the three main types of open PR-list electoral systems, the voter may choose either:
 (i) One party or one candidate of that party, as in Bosnia;
 (ii) One or more candidates of one party only, as in Belgium;
 (iii) One or more candidates of one or more parties, as in Switzerland.

Profile A voters' profile is the set of first and subsequent preferences of all concerned.

PR-STV *Proportional representation – single transferable vote* is based on AV§. The quota§ is set at x per cent + 1 depending on the number of persons to be elected. (Table 4.1) Transfers take place, not only from candidates eliminated, but also from those elected with a surplus over and above the quota. PR-STV constituencies§ usually have from three to six elected representatives.

QBS The *quota Borda system* is a PR§ electoral system based on an MBC§. The electorate votes by casting preferences, 1, 2, 3... as in AV§. In a multi-member constituency§ of four representatives, the count consists of two Parts, with two stages in each. If, at any stage, seats are still to be filled, the count proceeds to the next stage.

In Part I stage (i) of the count, any candidate gaining the quota§ is elected. In Part I stage (ii), any pair of candidates getting two quotas are both elected.

In Part II, only unelected candidates are taken into consideration. In Part II stage (iii), any pair of candidates getting one quota is 'elected', the seat going to whichever candidate of the pair has the higher MBC§ score. Finally, in Part II stage (iv), seats go to those candidates with the higher/highest MBC scores.

Qualified majority See majority.

Quorum A minimum number or percentage required for a sitting to be regarded as valid.

Quota In an electoral system, a quota is a specified number of votes which, if attained, ensures the election of the candidate concerned. The most common quotas are the Hare (which is defined as V, the valid vote§ divided by n, the number of seats), V/n; and the Droop (which divides V, the valid vote by $(n+1)$ the number of seats plus one), $V/(n+1)$. (See also divisor systems.)

Quotas can also apply to a minimum number of persons from a specific gender or ethno-religious group.

Referendum A referendum is usually a two-option but sometimes a multi-option vote by which the electorate may decide a matter of policy. A multi-option referendum can be conducted under the rules of any of a number of methodologies.

St. Laguë See divisors.

Serial voting A decision-making voting mechanism in which options are placed in order, say, from cheap to expensive. A majority vote is taken between the two extremes and the loser is eliminated; a second vote is taken between the winner and its new extreme opposite; the process continues until there is an overall winner. In theory, and if people vote sincerely§, the outcome will be the Condorcet§ winner.

Sincere voting A voter is said to vote sincerely when she votes for those options/candidates in her order of preference, without taking any tactical§ considerations into account.

Glossary

Single-peaked preferences A voter's preferences are said to be single-peaked if, when the options are laid out on, say, a cheap-expensive axis, his second and subsequent preferences lie in descending order to one side and/or the other of his first preference.

SNTV *Single non-transferable vote.* This electoral system is semi-proportional. The voter casts only one preference, but the constituencies§ are multi-member.

Special voting The term used in Belgium for consociationalism§.

STV *Single transferable vote* is another name for AV.

Suffrage See franchise.

Tactical voting A voter is said to vote tactically (as opposed to sincerely§) if, instead of voting for her preferred option(s) or candidate(s), she chooses option(s) or candidate(s) that may result in what she judges to be her best possible outcome.

Threshold The threshold of an electoral system is the minimum percentage of votes required for a candidate to be elected; this is usually the logical consequence of the mathematics of the specific electoral system concerned, but there can also be a laid-down minimum of, say, 5% as in Germany or 7% in Russia.

Top-up A top-up is the second part of an election count, applicable to some electoral systems like AMS§, in which votes are counted either in a different way and/or in a bigger constituency, to ensure a greater degree of overall proportionality.

Transitive order If a voter prefers option F to option C, and option C to option D, then, if her preferences are transitive, she also prefers F to D.

TRS The *two-round system* of voting can be used in decision-making or in a (non-PR) election. The first round is a plurality vote§, and, if nothing gains more than 50% support, the second round is a majority vote between the two leading options/candidates from the first round.

Turnout The number of people who, literally, turn out to vote; it is normally expressed as a percentage of the total electorate§.

Two-tier A two-tier electoral system consists of one election (which may be PR§) in small constituencies and a second election (which is PR) in larger regional or national constituencies. Examples include Austria, which has a two-tier system based on closed list PR; the Swedish version is open list PR; while Germany's MMP consists of two votes, one under FPP and the other under list PR.

Universality If a voting methodology has the condition of universality, then in exercising his vote on the options/candidates listed, a voter may express any number of preferences, in any order he likes. (See also impossibility theorem.)

Valid vote The number of voters deemed to have handed in a proper, valid vote, be it full or partial.

Veto The ability to prevent a vote being passed.

Weighted majority See majority.

Whip A party whip is an instruction from the party's leadership to its elected representatives to vote in a certain way. It may also be used to describe the functionary who issues such orders. Those who disobey may, as a result, lose the party whip and thus put their careers at risk.

Win-win A win-win decision is one in which (nearly) everybody wins something but nobody wins everything. It is the opposite of a zero-sum decision§.

Zero-sum A zero-sum decision-making process places voters in a win-or-lose situation: some win everything, and others lose everything.

Index

A
Abhazia, Georgia
   decision-making, 18, 21
   elections, 18n
Abyei, Sudan, 19, 21
ACE (Administration and Cost
      of Elections), 64n, 132
Adams, J.Q., President, USA, 55
Adande, A., Dahomey, 118
Adenaur, K., Chancellor, Germany, 160
Afghanistan
   decision-making, 128
   elections, 73, 84
   governance, 109
Africa, 4, 16, 19, 102
   decision-making, 6, 8, 20, 43
   elections, 76, 78
   governance, 102, 105, 107
Ajaria, Georgia, 21
Ahern, B., Premier, Ireland, 151n
al-Bashir, O., President, Sudan, 105
al-Gaddafi, M., Col. Libya, 105, 143
al-Maliki, N., Premier, Iraq, 72, 161
Aldrich, R.J., 62
Alexander II, Tzar, Russia, 101n
Algeria
   decision-making, 10, 128
   elections, 57, 69
Allawi, A., Iraq, 72
Althusius, Johannes, 169
American Samoa, decision-making, 152
Amin, I., Gen., Uganda, 102, 103
Andorra
   decision-making, 165
   elections, 95
Andrae, C., Denmark, 170
ANP (Awami National Party), Pakistan, 108

Antonescu, I., Premier, Romania, 147
Aristide, J.-B., President, Haiti, 147
Aristotle, 3, 52, 125, 126, 168, 171
Arman, Y., South Sudan, 105
Armenia, 159
   decision-making, 152, 173
Arrow, K., 171
Arthur, King, England, 53, 168
Ashdown, P., Lord, UK, 137
Australia
   decision-making, 132, 151, 163
   elections, 58, 66, 83, 84, 132, 161, 171
   governance, 130, 170
Austria
   decision-making, 29, 132, 145, 152, 159
   elections, 132, 180
   governance, 130, 131, 170
Azerbaijan, decision-making, 18, 21
Aziz, T., Foreign Minister, Iraq, 7

B
Baako, K., Ghana, 106
Badinter Commission, 138
Badinter, R., France, 138
Baker, J., xiii, xiv, 77, 103, 140
Bandaranaike, S., Premier, Sri Lanka, 172
Barrington, J., 155
BBC, 21n, 47, 137, 139, 150
Behan, Brendan, 13
Belarus, governance, 106
Belgium, 16
   decision-making, 6, 29, 37, 132, 180
   elections, 83, 132, 170, 179
   governance, vii, 30, 109, 130, 131, 150, 173
Belloc, H., 56
Bemba, J.-P., DRC, 69

184

Ben Ali, President, Tunisia, 71, 106
Benin, decision-making, 165
Berdimuhamedow, G., President, Turkmenistan, 106
Bhutan, governance, 112
BJP (Bharatiya Janata Party), India, 62, 109, 157
Black, D., 42n, 54, 171
Blair, T., Premier, UK, 7, 10, 59, 60, 144
Bogdanor, V., 53, 66, 117, 118
Bolivia, decision-making, 163
Bolshevik Party, Russia, 59n, 102, 143, 146
Bose, N.K., 75
Bosnia, 149
    Dayton Accords, 18, 71, 111, 112, 126
    decision-making, 9, 18, 21, 29, 30, 45
    elections, 13, 71–73, 75, 77, 84, 90, 179
    governance, 109, 111, 137, 175
Brams, S., 172
Brandt, W., Chancellor, Germany, 159
Brazil
    decision-making, 172
    elections, 61
Brezhnev, L., Gen. Sec., USSR, 102, 144n
Brown, G., Premier, UK, 60
Bruton, J., Premier, Ireland, 151n
Bulgaria
    decision-making, 159
    elections, 81, 172, 173
Burundi, governance, 102
Bush, G.W., President, USA, 55, 63, 141, 157
Butler, D., 66, 117, 118, 129n, 151n

C

Callaghan, J., Premier, UK, 156
Cambodia, decision-making, 163, 171
Cameroon, governance, 107
Canada, 164
    decision-making, 11, 21, 132, 152, 159
    elections, 132
    governance, 109, 113, 129, 130
Carol II, King, Romania, 146
Carter, J., President, USA, 62
Cassel, A., 78
Castro, F., President, Cuba, xi, 172
Caucasus, decision-making, 18
Cayman Islands, governance, 104
CDP (Conservative Democratic Party), Switzerland, 110n
CDU (Christian Democratic Union), Germany, 108, 132, 159
Centre Party, Germany, 146
Chávez, H., President, Venezuela, 152

Index

Cheney, D., Vice President, USA, 157
Chernomyrdin, V., Premier, Russia, 19
Chesterton, C., 56
Chile
    decision-making, 11, 148, 149, 163, 170
    elections, 148
China
    decision-making, 4, 45
    elections, 171
    governance, 55n, 105, 172, 173
Chirac, J., President, France, 82
Chomsky, N., 58, 147
Churchill, W.S., Premier, UK, 53, 62n, 95, 101
Cicero, M., Roman Republic, 168
Citizens' initiative, 27, 117, 122, 132, 134, 168
Citrine, N., 33, 67
Clinton, B., President, USA, 111
Clones, 44n
Co-habitation, 114
Composite, 123, 124
Condorcet, Le Marquis de, 30, 54, 95, 170
Confidence votes, 6–7, 28, 61, 113, 156–159
Consensors, 46, 123, 124, 127, 128, 135
Consensus coefficient, 46, 124, 126
Cook Islands, decision-making, 165
Cook, R., MP, UK, 23
Cosgrave, W., Premier, Ireland, 158
Costa Rica, governance, 171
Côte D'ivoire, elections, 20, 69–70
CPA (Comprehensive Peace Agreement), Sudan, 19
CPC (Communist Party of China), 105
CPSU (Communist Party of the Soviet Union), 56, 102, 144
Crawford, M., 168
Croatia
    decision-making, 9, 21, 149
    elections, 71
    governance, 126
CSU (Christian Social Union), Germany, 108, 132
Cuba, 172
Cusanus, N., Cardinal, 60, 169
CVP (Christian Democratic People's Party), Switzerland, 110n
Cyprus, decision-making, 7
Czechoslovakia
    decision-making, 29
    governance, 172, 173, 175

D

Dagestan, elections, 80, 81, 90
Dahl, R.A., 55, 104

Dahomey, decision-making, 118
Dalbakk. S., 79n
DAP, German Workers' Party, 145
Darfur, 9, 12, 19, 21, 105n
Davies, J.K., 4
de Borda, J.-C., 42, 54, 58, 76, 158, 170
de Gaulle, C., President, France, 10, 144
de Klerk, F.W., President, South Africa, 112
de Mac-Mahon, P., President, France, 158
de Valera, E., President, Ireland, 11, 95
de Waal, A., 12
Decision-making, 3, 25–27
 approval voting, 36–38, 172
 AV, 36, 37, 39, 83
 BC, 23, 36, 37, 39–40, 42, 172
 binary, 4, 31, 37, 115, 141
 Condorcet, 36–39, 44
 consensus voting, 25, 40–42, 44, 134, 139
 consociational majority, 37, 111, 169
 consociationalism, 29–30
 IRV, 39
 majority voting, xii, 3, 5, 7n, 37, 51–54, 56–58, 102, 106, 110, 111, 113–117, 122, 132, 137, 138, 142, 144, 155, 167, 171, 173
 MBC, 36, 37, 40–44, 46, 121, 123, 126, 135, 138, 172
 plurality voting, 7n, 36–38, 54, 168
 qualified majority, 117n, 169
 serial voting, 36–38
 STV, 39
 TRS, 36–38, 163, 164
 weighted majority, 28, 37, 46
Deliberative democracy, 44
Democracy
 consensual, x, xi, 26, 42, 48, 101, 112, 127, 132
 consensus, 140
 consensus voting, 46
 consociational, xi, 101, 110, 140
 majoritarian, ix–x, xi, 3, 16, 42, 48, 57, 101, 104, 108, 127, 137, 140, 155
Democratic Party, USA, 55, 59, 62, 157, 160
Democratic-Republican Party, USA, 55
Denmark
 decision-making, 21, 29, 132, 152, 159
 elections, 66, 84, 132, 170
 governance, 109, 130, 131, 149
Dermot, King, Ireland, 168
Desai, M., Lord, UK, 22
Deutscher, I., 14, 156
d'Hondt, 67, 85, 111, 131
Diamond, L., 140n

Dodgson, C. Rev., UK, 170
Dole, R., USA, 58
Donor democracy, 105
DOS (Democratic Opposition of Serbia), 129
Dowdall, D., Ireland/Nauru, 58n, 172
Doyle, W., 26
DRC (Democratic Republic of the Congo), 20
 elections, 69
 governance, 102
Droop, quota, 85
Droop, H.R., Belgium, 170
Dummett, M., xii, 42, 53, 63, 102, 138, 172
Dunne, B., Ireland, 63
DUP (Democratic Unionist Party), NI, 13, 110, 111n, 138, 161
Duvalier, F., President, Haiti, 147
Duverger, M., 13, 57, 65, 106, 141n

E
Eban, A., 20n, 115
Ecuador, decision-making, 152
Egypt
 decision-making, 153
 governance, 104
Electoral systems, 121, 127, 129
 AMS, 84, 87n, 164
 approval voting, 81, 83, 84, 90, 169, 172
 AV, 58, 80–85, 90, 131, 132, 164, 171
 BC, 54, 58, 60, 84, 86, 169, 170, 172, 173
 Condorcet, 82, 84, 86, 169, 170
 consensus voting, 75, 80, 87–94
 FPP, 11, 53, 56–60, 62–65, 67–69, 71–73, 77, 80–84, 87, 95, 106, 131, 132, 160, 164, 171, 173
 majority voting, 60, 67, 70, 131, 167, 168
 matrix vote, 91–94, 121, 125, 134, 139, 172
 MBC, 82, 86–88, 90, 92, 94, 134
 MMP, 72, 87, 131, 132, 164, 171, 173
 plurality, 79
 PR, x, 65, 67, 72, 76, 77, 80, 93, 96, 113, 144, 168, 173
 PR-list, 57, 64, 68, 71–72, 75–77, 81n, 82–85, 87, 131, 132, 170, 173
 PR-STV, 11, 66, 76, 77, 81, 82, 84–87, 90, 91, 95, 113, 132, 164, 170, 171
 QBS, 72n, 76, 81, 82, 84, 87–94, 121, 135, 139, 170, 172
 SNTV, 68, 73, 81, 83, 84, 131
 top-up, 72, 78, 80, 82, 84, 87, 91, 96
 TRS, 57n, 68, 69, 71–73, 80–84, 131, 132, 163–164, 170
 two-tier, 84, 87, 96, 131, 132

Electoral systems (*cont.*)
  weighted majority, 60, 169
Electronic voting, 56, 138–139
el Khazen, F., 80n
Ellis, G., 144
Emerson, R., 10, 22, 57, 104, 118
Emmanuel, V., King, Italy, 145
England. *See* UK
EP, United Russia Party, 106
Estonia, decision-making, 151, 156n, 159
Ethiopia
  elections, 105
  governance, 105
EU, xiii, 103
  decision-making, 17, 117n, 159, 177
Europe, governance, 3, 51

F
Falklands, governance, 104
Faroes, decision-making, 151
Fascist Party, Italy, 145
FDP (Free Democratic Party),
  Germany, 108
FDP (Free Democratic Party),
  Switzerland, 110n
Fianna Fáil, Ireland, 59n, 63n, 95, 158, 159
Filibuster, 115, 171
Fine Gael, Ireland, 63n, 132, 159
Finland, 164
  decision-making, 28, 37, 38, 132, 159, 163
  elections, 132, 160
  governance, 130, 131
Fishburn, P., 172
Fishkin, J.S., 64
Fisk, R., 110, 160
FitzGerald, G., Premier, Ireland, 140
Flint, J., 12
Focus groups, 116
Fontana, B., 170
France, 171
  decision-making, 12, 13, 43, 132, 144, 152, 158, 170
  elections, 72, 82, 84, 132, 170
  governance, 53–54, 93, 114, 130–131, 149, 168–170
Franco, F., Gen., Spain, 171
Frenjieh, S., President, Lebanon, 160
Fulbrook, M., 146

G
Gallagher, M., 14, 138
Gandhi, M.K., India, 25, 75
Gbagbo, L., President, Côte d'Ivoire, 69
Gender balance, 47, 57, 66, 76, 78, 79, 168

General will, 25, 26, 28, 54, 64
George, I., King, England, 170
Georgia, 103
  decision-making, 18n, 21
  governance, 173
Germany, 20n, 55, 132, 146, 172
  decision-making, 6, 43, 61, 108, 113, 145, 159
  elections, 14, 72, 84, 87, 132, 145, 160, 171, 180
  governance, 113, 130, 132, 169, 171
Gerry, E., Governor, USA, 64
Gerrymander, 64, 76
Ghana
  elections, 160
  governance, 106
Gibraltar, decision-making, 7
Gilgamesh, King, Uruk, 167
Gillard, J., Premier, Australia, 161
Gilpin, T., USA, 170
Gittings, J., 173
Glenny, M., 30, 71, 149
Gorbachev, M., Gen. Sec., USSR, 9, 56, 59, 62, 63, 102, 143, 172
Gore, A., Vice President, USA, 157
Governance, 101, 102, 121, 129
  all-party coalition, 101, 107, 110, 114, 118, 125, 132, 133, 171
  all-party state, 109, 122
  coalition, 48, 57, 113, 117, 125, 129, 150
  consensus, 104
  consociationalism, 109–112, 118
  GNU (government of national unity), 56, 101, 109, 110, 114, 122, 161
  grand coalition, 108, 129, 130
  majority coalition, 107, 108, 110, 113, 114, 122, 130, 131
  minority administration, 113, 129, 131
  minority rule, 4, 16
  multi-party state, x, 68, 85, 103, 105, 107, 118, 129
  no-party state, 54, 56, 57, 102, 114, 122
  non-partisan, 78, 104, 112, 113
  one-party state, 55, 62, 68, 101, 102, 113, 141
  one-party-dominant state, 55, 105, 131
  parliamentary, 107, 114, 134
  presidential, 107, 114
  single party majority rule, 113–115, 122, 130
  two-party state, 13, 53–56, 59, 62, 63, 82, 103, 106, 109, 128, 129, 131, 141, 142
  two-party system, 65
GP (Green Party)
  in Australia, 161
  in Britain, 60n, 161

Index 187

in Germany, 55, 108
in Ireland, xiv, 60n, 96n, 104
Greece
 decision-making, 4, 5, 33, 51, 114, 132, 167, 168
 elections, 51, 52, 79, 132, 167, 168
 governance, 3, 51, 52, 54, 57, 130, 167, 168, 171, 175
Guam
 decision-making, 152, 163–164, 172
Guardian, The, 8, 13, 17, 19, 45, 103, 105, 106
Guernsey, governance, 104
Guillotine, 115
Guyana
 decision-making, 129n
 elections, 57, 85n

H

Hage, H., Denmark, 170
Hailsham, Lord, 66
Haiti, decision-making, 147
Hamilton, A., President, USA, 170
Hansard, 7n, 22, 127, 158
Hare, quota, 85
Hare, T., MP, UK, 170
Hariri, R., Premier, Lebanon, 110
Harris, R., 168
Haughey, C., Premier, Ireland, 159
Havel, V., 51, 119
Hayes, R., President, USA, 160
HDZ, Croatian Democratic Party, 71
Hill, T., 170
Hillygus, D.S., 58, 62
Hitler, A., Führer, Germany, 10, 14, 143, 146, 149, 157, 171
Holy Roman Empire, decision-making, 169
Honduras, governance, 109
Horowitz, D., 67
Hoxha, E., First Sec., Albania, 143, 172
Hú, J., President, China, 105
Humphrys, J., UK, 137
Hung parliament, 12, 115
Hungary, 141n, 146
 decision-making, 152
 governance, 171
Huntington, S.P., ix, 47, 104
Hussein, S., President, Iraq, 8, 149

I

ICC (International Criminal Court), 105n
Iceland
 decision-making, 132
 elections, 132
 governance, 130, 166

IDEA (Institute for Democracy and Electoral Assistance), 64, 77, 106, 132
IFES (International Foundation for Electoral Systems), 72
IMF (International Monetary Fund), 14, 22, 117n, 118
INC (Indian National Congress), 109
India
 decision-making, 157
 elections, 62, 65, 68, 157, 171, 173
 governance, 108, 171
Indonesia, decision-making, 8, 18, 21, 45
IOC (International Olympic Committee), 7
IRA (Irish Republican Army), 115n
Iran, 62
 decision-making, 148, 153
 elections, 148
Iraq, 7, 43
 decision-making, 8, 45, 149
 elections, 72–73, 84, 160, 161
 governance, 109, 173
Ireland
 decision-making, 11, 12, 14, 21, 43, 132, 151n, 152, 155–156, 158, 159, 172
 elections, 84, 85, 94, 132, 159, 171, 172
 governance, 63, 114, 115, 119, 130, 132, 137, 150, 168, 169
Irrelavant alternative, 44n
Israel
 elections, 14, 84, 85
 governance, 17
Italy
 decision-making, 27, 132, 145, 152, 159
 elections, 87, 95, 131, 132, 145, 169
 governance, 130, 131, 132, 169, 171
 Roman Republic, 52, 168
Ivan IV, Tzar, Russia, 169
Izetbegović, A., President, Bosnia, 111

J

Jaafari, I., Premier, Iraq, 160
Jacobsen, T., 167
Jagan, C., Premier, Guyana, 57
James, I., King, England, 101
Japan
 decision-making, 132
 elections, 131, 132
Jaruzelski, W., President, Poland, 160
Jefferson, F.T., President, USA, 55, 160, 170
Jenkins, P., 54
Jenkins, R., Lord, UK, 27n, 139, 140
Jersey, governance, 104
Johnson, A., President, USA, 158

Jordan, A.J., 158
Jospin, L., France, 82

K
Kabila, L.D., President, DRC, 69
Kapuściński, R., 4, 133
Kashmir, 157
   decision-making, 45
Katz, R., 87
Kekkonen, U., President, Finland, 160
Kelly, P., GP, Germany, 55, 95
Kennedy, J.F., President, USA, 62
Kenya
   decision-making, 132
   elections, 68–69, 84, 106
   governance, 102, 103, 109, 114, 130–132
Kenyatta, M., President, Kenya, 68
Ketcham, R., 55, 140
Khomeini, R., Ayatollah, Iran, 148
Khrushchev, N., Gen. Sec., USSR, 55n, 102
Kibaki, M., President, Kenya, 68
Kigame, P., President, Rwanda, 69
Kiribati, governance, 104
KLA (Kosova Liberation Army), 62
Klein, N., 22
Koback, K.W., 14, 27
Kosova
   decision-making, 9, 18–19, 21, 28, 45
   elections, xiii, 62, 72, 103, 172
Koštunica, V., President, Serbia, 19
KPD, Communist Party, Germany, 14, 146
Kriesi, H., 66
Kuwait, 8
Kyrgyz Republic
   elections, xiii
   governance, 173

L
Labour Party
   in Australia, 161
   in Britain, 60, 63n, 82, 83n, 107, 161
   in Ireland, 132, 159
Lahoud, E., President, Lebanon, 110
Lakeman, E., 11, 79n
Larsen, J.A.O., 33, 167, 168
Latov, V., 126
Latvia, 156n
Le Pen, J.-M., France, 82
League of Nations, 171
Lebanon, xii, 102
   elections, 80, 81, 84, 90, 160
   governance, 109, 110, 173
   Taif Agreement, 126

The Left, Germany, 108
Lenin, V., Chairman, USSR, xi, 101, 102, 143, 156, 171
Lesotho, elections, 173
Lewis, Sir A., 78, 102, 104, 106, 113, 121, 133
Liberal Party, Australia, 161
Liberal Party, Lib-Dems, UK, 82, 156, 161
Liberia, elections, 172
Libya
   decision-making, 143n
   governance, 105
Liechtenstein, decision-making, 117, 151, 163
Lijphart, A., xiii, 6, 27, 77, 85, 103, 106, 109, 131, 133, 140, 141
Lincoln, A., President, USA, 25
Lithuania, 156n
Little, A., 29n, 149
Lloyd, G.E.R., 4, 5
Logrolling, 12, 13, 144, 155
Lottery, 51, 52, 60, 79, 167–169
Louis xiv, King, France, 169
Lucas, C., MP, UK, 13
Lukashenko, A., President. Belarus, 106
Lull, R., Spain, 169
Luxembourg
   decision-making, 132, 151
   elections, 85, 132
   governance, 130
Lyons, F.S.L., 119

M
Macedonia
   decision-making, 9
   elections, 13, 71
Madagascar
   decision-making, 152
Maguire, F., MP, NI, 156
Maher, J., 104
Major, J., Premier, UK, 59
Majority rule, xii, 4–6, 16, 17, 22, 25, 47, 56, 58, 65, 102, 106, 109, 111, 117, 122, 132, 137, 138, 144
Malta
   decision-making, 132
   elections, 85, 132
Malvinas. *See* Falklands
Mandela, N., 4, 112
Mandela, N., President, South Africa, 112
Máo, Z., Chairman, China, 101, 143
Marković, A., Premier, Yugoslavia, 9
Martinique, decision-making, 152
Matlosa, K., 105
Matveeva, A., 81

Index

McLean, I., 30, 33, 54, 65, 76, 95, 101
Medvedev, D., President, USSR, 102
Menang, T., 107
Menshevik Party, Russia, 143, 156
Michael, King, Romania, 146
Micronesia
  decision-making, 152
  governance, 104
Mill, J.S., 137
Mills, J.A., President, Ghana, 160
Milošević, S., President, Yugoslavia, 10, 19, 111, 129, 149
Miłosz, C., xi
Mobutu, S.-S., President, Zaire, 69, 102
Moi, A., President, Kenya, 68
Moldova, decision-making, 21, 159
Monbiot, G., 22
Monroe, J., President, USA, 55
Montenegro, elections, 71n, 85n
Morales, J., 65, 76
Mossadegh, M., Premier, Iran, 148
MQM (Muttahida Qaumi Movement), Pakistan, 108
Mugabe, R., President, Zimbabwe, 11, 57, 68
Munro, N., 71n, 81, 91n, 173
Museveni, Y., President, Uganda, 11, 103
Musharraf, P., President, Pakistan, 108
Mussolini, B., Il Duce, Italy, 10, 131, 145, 171

N

Nagorno-Karabakh, Azerbaijan, 18, 21
Namboodiripad EMS, India, 171
Napoleon Bonaparte, Emperor, France, 10, 54, 144, 170
Nasser, G.A., President, Egypt, 104
National Peasant Party, Romania, 146
NATO (North Atlantic Treaty Organisation), 19, 62
Nauru
  elections, 58, 84, 86, 172, 173
  governance, 104
Nehru, J., Premier, India, xi, 101
Nerburn, K., 4
Netherlands, 56
  decision-making, 129n, 132, 158, 159
  elections, 84, 85, 132
  governance, x, 48, 113, 122, 130, 131, 150, 173
New Zealand, 164
  decision-making, 27n, 45, 66, 132, 140, 151, 163
  elections, 27n, 47, 84, 95, 131, 132, 140

governance, ix, 84, 95, 131, 140
Nicholas II, Tzar, Russia, 171
NIG (New Ireland Group), xiv, 104, 138
Nigeria, decision-making, 20
Nkomo, J., Zimbabwe, 68
No-confidence. *See* Confidence votes
Norfolk, governance, 104
North Korea, governance, 105
Northern Ireland, 16
  Belfast Agreement, 6, 21, 28, 30, 110–113, 126, 138
  decision-making, 6, 7, 9, 13, 14, 18, 21, 28–30, 37, 45
  elections, 61, 66, 73, 76, 79, 80, 90, 160
  governance, 67, 79, 109, 110, 113, 127, 137, 138, 175
Northern Mariana Islands, decision-making, 163, 172
Norway
  decision-making, 28, 37, 38, 132, 153, 158
  elections, 79, 132
  governance, 129, 130, 149
NSDAP (National Socialist DAP), Nazi, Germany, 145, 146
Nunavut, governance, 104
Nurmi, H., xiv, 38, 104
Nyerere, J., President Tanzania, 8, 102

O

Obama, B., President, USA, 13
Obote, M., President, Uganda, 103
Odinga, R., Premier, Kenya, 68
O'Higgins, B., El Supremo, Chile, 170
O'Higgins, K., Ireland, 119
Opinion polls, 116
Opsahl Commission, 139
Opsahl, T., Norway, 139
Orlovsky, S., 149
OSCE (Organization for Security and Co-operation in Europe), xiii, 70, 72, 75, 103, 115, 117, 173
Oslobodjenje, 17
Othieno, T., 19
Ouattara, A., President, Côte d'Ivoire, 69

P

Pahlavi, R., Shah, Iran, 148
Paine, T., 12
Paisley, Rev I, NI, 7, 14
Pakenham, T., 16
Pakistan, 157
  governance, 108

Palau, governance, 104
Palestine
  elections, 14
  governance, 17
Paradox of voting, 31, 36, 38, 39, 40n, 170
Parizeau, J., Quebec, 11
Parti Socialiste, France, 82
Partial voting, 89–90, 172
Pinochet, A., President, Chile, 10, 11, 148
Plaid Cymru, Wales, 10, 35, 161
Plato, 58, 168
Pliny the Younger, 33, 67, 123, 168
PML (Pakistan Muslim League), 108
PNG
  decision-making, 6, 132
  elections, 63, 131, 132, 173
  governance, 130, 131
Poland
  decision-making, 132
  elections, 132, 160
  governance, 130
Pollak, A., 139
Pope, 60, 169
Portugal
  decision-making, 132, 152
  elections, 131, 132, 160
  governance, 130, 131, 172
Power-sharing, 92, 95, 101, 109–112, 114, 118, 121, 122, 125, 126, 131–133
PPP (Pakistan People's Party), 108
Préval, R., President, Haiti, 147
Prodi, R., President, Italy, 159
Prunier, G., 16, 19
Puerto Rico, 164
  decision-making, 37, 163
Putin, V., President/Premier, Russia, xiii, 57, 102, 103, 106, 131

Q
Quebec, 11, 21, 152
Quota, 77–78, 83, 85, 87, 89, 170

R
Ranney, A., 66, 117, 118, 129n, 151n
Reader, J., 16
Reagan, R., President, USA, 62
Referendum, 7, 9–11, 14, 15, 17–22, 27–30, 45, 65, 66, 82, 103, 111, 117, 128, 132, 133, 138, 140, 143, 151, 153, 159, 164, 169, 170, 173. *See also* Decision-making

abrogative, 27
multi-option, 27n, 28, 36, 45, 79, 95, 138, 140, 158, 163-165, 171, 173
Reilly, B., 43, 86n
Republican Party, USA, 55, 58, 59, 62, 63n, 157, 160
Rhodes, P.J., 168
Riasanovsky, N.V., 171
Rights
  democratic, 103, 128, 132, 133
  divine, 3
  human, 1n, 73, 95, 122, 123, 128, 133, 134, 138, 158
  Human Rights Watch, 103
  majority rule, 4, 9, 132
  self-determination, 3, 17–18, 20, 21, 138, 153
  UN Charter, 40, 171
Riker, W.H., 5
Rodgers, B., NI, 111
Romania
  decision-making, 147
  elections, 146
Roosevelt, T., President, USA, 95, 140
Rose, R., 71n, 81, 91n, 173
Rousseau, J.-J., 25, 56, 140
RPF (Rwanda Patriotic Front), 69
RTÉ (Radio Telefís Éireann), 139
Rugova, I., President, Kosova, 62
Russia, 19, 20n, 101n, 103
  decision-making, 132, 152, 156
  elections, 69, 84, 91n, 131, 132, 143, 173, 180
  governance, 55, 57, 103, 105, 106, 114, 130, 131, 132, 169, 171
Russian Social Democratic Workers' Party, 156
Rwanda, 16, 69
  decision-making, 4, 6, 16
  governance, 102, 103

S
Saakashvili, M., President, Georgia, xiii, 103
Saari, D.G., xiv, 33n, 42, 104, 139n
St. Aquinas, T., 52
St. Laguë, 85
Sakharov, A., 55, 56, 79
Salazar, A., President, Portugal, 172
Sartori, G., 65
Scandinavia
  decision-making, 173
  governance, 168
Scotland

decision-making, 45
governance, 113
SCW (Society for Social Choice and Welfare), xiv, 104, 138
SDA, (Party of Democratic Action), Bosnia, 71
SDLP (Social Democratic and Labour Party), NI, 9, 13, 110, 111n, 161
SDP (Social Democratic Party), Germany, 108
SDS (Serbian Democratic Party), Bosnia, 71
Secret vote, 158, 168, 170
Šedo, J, 13, 71, 72
Serbia
   decision-making, 9, 21, 149
   elections, 71, 160
   governance, 129, 132
Serfaty A, Morocco, 45
Šešelj, V., Serbia, 160
SF (Sinn Féin), Ireland and NI, 13, 110, 111n, 138, 139, 161
Sharif, N., Premier, Pakistan, 108
Sheeran, M.J., 56, 124
Shehu, M., Premier, Albania, 172
Shields, T.S., 59, 62
Sierra Leone, elections, 67
Sigmund, P.E., 8, 25, 102, 106
Silber, L., 29n, 149
Simeon II, Czar/Premier, Bulgaria, 173
Sincere voting, 15, 17, 22, 78, 96, 124
Singapore, decision-making, 163
Singh, M., Premier, India, 109
Single-peaked preferences, 35, 39, 124, 171
Skinner, Q., 52
SLA (Sudan Liberation Army), 19
Slovenia
   decision-making, 9, 20, 152, 165
   elections, 58, 84, 86, 95, 173
SNP (Scottish National Party), 161
Solon, Greece, 167
Somaliland, decision-making, 20
South Africa, 20
   decision-making, 37
   elections, 84, 85n
   governance, 109, 112
South Ossetia, Georgia, 18, 21
Spain
   decision-making, 6, 132
   elections, 131, 132, 169
   governance, 113, 130, 131, 171
SPD (Social Democratic Party), Germany, 14, 146
Speaker, 66, 122, 158, 159, 169
SPLA (Sudan People's Liberation Army), 19

SPS (Social Democratic Party), Switzerland, 110n
SR (Socialist Revolutionaries), Russia, 143
Sri Lanka
   decision-making, 159
   governance, 170
Stalin, J., Generalissimo, USSR, 14, 29n, 81, 95, 102, 141, 143, 146, 149, 171
Stanishev, S., Premier, Bulgaria, 159
Ste Croix, de, G.E.M., 52, 167
Sudan, 19–20
   decision-making, 4, 9, 12, 18–21, 45
   elections, 105
   governance, 105
Sukarno, K., President, Indonesia, 8
Sumer, decision-making, 167
SVP (Swiss People's Party), 110n
Sweden, 16n
   decision-making, 15, 28, 37, 38, 132, 151, 158, 159, 163–164
   elections, 61, 84, 87, 180
   governance, 130, 149
Swift, J., 56
Switzerland
   decision-making, 14, 22, 27, 29, 37, 117, 132, 151, 163, 169, 170
   elections, ix, 47, 66, 84, 85, 132, 170, 179
   governance, 101, 109, 117, 126, 129, 130, 150, 171
Syria, 110
   decision-making, 43, 149, 153

T
Tactical voting, 13, 15, 22, 40, 65, 78
Tadić, B., President, Serbia, 160
Tanzania
   decision-making, 102n, 132
   elections, 102n
   governance, 102, 105, 130
Tasmania, elections, 85
Taylor, R., 111
Thailand, governance, 112
Thatcher, M., Premier, UK, 62, 66, 157
Thorley, J., 168
Threshold, 62, 77–78, 80, 96, 126, 129, 131
Tibet, decision-making, 45
Timor-Leste, decision-making, 18, 21
Timoshenko, J., Premier, Ukraine, 70
Tito, J., President, Yugoslavia, 172
Tokelau, governance, 104
Tolstoy, L.N., 56, 61

Tory Party, UK, 53, 63n, 156, 161
Touré, S., President, Guinea, xi
Trans-Dnestr, Moldova, 21
Trechsel, A., 66
Trimble, D., First Minister, NI, 160
Trinidad and Tobago, elections, 160
Tubman, W., President, Liberia, 172
Tudjman, F., President, Croatia, 111, 149
Tunisia
    elections, 71
    governance, 105, 106, 109
Turkey, decision-making, 152
Turkmenistan, governance, 106
Turner, B., 168
Tuvalu, governance, 104

U
Uganda, 16
    elections, 103
    governance, 102, 103
UK, 16n, 155, 170
    decision-making, 7n, 13, 15, 21, 22, 43, 132, 156–158, 169, 171
    elections, 27n, 52, 53, 59, 62, 68, 82, 84, 110, 132, 139, 161, 169–171
    governance, 52 -54, 56, 66, 93, 104, 106, 107, 110, 122, 130, 149, 157, 168–170
Ukraine
    elections, 69, 70, 85n
    governance, 173
UMP (Union pour un Mouvement Populaire), France, 83
UN, 22, 95, 147, 172
    Charter, 171
    decision-making, 7, 45n, 115, 117
    High Representative, Bosnia, 135
    Security Council, 7, 43, 117
UPA (United Progressive Alliance), India, 109
Urken, A.B., 30, 33, 54, 65, 76, 95, 101
Uruguay, decision-making, 152, 163
USA, xiii, 103, 147, 158
    decision-making, 12, 13, 22, 27, 43, 128, 132, 157, 158, 170, 171
    elections, ix, 47, 54, 59, 62 -65, 68, 69, 77, 78, 132, 157, 160, 170, 172
    governance, 4, 51, 54 -57, 63, 104, 106, 107, 114, 126, 128, 130, 169–171
USSR, 146, 169, 170
    decision-making, 9, 21, 173
    elections, 55, 70, 79, 126, 143, 172
    governance, 63, 102, 139, 143, 172
UUP (Ulster Unionist Party), NI, 6, 13, 107, 110, 111n, 138, 139, 156

V
Vajpayee, A.B., Premier, India, 157
van Holsteyn, J., 129n
Vatican, elections, 169
Venezuela, decision-making, 152
Veto, 9, 22, 29, 30, 110, 111, 117
Vietnam, 62
von Hindenburg, P., President, Germany, 145, 146
von Papen, F., Chancellor, Germany, 145

W
Wales, decision-making, 10, 13, 22, 34, 65, 152
Walpole, R., Premier, UK, 170
Washington, G., President, USA, 54, 170
Weimar Republic, Germany, 171
West, R., 126
Western Sahara, decision-making, 45
Whig Party, UK, 53
Whip, party, 11, 46, 61, 93, 119
Wigley, D., 10
Woodward, S.L., 9, 17, 118
Wootton, D., 169
World Bank, 14, 22
Wright, J.F.H., 66

Y
Yanukovich, V., President, Ukraine, 70
Yeltsin, B., President, Russia, 102, 172
Yuán, S., President, China, 171
Yugoslavia
    decision-making, 9, 17, 20, 21, 45, 138, 149
    elections, 76, 80, 172
    governance, 117n, 118n, 172

Z
Zaire. *See* DRC (Democratic Republic of the Congo)
Zanzibar
    decision-making, 102
    elections, 160
Zhvania, Z., Premier, Georgia, 18n
Zimbabwe
    decision-making, 11
    elections, 68
    governance, 109
Zinoviev, G.Y., USSR, 59